THE SCOTTISH SOLDIER AND EMPIRE, 1854–1902

The Scottish Soldier and Empire, 1854–1902

Edward M. Spiers

Edinburgh University Press

Figures 2–5, 7–8 are reproduced by permission of Anne S. K. Brown Military Collection, Brown University, Providence, RI.

Edinburgh University Press Ltd
22 George Square, Edinburgh

Typeset in Adobe Sabon
by Servis Filmsetting Ltd, Manchester, and
printed and bound in Great Britain by
The Cromwell Press, Trowbridge, Wilts

A CIP record for this book is available from the British Library

ISBN-10 0 7486 2354 X (hardback)
ISBN-13 978 0 7486 2354 9 (hardback)

CONTENTS

MAPS

FIGURES

ACKNOWLEDGEMENTS

I should like to acknowledge the British Academy for its willingness to award me a Small Research Grant to facilitate the research on this book.

Quotations of Crown copyright material in the Public Record Office appear by permission of The National Archives as the custodians of the records. I should like to acknowledge permission of the Trustees of the National Library of Scotland for permission to quote from papers in their possession and to the Rt Hon. Earl Haig as holder of his father's copyright. I am particularly grateful to Dr A. Massie for permission to quote from numerous archival collections in the National Army Museum and for every effort made to trace the owner of the copyright of John Paterson's photocopied MS. I am also obliged to the Rt Hon. Lord Monro of Langholm, AR, DL for permission to quote from material in the Monro of Williamwood Muniments and to Mr James Methuen Campbell for permission to quote from the papers of 3rd Baron Methuen in the Wiltshire and Swindon Record Office. Quotations from the Campbell-Bannerman and White papers appear by permission of The British Library.

I should like to acknowledge the assistance of Professors I. F. W. Beckett, K. Jeffery, J. Gooch and S. M. Dixon, Drs Stephen Miller and Roger T. Stearn; Mr P. Harrington (A. S. K. Brown Collection, Brown University); Dr P. B. Boyden and Dr A. Massie (National Army Museum); Allan Carswell and Stuart Allan (National War Museum of Scotland); Helen Osmani (National Museums of Scotland); Lieutenant-Colonel C. G. O. Hogg, DL (Regimental Headquarters, The King's Own Scottish Borderers); Mr T. B. Smyth (The Black Watch Archive); Lieutenant-Colonel A. A. Fairrie, DL and Lieutenant-Colonel A. M. Cumming, OBE (The Highlanders Museum); Mr R. McKenzie (Regimental Headquarters, The Argyll and Sutherland Highlanders); Mrs Sarah MacKay, Major M. Ross and Mr W. Smith (The Gordon Highlanders Museum); Miss Tessa Spencer (National Register of Archives for Scotland); Mr John D'Arcy (principal archivist, Wiltshire and Swindon Record Office); Ms Z. Lubowiecka (Hove Library); Mr Brian J. Newbury (chairman and managing director, The Parker Gallery); Mr Norman Newton and Ms Edwina Burridge (Inverness Reference Library); the inter-library loan staff of Leeds University.

I am much obliged to Dave Appleyard (Graphics Unit, University of Leeds) for preparing the maps and Ms Roda Morrison (Edinburgh University Press) for all her advice and assistance in preparing the book. As ever, I am deeply indebted to Fiona, my wife, for all her support and to Robert and Amanda for enduring the writing of another work.

Edward M. Spiers
December 2005

ABBREVIATIONS

ASH	Argyll and Sutherland Highlanders
BL	British Library
BOP	*Boy's Own Paper*
BWRA	Black Watch Regimental Archive
GH	Gordon Highlanders
HLI	Highland Light Infantry
JSAHR	*Journal of the Society for Army Historical Research*
KOSB	King's Own Scottish Borderers
MP	Member of Parliament
NAS	National Register of Archives for Scotland
NLS	National Library of Scotland
Parl. Deb.	*Parliamentary Debates*
PP	Parliamentary Papers
PRO	Public Record Office
REJ	*Royal Engineers Journal*
THM	The Highlanders Museum
TNA	The National Archives
WO	War Office

GLOSSARY

ansar	armed followers of the Mahdi
assegai	a slender spear of hard wood used in South Africa
bey	a Turkish governor
commando	a Boer military unit
donga	a gully
fencible	a militiaman or home defence soldier raised in a crisis
hackle	a scarlet plume that adorned the bonnets of the Black Watch
hummle	a bonnet or cap worn by Scottish regiments before the introduction of the glengarry
impi	a body of armed natives
khedive	the viceroy of Egypt
khor	a dry watercourse
knoll	a round hillock
kopje	a low hill
kotal	a pass
kraal	a native village or corral for animals
on commando	military service in the field
pasha	a Turkish title given to governors and military and naval officers of high rank
sangar	a stone breastwork
sepoy	Indian infantry private soldier

sirdar	commander-in-chief
sjambok	a whip of dried hide
veld	open, unforested grass country

1

THE IMAGES AND SELF-IMAGE OF THE SCOTTISH SOLDIER

❦

During the late nineteenth century – a period in which British imperial expansion reached its zenith – Scottish, and in particular Highland, regiments earned accolades as empire-builders. Richard Finlay argues that 'the military contribution of the Scottish regiments was the most important factor in the propagation of a distinctive Scottish input into British imperial activity'.[1] John M. MacKenzie agrees that Scottish regiments, especially the kilted regiments, had on account of their conspicuous prominence 'become one of the principal icons of the imperial enterprise', and that imperial service, so popular across the political spectrum in Scotland, had not only enhanced a sense of British national identity but had also preserved and strengthened 'the distinctive identities of the Scots and the other ethnicities of Greater Britain'.[2] This work will seek to amplify these arguments by reviewing the imperial experience from the perspective of the soldiers themselves and by evaluating perceptions of their achievements in Britain. It will build on previous studies of imperial campaigns,[3] and the Victorian campaigning experience in Africa,[4] by incorporating material from the campaigns waged on the North-West Frontier and by assimilating both the interpretations of military campaigning in the press and in popular writing, as well as the images composed by war-artists, battle-painters and sculptors.

By reviewing this imperial experience from the perspective of the soldiers themselves, this work aims to provide a fresh perspective on the Scottish military experience in the late nineteenth century. Recent writing on this period can be found in biographies of Scottish soldiers, in regimental histories, and an excellent account of the social origins of the Highland regiments.[5] There are also wide-ranging studies of the Scottish soldier, serving not only in Scottish regiments but also in non-Scottish regiments, the East India Company, and the many units raised for home defence – fencibles, Militia (conscripted and later voluntary), Yeomanry and Volunteers – and of the impact of Scottish military service upon Scottish society.[6] Yet few studies have used the campaign correspondence of Scottish soldiers, much of it published in the provincial press on both sides of the border, to illustrate their findings. These writings, it will be argued, contributed to an evolving image of the Scottish soldier by complementing the sketches and reports of war correspondents, the works of contemporary battle-painters (such as Elizabeth Thompson, later Lady Butler, Robert Gibb and Vereker Hamilton), poets and song-writers. It was an image of the Scottish soldier that would be disseminated widely in popular art, imperial iconography and in the illustrations of children's books.[7] It will be argued that this image appealed broadly, if not universally, across classes and regions in Scotland, that it strengthened a sense of Scottish national identity, and that it enhanced the popularity of the imperial mission in Scotland.

Institutionally, the Highland regiments had already played a pivotal role in sustaining Highland traditions and clan feeling, the only Highlanders allowed to carry arms and wear Highland dress under the Disarming Act, imposed in 1746 after the battle of Culloden (and not repealed until 1782). Over the period from 1739 to 1800 some fifty-nine marching and fencible Highland regiments were raised, with fencible regiments undertaking home defence duties, including service in Ireland. In spite of occasional mutinies, Highland regiments served throughout the empire, fighting in North America, India, and in the French Revolutionary and Napoleonic Wars. The 42nd, 79th and 92nd Highlanders, like the Scots Greys, would be fêted and honoured for their achievements at the battle of Waterloo (1815). As many regiments were disbanded after major wars, only eleven survived the Napoleonic Wars, with a mere five wearing the kilt.[8] Although older units such as the 42nd (originally the 43rd in order of precedence) had worn the belted plaid, Highland regiments adopted the more convenient kilt, generally wearing the government or Black Watch tartan (with variations in some cases, including a red and white stripe for the 78th, a yellow stripe for the 92nd and the Cameron tartan for the 79th). Major-General David Stewart of Garth, formerly of the 42nd Highlanders, who founded the Celtic Society of Edinburgh in 1820 and wrote a major work on the clans, advised Sir Walter Scott on matters of ceremony and dress before the first visit of a Hanoverian monarch to the Scottish capital in 1822. On that occasion the elite of Scottish society wore Highland dress, as did King George IV, during an extravaganza of tartan in Edinburgh.[9]

It was during the aftermath of this visit and through much of the early to mid-nineteenth century that Scotland, as Finlay argues persuasively, underwent a 'reinvention', whereby many recoiled from the squalor of rapid urbanisation and industrialisation to regard the essence of the nation as located in a mythical rural past, increasingly associated with Highland symbolism. The purportedly innate qualities of the Highlander – stoicism, loyalty and martial prowess – qualities supposedly forged amid a rugged, unspoiled landscape – were transposed onto Scotland generally. They complemented the values of an increasingly pervasive ideology in the Lowlands, namely individual advancement through thrift, hard work, respectability and meritocratic recognition. If these values were gathering adherents across Victorian Britain,[10] they accorded with the prevailing political and religious traditions of mid-nineteenth-century Scotland, notably those of the Liberal party that dominated Scottish politics from 1832 until 1900 and Presbyterianism. Scots found an outlet for these values in the imperial mission, serving as pro-consuls, missionaries, entrepreneurs, merchants, engineers, imperial civil servants and as soldiers in far-flung parts of the empire. Far from serving as 'the colonised in the colonies',[11] Scots (or at least those who had profited from the Union and empire) saw imperial service as a matter of historic destiny, a means of bolstering their self-esteem by accommodating their national identity with the purposes and mission of the British state. As the 8th Duke of Argyll asserted, Scots 'saw that the interests of their country, and its glory, lay in assuming its full share of imperial duties under one Imperial Crown'.[12]

Military service, with an increasingly prominent Scottish dimension, represented part of these duties. Unlike the five kilted regiments that survived the Napoleonic Wars – the 42nd (Royal Highland Regiment or the Black Watch), the 78th (Ross-shire Buffs), 79th (Cameron) Highlanders, the 92nd (Gordon) Highlanders and the 93rd (Sutherland) Highlanders – six regiments had lost their Highland status on account of recruiting difficulties in 1809. They struggled thereafter to regain their tartan, pipers and Highland designation. In 1820 the 91st took the title 'Argyllshire', and in 1823 the 72nd regained a 'Highland' title as the '72nd or the Duke of Albany's Own Highlanders' and wore tartan in the form of trews. In 1845 the 74th regained its 'Highland' title and trews. In 1862 the 73rd assumed the title 73rd (Perthshire) Regiment while the 75th became the 'Stirlingshire' Regiment, and, in 1864, the 91st became the 'Argyllshire Highlanders' and went into tartan trews. Only in the amalgamations of 1881 did the 72nd, 73rd, 75th and 91st regain their full Highland status and dress (while the 74th were linked with the 71st as the Highland Light Infantry and wore trews).[13]

Scottish regiments also prospered under royal patronage, as they had done in the eighteenth century.[14] Queen Victoria, and her consort, Albert, regularly alluded to their bond with the military as they struggled to preserve the royal prerogative in the command of the army (ultimately failing when the office of commander-in-chief was subordinated to ministerial control in July 1855). Proud of her father's military background, Victoria informed the Royal Scots as she presented them with new colours: 'I have been associated with your regiment from my earliest infancy, as my dear father was your Colonel. He was proud of his profession, and I was always taught to consider myself a soldier's child.' She described soldiers as 'my dear noble Troops' or 'my own children' and 'trembled with emotion, as well as pride' when reading about the 'heroism of these devoted men' in the Crimean War. When a new gallantry medal was struck, she ensured that it would reaffirm her bond with the armed services by being known as the Victoria Cross.[15]

Queen Victoria's fascination with Scotland and its people developed from her first visit to the country in 1842, followed by her first sight of Balmoral six years later, and by long and frequent visits thereafter. From the outset she was impressed by the appearance of her Highland soldiers, men of the 42nd who 'looked very handsome in their kilts' and enthused about Highlanders in general: 'they are such a chivalrous, fine, active people'.[16] Throughout her reign she took a close interest in her Highland guards of honour, and, as a reflection of her well-known affection for Scotland, this enhanced her popularity north of the border and strengthened the monarchical connection with Scotland. She asked after individual Scottish soldiers, bestowed a royal title on the 79th in 1873 (whereupon the regiment became known as the 79th Queen's Own Cameron Highlanders), presented regimental colours to Highland regiments at Balmoral, and recalled the emotional departure of her guard of Gordon Highlanders for the South African War: 'I felt quite a lump in my throat as we drove away, and I thought how these remarkably fine men might not all return.'[17]

The queen's pride in her Highland regiments was underpinned by their spectacular achievements in the Crimean War (1854–6) and the Indian Mutiny (1857–9). In dispatches and reports from the Crimea (notably those of William Howard Russell of *The Times*), Highland soldiers gained further accolades and renown. Their offensive zeal was highlighted when the Highland Brigade (42nd,

79th and 93rd Highlanders), commanded by Sir Colin Campbell, stormed the heights of Alma (20 September 1854). Advancing on the left flank of the British assault, their rapid ascent, led by their regimental officers, proved decisive in the battle. When they reached the summit, 'the Russians', as Private Donald Cameron (93rd) recalled, 'not caring for cold steel turned heel and fled'.[18] The brigade lost only one officer and about 100 men: 'Our getting off so easily', claimed Lieutenant-Colonel Anthony Sterling, 'was mainly owing to the admirable leading of C.[ampbell] and the pace we went . . .', while Campbell reported that 'I never saw officers and men, one and all, exhibit greater steadiness and gallantry, giving evidence of their high state of instruction and discipline, and of the noble spirit with which they were animated . . .'[19] Very different qualities were in evidence on 25 October 1854 when six companies of the 93rd, 550 men and one hundred invalids, deployed in two lines at Balaclava to repel the advance of Russian cavalry with three volleys from their Minié rifles. This resolute stand assumed legendary proportions, following Russell's famous report on the 'thin red streak tipped with a line of steel' (later misquoted as the 'thin red line'), as did Campbell's famous exhortations, first before the attack: 'There is no retreat from here men! You must die where you stand!' and later, when the Highlanders showed signs of moving forward: 'Ninety-Third! Ninety-Third! Damn all that eagerness.'[20]

In a war that highlighted both the privations of the ordinary soldier, especially in the first winter, and the failings of the high command, Highlanders earned plaudits for their stoicism and confidence in Campbell's leadership. Both on the line of march, where far fewer Highlanders fell out than Guardsmen in the accompanying brigade, and in the camp at Balaclava, Highlanders displayed considerable hardiness and resolve. They endured the miseries of the first winter in which men laboured often up 'to the knee in mud',[21] and sheltered in tents that offered 'poor protection against the piercing cold, the boisterous wind, and driving rain'. They lived off salt beef or pork and hard dry biscuit; many succumbed to dysentery and cholera but the Highland regiments, as Sterling claimed, 'never broke down at all, like so many others . . .'[22] Admittedly, conditions in Balaclava were less severe than those experienced on the heights before Sevastopol and the brigade was spared the carnage of the battle of Inkerman. So, when Highlanders were sent under Sir George Brown to storm Kerch and open the Sea of Azov to allied shipping (May 1855), signs of resentment crept into the correspondence from

Crimea. As Lieutenant-Colonel Charles Lygon Cocks (Coldstream Guards) observed:

> I am glad that the Highlanders have at last done something as the army were beginning to throw stones at them for doing nothing, as from having been here at Balaclava they have nearly escaped the trenches and were not present at Inkerman so that all they have done was at Alma and the 93rd receiving a Charge at Balaclava, though according to the newspapers and common report in England, they have been everywhere & done everything . . .[23]

Captain R. B. Hawley (89th) was equally caustic about the brigade on its return when it was reassigned to support the Sardinians near Kamara. 'They are in a pleasant camp', he wrote, 'on the plain. They did so *much* trench-duty in the winter . . . they deserve such care'.[24]

If this was a foretaste of the enmity that the Highlanders would arouse periodically, it was also testimony to the widespread coverage of their exploits in the field. Some English observers strongly commended Campbell and his Highlanders. William Govett Romaine, the Deputy Judge-Advocate to the Army of the East, and the senior civilian at headquarters, became a close friend of Campbell. He regarded Sir Colin as 'an iron man and a good general', the general most qualified to assume overall command after the resignation of General Sir James Simpson. Romaine had been appalled when the Highland Brigade was removed from Campbell for the Kerch expedition as 'The Highlanders worship him [Campbell] & w[oul]d have fought twice as well under him as under anyone else'; he now feared that Campbell had become the victim of 'abuse' from 'the Guards & their friends' at Court. In the final storming of Sevastopol, where the French succeeded while the British assault failed, Romaine was in no doubt that 'had Sir C. Campbell and his 2000 Highlanders been sent at the Redan they would have marched into it as a body and driven out the defenders like rats'.[25] For their part, the Highlanders acknowledged that they relied upon the leadership skills of Campbell, a veteran commander, who had served in the Peninsular War. They claimed that he possessed a 'true tactical eye' and would not lead them into impossible positions. Sir Colin, who had never commanded Highlanders before the Crimean War, reciprocated this feeling and declared in his farewell address: 'Our native land will never forget the name of the Highland Brigade, and in some future war the nation will call for another one to equal this, which it never can surpass.'[26]

The Indian Mutiny, though, left a more durable legacy. As MacKenzie argues, it 'thoroughly established the iconic significance of the Scottish soldier, and the musical resonance of his bagpipes, in the representations of the military in the nineteenth century'.[27] This derived partially from the sheer enormity and nature of threat posed by the sepoy revolt, partially from the response of the press in Britain, and partially from the manner in which the revolt was suppressed (with Scottish regiments prominent among the ranks of the European and loyal native forces involved). The bloody revolt in Meerut had provoked a widespread orgy of looting, arson and murder of Europeans, with the treacherous Nana Sahib ordering the massacre of seventy-three women and 124 children at Cawnpore and the throwing of naked corpses down a well. The lurid reports from India, exploiting fears of rape of white women, aroused demands for vengeance in Britain, feelings shared by the many soldiers, including Highlanders, who visited the slaughter house in Cawnpore.[28] Eager to take the offensive, most Highland units (if not the 79th initially) assumed the role of assault troops, following up artillery bombardments of enemy defences often with bayonet charges and repeatedly claiming the credit for being the first to breech the enemy's positions.[29] When the 78th Highlanders fought their way into the Residency at Lucknow (25 September 1857), Mrs Harris recalled:

> We had no idea that they were so near . . . when suddenly, just at dark, we heard a very sharp fire of musketry quite close by, and then a tremendous cheering; an instant after, the sound of bagpipes, then soldiers running up the road, our compound and verandah filled with our *deliverers*, and all of us shaking hands frantically and exchanging fervent 'God bless you's [sic]!' with the gallant men and officers of the 78th Highlanders . . . the state of joyful confusion and excitement is beyond all description. The big, rough, bearded soldiers were seizing the little children out of our arms, kissing them with tears rolling down their cheeks and thanking God they had come in time to save them from the fate of those at Cawnpore.[30]

Despite the heroics of the 78th, for which they would earn eight Victoria Crosses, the small column commanded by Sir Henry Havelock could neither raise the siege nor break out of Lucknow. The epic struggle continued with the relief of Lucknow only accomplished on 17 November 1857 by a small army under Sir Colin Campbell's command (whereupon the women, children, sick and wounded were evacuated). Campbell then routed a rebel force at Cawnpore on 6 December but had to raise a much larger army with many more guns before he could capture the city of Lucknow on 21 March 1858. In all these actions Highlanders proved conspicuous, with regiments like the 93rd fighting in feather bonnets and kilts and earning a formidable reputation for hand-to-hand fighting as they led the storming of Sikandarbagh (where some 2,000 sepoys were slain) and penetrated the defences of the Shah Najaf mosque. As Campbell informed W. H. Russell, these troops could 'strike terror' into the enemy.[31] The Highlanders were known to complain that some rebels, usually after a heavy pounding from the guns, showed 'little disposition for fighting'.[32]

Highlanders did not always conform to the heroic, picturesque and triumphant image of their services during the Mutiny. They participated in the extensive looting within Lucknow when Russell described the men as 'literally drunk with plunder'.[33] Some units fought in more serviceable kit and especially in the hot season after Lucknow – ship smocks dyed dark blue and covered hummle bonnets with flaps hanging over the nape of the neck – although many men preferred to retain their feather bonnets.[34] Highland offensives also foundered if poorly led as at the fort of Ruiya (15 April 1858), where Major-General Robert Walpole launched the 42nd, later reinforced by the 4th Punjab Rifles, in a frontal assault without proper reconnaissance. Brigadier Adrian Hope, the revered colonel of the 93rd, was killed and another five officers and 112 men were killed and wounded before the force was withdrawn and the rebels allowed to escape. At the order to retire, Colour-Sergeant Quibell Cooper of the 42nd recalled that 'nothing was heard but loud and deep cursing at him [Walpole]', while the officers of the 42nd and 93rd later told Russell that 'they were afraid of mutiny, or worse, when poor Hope was buried!'[35]

Campbell, who was criticised for his cautious tactics and operational movements in suppressing the mutiny, was determined not to risk his men unnecessarily. Facing a much larger if less well equipped enemy, he relied on artillery and the Enfield rifle, which had a longer range than the sepoy weapons, and tried to avoid street fighting if possible. By careful artillery preparation he sought to maximise the impact of his Highland assault forces: 'The difficulty with these troops', he informed Russell, 'is to keep them back: that's the danger with them. They will get too far forward.'[36] Nevertheless, with reinforcements, he was able to move on Bareilly, the capital of Rohilkand, and defeat the army of Khan Bahadur Khan (5 May 1858) with a Highland Brigade of the 42nd, 79th and 93rd comprising the first line of attack. Thereafter Campbell's Highlanders mounted patrols in pursuit of the rebels in the Ganges valley, while other Highland units (71st, 72nd and 92nd) served in central India. Overall, the Scottish units earned accolades for their extensive duties (the 42nd won eight Victoria Crosses, the 93rd seven), and the 78th, on returning to Scotland, were dubbed the 'saviours of India'. Fêted in the Highlands, the regiment enjoyed banquets in Edinburgh and Hamilton, received campaign medals from Lady Havelock (the widow of their former commander), and, in 1861, had a monument in the form of a runic cross erected on the esplanade of Edinburgh Castle. On 2 April 1872 a memorial tablet to the fallen of the 42nd (the Black Watch) from the regiment's inception to the end of the Indian Mutiny was unveiled in Dunkeld Cathedral.[37]

The values associated with Highland soldiery were bound inextricably with the images generated during and after these two conflicts. As Peter Harrington has shown, the mutiny produced a surge of illustrative material in 1858 – songs, poems, sketches in the illustrated press (based on materials supplied by serving soldiers and amateur artists), illustrated engravings, lithographic works, dioramas of Delhi and Lucknow, public amusements, a dramatic re-enactment of 'The Storming and Capture of Delhi' and numerous porcelains, figurines and penny novels. One of the earliest paintings was *The Campbells are coming: Lucknow, September 1857* by Frederick Goodall (1858), more popularly known as *Jessie's Dream*, which commemorated the arrival of the 78th Highlanders at Lucknow. It depicted Jessie Brown, a corporal's wife, apparently hearing the bagpipes from the approaching force. Despite doubts about its authenticity, this romanticised scene was reproduced in prints, porcelains and poetry. More detailed and accurate paintings would soon appear, notably *The Relief of Lucknow* by Thomas Jones Barker, exhibited in 1859.[38] The latter represented the meeting of three of the most popular commanders of the mutiny, Havelock, Campbell and Sir James Outram, and, as Joan Hichberger argues, Campbell's nonchalant shaking of Outram's hand passed into 'national mythology as an example of British *sangfroid*'.[39]

The imagery associated with the Crimean War and the Mutiny was not confined to the 1850s, but recurred periodically throughout the century with the dedication of memorials, the publication of memoirs, histories including *Invasion of the Crimea* by Alexander Kinglake (1863–7), and later interviews with surviving veterans of the conflicts. The twentieth anniversary of the Crimean War was marked by the highly acclaimed paintings of Elizabeth Thompson, *The Roll Call* (1874) and *Balaclava* (1876).[40] The Scottish painter Robert Gibb followed suit. In *Comrades* (1878) he captured the close personal bonds within Highland regiments by depicting a dying Highlander in the Crimean snow, whispering to his comrade while another watches over the scene. In *The Thin Red Line* (1881) Gibb used the rise and fall of undulating ground to portray the continuous line of the 93rd, isolated at Balaclava. Even if his Russian troopers fell far too close to the line, he captured the look of resolute defiance on the faces of the Highlanders. When unveiled in Edinburgh, the painting received plaudits from both the general public and art critics. *Alma: Forward the 42nd* (1889) did not receive quite so much critical acclaim (it exploited the same use of undulating ground to portray the advancing Highlanders), but it reminded observers of the distinguished deeds of the Highlanders under Campbell's leadership.[41] Even in the late 1890s memories of the Crimean War and the Mutiny would be revived by interviews with the last-surviving veterans of the Thin Red Line.[42]

The martial qualities and values reflected in the reportage and imagery generated by these wars, especially the gallantry, comradeship, resolve, offensive zeal, esprit de corps and good officer/man relations, were not the exclusive preserve of the Highland regiments. Any proficient Lowland, English, Welsh or Irish regiment claimed similar qualities, and, if the opportunity arose, displayed them (as the 4th, 33rd and 45th regiments would do in storming the fortress of Magdala during the Abyssinian campaign of 1867–8, when the sole Scottish unit, the 26th, served on the line of communications).[43] Yet Surgeon William Munro, who served with the 93rd throughout the Crimean War and the Mutiny, maintained that there was more than the normal camaraderie in 'Scotch or Highland regiments':

> In these there was a friendly intimacy between officers and men . . . evidence of esteem and confidence in each other which knew no fear, and was the result not only of long companionship but of a feeling of nationality. In those days . . . Scotch regiments were intensely national . . . the 93rd Sutherland Highlanders, which, on embarkation for India in 1857, out of a strength of one thousand and seventy men, had nine hundred and forty-four Scotchmen in the ranks, and the great majority of these were Gaelic-speaking Highlanders.[44]

The 93rd, though, was hardly representative of all Highland regiments: by 1854, the 42nd was attracting less than 20 per cent of its

Figure 1   The Thin Red Line *(Robert Gibb, reproduced by permission of Diageo on loan to the National Museums of Scotland)*

recruits from the Highlands or its designated recruiting area, and in 1854–5 the 78th found barely 50 per cent of its recruits from Scotland.[45] As H. J. Hanham has shown, Scottish recruiting patterns were undergoing considerable change in mid-Victorian Britain: by 1878 there were only nineteen nominally Scottish regiments, four of them with two battalions each, and of these only the 42nd, 79th and 92nd Highlanders drew over 60 per cent of their officers and men from Scotland. Another four Highland regiments, the 71st, 72nd, 78th and 93rd, drew 40 to 60 per cent of their officers and over 60 per cent of their men from Scotland. Conversely five nominally Scottish regiments (1st, 25th, 73rd, 75th and 99th) found less than 15 per cent of their non-commissioned officers and men from Scotland. The depopulation of much of the eastern and northern Highlands, emigration to North America, competition from better-paid industrial employment and prejudice against military service among the respectable working class in the Lowlands were all taking their toll. 'Scottish recruiting', argues Hanham, 'was clearly unable to keep up with the demand for Scottish soldiers. Highland regiments did better than Lowland regiments, partly because their traditions were stronger.'[46] Broadly this was true but even some Highland regiments, despite their high standing and popular esteem, struggled to find recruits locally: by 1892 Lieutenant-Colonel A. Y. Leslie (Queen's Own Cameron Highlanders) complained that his recruiting district of Inverness-shire was 'miserable in its unproductiveness', and when a second battalion of the regiment was raised in 1897 it was given the whole of Scotland as its recruiting area.[47]

Scottish military participation, nonetheless, extended beyond the regular army with a significant number of Scots serving in the auxiliary forces from the mid-century onwards. Some served in the mounted Yeomanry, a predominantly rural body, which had survived since the Napoleonic Wars (with the Kilsyth troop of the Stirlingshire Yeomanry helping to maintain public order at Bonnymuir near Falkirk in April 1820). Others joined the voluntary Militia, reconstituted after the invasion scare of 1852, and had to complete twenty-one days' training each year. Even more enrolled in the Volunteer movement reconstituted after the invasion panic of 1859, joining the uniformed rifle clubs (and some artillery units) that flourished throughout Scotland. The Volunteers had considerable appeal in the cities and industrial Lowland areas like Lanarkshire, but even Lowland units often contained 'Highland companies', wearing full Highland military costume, or a group of Highland Volunteers. Under the amalgamations of 1881, Militia and Volunteer battalions were attached to the double-battalion infantry regiments in their respective territorial districts.[48]

Another legacy of the Mutiny was the special bond between Sir Colin Campbell and his Highlanders. Campbell, wrote Munro, 'was of their own warlike race, of their own kith and kin, understood their character and feelings . . .' Leading from the front, he had a capacity to rouse or quieten his men 'with a few words, sometimes spoken kindly, but at other times sharply and emphatically'. He lived among his men, knew many of them individually, often addressing them by name, and visited the sick and wounded in hospital frequently. The men of the Highland Brigade had 'such confidence in and affection for him' that 'they would have stood by or followed him though any danger.'[49] Apart from his leadership qualities, the popular version of Campbell's life-story had considerable appeal in contemporary Scotland, chiming with the predominantly meritocratic and anti-aristocratic sentiments. The son of a Glaswegian carpenter, Campbell was relatively poor and cared for his father and unmarried sister for much of his life. His military career advanced slowly despite his bravery as a subaltern in the Peninsular War and distinguished service in China and the Second Anglo-Sikh War. After forty-six years of military service he was only a half-pay colonel when the Crimean War erupted. Within four years he became a full general and a peer of the realm (Baron Clyde of Clydesdale), and four years later a field marshal. A critic of the purchase system, and of the privileges enjoyed by the Guards, he favoured the principle of promotion by merit. When he died in 1863, his grave inscription stated 'by his own deserts' and statues were erected to him in London and Glasgow.[50]

In fact, Campbell, whose family name was Macliver, came from distant gentry stock (his grandfather's estate had been forfeited after the rising of 1745). An uncle paid for his school and military education, with Campbell adopting his uncle's surname when applying for a commission; wealthy friends and relatives helped him to purchase promotions to a majority and a lieutenant-colonelcy. After suffering from criticisms in *The Times* when he was being considered as a possible successor to Lord Raglan as commander-in-chief of the Army in the Crimea, he took Russell into his confidence in India, invited him to dine in the mess and facilitated his reporting in numerous ways (even offering him the use of his horse). This 'co-opting' of the press may have been advised by Sterling, Campbell's staff officer, who felt that the army had badly mishandled its relationship with Russell in the Crimea. The new relationship ensured that Campbell received largely positive reporting from Russell, despite the widespread criticisms of his cautious movements and partiality towards his 'pet' Highlanders.[51] Conscious of his place in history, Lord Clyde commissioned George Jones to paint *Lucknow-evening* and *Cawnpore, the passage of the Ganges at Cawnpore on the 29th and 30th November 1857*. Clyde supervised the artist in executing these works, but died before their completion. Both paintings were displayed in the Royal Academy in 1869 and both depicted Campbell in a prominent position.[52]

In manipulating the media and seeking to preserve his legacy, Campbell set an example that several Victorian generals would follow. In the process he added lustre to the reputation of his Highland soldiers, whose achievements would find reflection in the populist writings of James Grant (1822–87). A prolific novelist with pronounced Jacobite sympathies, Grant has been credited by Hichberger with providing the 'link between Scottish Romanticism, Scottish nationalism and Scottish militarism in the 1850s'.[53] Determined to show the debt that Scotland owed to the Highlands, he wrote numerous novels on military themes, elevating the martial qualities of the primitive Highland soldier, not least his devotion to duty and basic aggression.[54] This veneration of the Highland soldier, particularly the 93rd after Balaclava and later the Gordons after Dargai (see Chapter 6), found reflection on the popular stage and in the music hall. Military spectacles were standard fare on the popular stage, with theatres in Edinburgh and Glasgow staging versions of *The Battle of the Alma* during the Crimean War, while Arthur Lloyd sang a popular song in the music halls of 1878 about a young man seeking to impress a girl by joining the 'Gallant 93rd'.[55]

Highlanders, moreover, provided excellent 'copy' for the rapidly growing number of war correspondents, war-artists and photographers who accompanied the Victorian army on its expeditionary campaigns. They tended to follow Highland units into battle, especially after Winwood Reade of *The Times* 'scooped' his rivals by following the 42nd in the Asante War (see Chapter 2). Melton Prior of the *Illustrated London News* closely followed the tartan thereafter (see Chapters 3, 4 and 5), and when his rival, Frederic Villiers of the *Graphic*, decided to throw in his 'lot' with the 42nd at Tel-el-Kebir, he found that Prior was already following the advance of the Highland Brigade.[56] Several correspondents were proud of their Scottish heritage (notably Bennet Burleigh of the *Daily Telegraph*, Archibald Forbes of the *Daily News* and John Cameron of the *Standard*) but, more importantly, most though not all[57] were intensely patriotic and proud of Britain's military and imperial power. Like many Victorian officers, they embraced fashionable ideas of racial superiority and social Darwinism, and regarded moral and not matériel factors as the ultimate arbiter in battle. They applied this reasoning in accounts of colonial campaigns, where the British often found themselves fighting against superior numbers in unfavourable conditions. Correspondents argued that victory depended less upon superior organisation and weaponry than superior qualities of resilience, courage, morale and, above all, will. They eulogised the warrior ethos of the Victorian soldier, including the Highlander, in gallant assaults and defiant last stands; they described the heroism of Highlanders, their courage under fire, and their readiness to meet a noble death in battle. After Tel-el-Kebir, Villiers described the dead Highlanders as 'resting in easy attitudes on the desert as if in deep slumber shot through the brains'.[58]

Similarly, Highlanders continued to provide excellent material for battle-painters and the popular art market. Lady Butler delighted in making Highlanders the subjects of her paintings: 'these splendid troops', she wrote, were 'so essentially pictorial'.[59] Studio-based artists, such as Butler, Stanley Berkeley, Richard Caton Woodville and Vereker Hamilton, exploited the potential of Highland costume; the kilt added colour, especially when depicting khaki-clad soldiers serving in drab desert or mountainous locations; bagpipes highlighted the Scottish dimension, sometimes providing pivotal points of interest; and lines of kilted Highlanders dramatised motion in battlefield scenes. The kilted Highlander was also an excellent subject in poignant scenes of departure for active service, juxtaposed with anxious wives and children.[60] Kestner, though, possibly errs in claiming that Butler used her 'Celtic soldiers as paradigms of valiant masculinity to reinforce conceptions of white superiority' as Butler rarely painted scenes of conflict (in her *Rorke's Drift* she confined the Zulus to a shaded side of the painting other than 'one salient figure grasping a soldier's bayonet to twist it off the rifle, as was done by many of those heroic savages').[61] Most artists were less reticent than Butler and relished painting dramatic scenes of conflict, with prints and engravings based on their works, like those of Butler, adorning messes, clubs, schools and institutes. When coupled with the multitude of images in the rapidly expanding illustrated press, and derivative works in numerous forms including school textbooks and cigarette cards, popular art helped to define the image of warfare for Victorian Britain.[62]

Like other soldiers, Highlanders co-operated with the war-artists, photographers, correspondents and battle-painters at home. They often helped artists and correspondents in the field, providing them with drinks, transport and information; and they certainly appreciated those who fought alongside them (as Burleigh did when the square broke at the battle of Tamai).[63] Highlanders provided sketches and photographs from the front, particularly from the more remote campaigns on the North-West Frontier and the Sudan, where Lieutenant Angus McNeill (Seaforth Highlanders) and Corporal John Farquharson (Seaforth Highlanders) provided notable sketches.[64] Highland soldiers also served as models for battle-painters and advised on the details of uniform and the specific incidents in famous battles. Sometimes the painter exploited fortuitous local postings (like Butler, when she painted the Cameron Highlanders who were quartered at Parkhurst, near Ventnor), but on other occasions the artist sought and received more specialised support (notably Gibb, in obtaining the advice of Sir Arthur Halkett in painting the charge in *Alma: Forward the 42nd* and in using veterans of the 93rd in painting *The Thin Red Line*). The painter Allan Stewart knew Colonel Andrew Wauchope (Black Watch), who arranged for Stewart to observe a Highland regiment charging.[65]

Complementing the legacy of the Mutiny and these enduring visual images were the letters of soldiers on active service in Scottish regiments. Some of these letters were written for metropolitan or provincial newspapers, either pre-commissioned before particular campaigns or, during the South African War, sent for inclusion in 'Letters from the Front' columns. The vast majority, though, were sent to family and friends and then passed on by the recipients, with or without their author's consent, to the press. As uncensored, eye-witness accounts reflecting many (if by no means all) the feelings and concerns of regimental officers and men, they had an immediate appeal for newspaper editors. They were often promoted as letters of 'interest' on account of their personal insights, colour, detail and sometimes criticism that rarely appeared in official dispatches. If written by local soldiers, they were printed under headlines such as 'A Pitlochry Soldier's Baptism of Fire' or were published for local interest (after Tel-el-Kebir, a Scottish Royal Marine was able to pass on through his family in Stirling that nine specific rankers were safe, three from the 42nd, three from the 72nd, two from the 74th and one from the 79th).[66] More substantively, the letters represented first-hand commentary upon the challenges of colonial campaigning – the adaptation to new, exotic environments, the difficulties of moving across inhospitable terrain often in extremes of climate, and the demands of engaging more numerous adversaries, operating in their own localities. The letters gave insights, too, into how the Scottish battalions responded to their imperial commitments, serving in larger formations alongside English units or native auxiliaries and discharging their responsibilities in protracted operations. Above all, they recorded first-hand impressions of combat experience – the supreme test of the Highland warrior ethos – with graphic descriptions of assaults on fortified positions, of fighting in defensive squares (or sometimes in sieges and heroic last stands), and of hand-to-hand fighting with claymore or bayonet. These reflections in the wake of battle – whether exultation in the euphoria of victory or remorse at the loss of revered commanders and comrades in arms or, occasionally, bitter recriminations after humiliating defeat – all testified to the emotions stimulated by imperial service.

Although the volume of published correspondence was remarkable, particularly after notable triumphs or during lengthy campaigns, it represented the thoughts of only a minority of officers and men.[67] Some letters were published in their entirety but many were edited or abridged for publication. They bypassed the censors, who only reviewed copy from the war correspondents from the 1880s onwards, but they had a degree of self-censorship, with soldiers tending to avoid swear words in print or refraining from any mention of sexual liaisons in writing to friends and family. If they had to ask a literate friend to write these messages, they may also have been reticent in how they expressed themselves in public. Finally, all letters from the front reflected the limited perspectives of the regimental soldiers; they were often inexact in estimates of enemy numbers, distances travelled, casualties incurred or the duration of events.[68] In spite of all these limitations, and the tendency of many letters to arrive after the reports of 'special' correspondents or official dispatches, they had a personal quality that recipients, newspapers (and probably the newspaper-reading public) readily appreciated. The reflections of serving soldiers in Scottish units conveyed the feelings of men as they responded to immense physical and psychological challenges; they demonstrated that regimental cohesion, discipline and esprit de corps – factors inextricably connected with their warrior ethos – could be employed impressively in imperial missions.

Notes

1 R. J. Finlay, *A Partnership for Good? Scottish Politics and the Union Since 1880* (Edinburgh: John Donald Publishers, 1995), p. 27.

2 J. M. MacKenzie, 'Essay and Reflection: On Scotland and the Empire', *International History Review*, XV, no. 4 (1993), pp. 714–39 and 'Empire and National Identities: The Case of Scotland', *Transactions of the Royal Historical Society*, 6th ser., VIII (1998), pp. 215–31. On the popularity of imperialism in late nineteenth-century Scotland, see R. J. Finlay, 'The rise and fall of popular imperialism in Scotland, 1850–1950', *Scottish Geographical Magazine*, 113, no. 1 (1997), pp. 13–21.

3 E. M. Spiers, 'Campaigning under Kitchener', in E. M. Spiers (ed.), *Sudan: The Reconquest Reappraised* (London: Frank Cass, 1998), pp. 54–81 and 'The Scottish Soldier in the Boer War' in J. Gooch (ed.), *The Boer War: Direction, Experience and Image* (London: Frank Cass, 2000), pp. 152–65 and 273–7.

4 F. Emery, *Marching Over Africa: Letters from Victorian Soldiers* (London: Hodder & Stoughton, 1986) and E. M. Spiers, *The Victorian soldier in Africa* (Manchester: Manchester University Press, 2004).

5 L. Gordon-Duff, *With the Gordon Highlanders to the Boer War & Beyond* (Staplehurst: Spellmount, 2000); P. J. R. Mileham, *Fighting Highlanders!: The History of the Argyll & Sutherland Highlanders* (London: Arms and Armour Press, 1993); D. M. Henderson, *Highland Soldier 1820–1920* (Edinburgh: John Donald Publishers, 1989).

6 S. Wood, *The Scottish Soldier* (Manchester: Archive Publications, 1987); S. Allan and A. Carswell, *The Thin Red Line: War, Empire and Visions of Scotland* (Edinburgh: National Museums of Scotland Enterprises Limited, 2004).

7 J. M. MacKenzie, Introduction to *Popular Imperialism and the Military, 1850–1950* (Manchester: Manchester University Press, 1992), p. 20 and *passim*.

8 J. Prebble, *Mutiny: Highland Regiments in Revolt 1743–1804* (London: Penguin, 1975), pp. 496–501.

9 Ibid., p. 279; 'The Highland Regiments and Their Traditions', *Dundee Courier & Argus*, 26 March 1884, p. 4; Henderson, *Highland Soldier*, pp. 4–5, 306; Lieutenant-Colonel A. Fairrie, *'Cuidich 'N Righ': A History of the Queen's Own Highlanders (Seaforths and Camerons)*, (Inverness: Regimental HQ Queen's Own Highlanders, 1983), p. 25; H. Trevor-Roper, 'The Invention of Tradition: The Highland Tradition of Scotland', in E. Hobsbawn and T. Ranger (eds), *The Invention of Tradition* (Cambridge: Cambridge University Press, 1983), pp. 15–41; C. Withers, 'The Historical Creation of the Scottish Highlands', in I. Donnachie and C. Whately (eds), *The Manufacture of Scottish History* (Edinburgh: Polygon, 1992), pp. 143–56.

10 O. MacDonagh, *Early Victorian Government 1830–1870* (London: Weidenfeld & Nicolson, 1977), p. 9.

11 J. A. Kestner, 'The colonized in the colonies: representation of Celts in Victorian battle painting', in S. West (ed.), *The Victorians and Race* (Aldershot: Solar Press, 1996), pp. 112–27. For a major study of the Scots in imperial activity, see M. Fry, *The Scottish Empire* (East Linton: Tuckwell Press, 2001).

12 George Douglas Campbell, 8th Duke of Argyll, *Scotland as it was and as it is*, 2 vols (Edinburgh: David Douglas, 1887), 2, p. 166; Finlay, *A Partnership for Good?*, pp. 21–5.

13 Henderson, *Highland Soldier*, pp. 7–8 and 306; Fairrie, *'Cuidich 'N Righ'*, p. 7.

14 Allan and Carswell, *Thin Red Line*, pp. 28–9.

15 S. A. Tooley, *The Personal Life of Queen Victoria* (London: Hodder & Stoughton, 1896), pp. 3–4; C. Erickson, *Her Little Majesty: The Life of Queen Victoria* (London: Robson Books, 2004), pp. 130–2, 138; Queen Victoria's journal, 12 November 1854, quoted in M. Charlot, *Victoria, The Young Queen* (Oxford: Basil Blackwell, 1991), p. 352.

16 D. Duff (ed.), *Queen Victoria's Highland Journals* (Exeter: Webb & Bower, 1980), journal entries for 6 September and 3 October 1842, pp. 25 and 47.

17 Ibid., journal entries for 16 August 1872 and 19 October 1899, pp. 161, 223–4; 'The Seaforth Highlanders', *Highland News*, 7 October 1899, p. 2; Fairrie, *'Cuidich 'N Righ'*, p. 34.

18 Argyll and Sutherland Highlanders (ASH) Museum, N-B93.MOL, Private D. Cameron, diary transcribed by T. Moles (August 1986).

19 Lieutenant-Colonel A. Sterling, *The Highland Brigade in the Crimea* (Minneapolis: Absinthe Press, 1995), pp. 41 and 45.

20 'The War in the Crimea', *The Times*, 14 November 1854, p. 7; Sterling, *Highland Brigade*, p. 63; A. Forbes, *Colin Campbell, Lord Clyde* (London: Macmillan, 1895), p. 98; Lieutenant-Colonel P. Groves, *History of the 93rd Sutherland Highlanders now the 2nd Battalion Princess Louise's Argyll and Sutherland Highlanders* (Edinburgh: W. & A. Johnston, 1895), p. 22; ASH Museum, N-B93.MOL, Cameron diary and N-C93.STO, E. Stotherd to Dick and to his parents, 27 October and 1 November 1854, and N-C93.GRE, diary of Private George Greig (no. 2787) 93rd Highlanders, pp. 6–7; I. Fletcher and N. Ishchenko, *The Crimean War: A Clash of Empires* (Staplehurst: Spellmount, 2004), pp. 167–9.

21 ASH Museum, N-C93.H, Private Robert H., letter, 13 November 1854.

22 Surgeon-General W. Munro, *Reminiscences of Military Service with the 93rd Sutherland Highlanders* (London: Hurst & Blackett, 1883), p. 47; compare Sterling, *Highland Brigade*, p. 215 with Major C. Robins (ed.), *The Murder of a Regiment: Winter Sketches from the Crimea 1854–1855 by an Officer of the 46th Foot (South Devonshire Regiment)* (Bowden: Withycut House, 1994).

23 National Army Museum (NAM) Acc. No. 1988-06-29-2, Lieutenant-Colonel C. Lygon Cocks Mss., Lt-Col. C. Lygon Cocks to aunt, 27 May 1855; A. Massie, *The National Army Museum Book of the Crimean War: The Untold Stories* (London: Sidgwick & Jackson, 2004), p. 191; Major C. Robins (ed.), *Romaine's Crimean War: The Letters and Journal of William Govett Romaine* (Stroud, Gloucestershire: Sutton Publishing for the Army Records Society, 2005), p. 56.

24 Capt. R. B. Hawley to his father, 31 August 1855, in S. G. P. Ward (ed.), *The Hawley Letters: The Letters of Captain R. B. Hawley, 89th from the Crimea, December 1854 to August 1856* (Society for Army Historical Research), Special Publication No. 10 (1970), p. 79.

25 Robins (ed.), *Romaine's Crimean War*, pp. 185, 199, 204, 212, 234, 245.

26 ASH Museum, N-C93.GRA, 'Reminiscences of Charlie Gray Carlisle Express One of the Thin Red Line', and N-C93.TAY, Sergeant James Taylor, 93rd Sutherland Highlanders, diary, 9 May 1856; Sterling, *Highland Brigade*, p. 45; Forbes, *Colin Campbell*, p. 107.

27 J. M. MacKenzie, 'Heroic myths of empire', in MacKenzie (ed.) *Popular Imperialism*, p. 116.

28 S. David, *The Indian Mutiny* (London: Penguin, 2003), pp. 220–2, 254–8; W. Forbes-Mitchell, *Reminiscences of the Great Mutiny 1857–9* (London: Macmillan, 1893), pp. 16–19; Major H. Davidson, *History and Service of the 78th Highlanders (Ross-Shire Buffs) 1793–1881*,

2 vols (Edinburgh: W. & A. K. Johnston, 1901), 1, p. 193; Black Watch Regimental Archive (BWRA), 0421, Private A. W. McIntosh, diary, p. 134; Lieutenant-Colonel W. Gordon-Alexander, *Recollections of a Highland Subaltern* (London: Edward Arnold, 1898), pp. 35–7; Captain D. Wimberley, *Some Account of the Part taken by the 79th Regiment or Cameron Highlanders in the Indian Mutiny Campaign in 1858* (Inverness: private, 1891), p. 9.

29 For Delhi, see Gordon Highlanders (GH) Museum, PB 1657, 'The Assault of Delhi' (1857) transcribed from the diaries of Lieutenant-General R. Barter (75th Regiment), p. 3, and for Sikandarbagh, see Gordon-Alexander, *Recollections*, pp. 86, 91 and Forbes-Mitchell, *Reminiscences*, p. 64; on the 79th, see Wimberley, *Some Account*, pp. 23 and 26.

30 Mrs G. Harris, *A Lady's Diary of the Siege of Lucknow* (London: John Murray, 1858), pp. 119–20.

31 W. H. Russell, *My Diary in India, in the Year 1858–9*, 2 vols (London: Routledge, Warne & Routledge, 1860), 1, p. 311; see also ASH Museum, N-C93.WIS, Lieutenant-General S. Wiseman Clarke, 'A short personal narrative of the doings of the 93rd, Sutherland Highlanders from 1857 to 1st March 1859' (London: 1898), pp. 31–41; N-C93.GRE, Greig, diary, pp. 15–16; N-C.93. TAY, Taylor, diary, 16 November 1857.

32 ASH Museum, N-C93. TAY, Taylor, diary, 5 May 1858; Russell, *My Diary*, 1, p. 296.

33 Russell, *My Diary*, 1, p. 330; Wimberley, *Some Account*, pp. 35, 41.

34 Wimberley, *Some Account*, p. 42.

35 BWRA, NRA 0212, Sergeant Quibell Cooper, diary, p. 27; Russell, *My Diary*, 1, p. 393; Forbes-Mitchell, *Reminiscences*, p. 246: David, *Indian Mutiny*, p. 348; C. Hibbert, *The Great Mutiny India 1857* (London: Allen Lane, 1978), pp. 369–70.

36 Russell, *My Diary*, 1, pp. 211, 394; Gordon-Alexander, *Recollections*, p. 307.

37 Fairrie, *'Cuidich 'N Righ'*, p. 23; J. Cromb, *The Highland Brigade: Its Battles and its Heroes* (London: J. Shiells, 1896), frontispiece and p. 235.

38 P. Harrington, *British Artists and War: The Face of Battle in Paintings and Prints, 1700–1914* (London: Greenhill Books, 1993), pp. 162–5, 170–1, 184n.9. If the bulk of the Jessie Brown anecdote is probably spurious, Mrs Harris at least confirmed the sound of the bagpipes, see *A Lady's Diary*, p. 119.

39 J. W. M. Hichberger, *Images of the Army: The Military in British Art, 1815–1914* (Manchester: Manchester University Press, 1988), p. 61; Hibbert, *Great Mutiny*, p. 345.

40 P. Usherwood and J. Spencer-Smith, *Lady Butler: Battle Artist 1846–1933* (London: National Army Museum, 1987), pp. 28–36.

41 P. Harrington, 'The Man Who Painted THE THIN RED LINE', *Scots Magazine*, 130, 6 (1989), pp. 587–95.

42 'A Hero of the "Thin Red Line" ', *Aberdeen Journal*, 27 January 1898, p. 4; 'Balaclava Veteran in Belfast', *Belfast News-Letter*, 29 March 1898, p. 5; ASH Museum, N-C93.GRA, 'Reminiscences of Charlie Gray'.

43 The 26th (Cameronian) Rifles only arrived at Zula on 31 March 1868, never participated in the march to Magdala, and remained on the line of communications until 10 May when it began to withdraw. It earned a battle honour without any casualties. S. H. F. Johnston, *The History of the Cameronians (Scottish Rifles) 26th and 90th*, 2 vols (Aldershot: Gale & Polden, 1957), 1, p. 261.

44 Munro, *Reminiscences*, pp. 201–2.

45 E. and A. Linklater, *The Black Watch: The History of the Royal Highland Regiment* (London: Barrie & Jenkins, 1977), p. 227; Davidson, *History and Services of the 78th Highlanders*, 2, p. 168.

46 H. J. Hanham, 'Religion and Nationality in the Mid-Victorian Army', in M. R. D. Foot (ed.), *War and Society: Historical Essays in Honour and Memory of J. R. Western 1928–1971* (London: Paul Elek, 1973), pp. 159–81.

47 Lieutenant-Colonel A. Y. Leslie, q. 12,256 in evidence before PP, *Report of the Committee on the Terms and Conditions of Service in the Army*, C. 6582 (1892), XIX, pp. 416–18; E. M. Spiers, *The Late Victorian Army 1868–1902* (Manchester: Manchester University Press, 1992), p. 127; Fairrie, *'Cuidich 'N Righ'*, p. 51.

48 Henderson, *Highland Soldier*, pp. 30–1; Allan and Carswell, *Thin Red Line*, pp. 34–5, 65–6; see also Major-General J. M. Grierson, *Records of the Scottish Volunteer Force 1859–1908* (Edinburgh: Blackwood, 1909), pp. 4–5, 234–5; P. J. R. Mileham, *The Yeomanry Regiments: A Pictorial History* (Tunbridge Wells: Spellmount, 1985), p. 16.

49 Munro, *Reminiscences*, p. 37; see also Russell, *My Diary*, 2, p. 328.

50 Sterling, *Highland Brigade*, pp. 49–50; Russell, *My Diary*, 2, p. 22; L. Shadwell, *The life of Colin Campbell*, 2 vols (1881), 2, p. 478; Sir C. Campbell, q. 3,377 in PP, *Report of the Commission appointed to inquire into the system of purchase and sale of Commissions in the Army, with evidence and appendix*, C. 2267 (1857 Sess. 2), XVIII, p. 190; Massie, *NAM Book on the Crimean War*, pp. 213–14.

51 Sterling, *Highland Brigade*, pp. 178–9, 185; Russell, *My Diary*, 1, pp. 170–3, 177, 196–8, 380, 394; Field Marshal Lord Roberts, *Forty-One Years in India*, 2 vols (London: Richard Bentley & Son, 1897), 1, p. 383; *Oxford Dictionary of National Biography*, 9 (2004), pp. 754–7.

52 Harrington, *British Artists*, pp. 174–5.

53 Hichberger, *Images of the army*, p. 108.

54 Ibid.

55 B. Findlay (ed.), *A History of the Scottish Theatre* (Edinburgh: Polygon,

1998), pp. 172, 188–9; D. Russell, ' "We carved our way to glory" The British soldier in music hall song and sketch, c. 1880–1914', in MacKenzie (ed.), *Popular Imperialism*, p. 60.

56 F. Villiers, *Villiers: His Five Decades of Adventure*, 2 vols (London: Hutchinson, 1921), 1, p. 266; M. Prior, *Campaigns of a War Correspondent* (London: Edward Arnold, 1912), pp. 174–6; P. Johnson, *Front Line Artists* (London: Cassell, 1978), p. 121.

57 Arthur Aylward, employed by the *Daily Telegraph*, was a fervent Irish nationalist, with well-known anti-British feelings, R. Wilkinson-Latham, *From Our Special Correspondent: Victorian War Correspondents and Their Campaigns* (London: Hodder & Stoughton, 1979), p. 161.

58 Villiers, *Villiers*, 1, p. 270; on war correspondents and artists generally, see R. T. Stearn, 'War and the Media in the 19th Century: Victorian Military Artists and the Image of War, 1870–1914', *Royal United Services Institute Journal of Defence Studies*, 131, no. 3 (1986), pp. 55–62, 'G. W. Steevens and the message of empire', *Journal of Imperial and Commonwealth History*, 17 (1989), pp. 210–31, and 'War correspondents and colonial war, c. 1870–1900', in MacKenzie (ed.), *Popular Imperialism*, pp. 139–61.

59 E. Butler, *An Autobiography* (London: Constable, 1922), p. 99.

60 'Summoned for Active Service', *Graphic*, 11 June 1879, pp. 32–3.

61 Kestner, 'The colonized in the colonies', p. 117, see also pp. 113, 121, 125; Butler, *An Autobiography*, pp. 187–8.

62 J. O. Springhall, ' "Up Guards and at them!" British Imperialism and Popular Art, 1880–1914', in J. M. MacKenzie (ed.), *Imperialism and Popular Culture* (Manchester: Manchester University Press, 1986), pp. 49–72; R. T. Stearn, 'Richard Caton Woodville, 1856–1927', *Soldiers of the Queen*, 97 (1999), pp. 14–27; Harrington, *British Artists and War*, chs 9 and 11.

63 R. T. Stearn, 'Bennet Burleigh Victorian War Correspondent', *Soldiers of the Queen*, 65 (1991), pp. 5–10; Prior, *Campaigns of a War Correspondent*, pp. 188–9, 196, 304; W. Reade, *Story of the Ashantee Campaign* (London: Smith, Elder & Co., 1874), p. 312.

64 GH Museum, PB 75 'Extracts from Arbuthnott S. Dunbar's letters during the Afghan Campaign 1879', 29 January 1879, p. 6; P. Harrington, 'Images and Perceptions: Visualising the Sudan Campaign' in Spiers (ed.), *Sudan: The Reconquest Reappraised*, pp. 82–101; W. Trousdale (ed.), *War in Afghanistan,1879–80: The Personal Diary of Major-General Sir Charles Metcalfe MacGregor* (Detroit: Wayne State University Press, 1985), p. 103n.100.

65 Butler, *An Autobiography*, p. 99; ASH Museum, N-B93.PEA, 'Some Quotes about Robert Gibb (1845–1932) & THE THIN RED LINE'; Harrington, 'The Man Who Painted THE THIN RED LINE', p. 593, and *British Artists and War*, p. 246.

66 'A Pitlochry Soldier's Baptism of Fire', *Perth Constitutional & Journal*, 8 January 1900, p. 8; 'Letter from a Son of the Rock', *Stirling Observer*, 28 September 1882, p. 4.

67 On the literacy of the rank and file, see A. R. Skelley, *The Victorian Army at Home: The Recruitment and Terms and Conditions of the British Regular, 1859–1899* (London: Croom Helm, 1977), pp. 86–90.

68 Spiers, *Victorian soldier*, pp. 9–12, 180.

2

THE BLACK WATCH IN WEST AFRICA

_෧_

In the late nineteenth century the Asante War (1873–4) provided the first opportunity for a Scottish battalion, specifically the 42nd Highlanders (later the 1st Battalion, the Black Watch), to engage in front-line fighting in Africa. The Asante (pronounced Ashanti) had invaded the Gold Coast in 1873, an area over which Britain had exercised an informal protectorate since the 1830s. As two previous British expeditions to the Gold Coast had suffered serious losses, the Colonial Office resolved not to send another British expedition to a region infamously known as 'the white man's grave'. Initially it had hoped that a composite force of local troops, some Royal Marines and the 2nd West India Regiment could control the invaders, but the continuing reports from the panic-stricken authorities at Cape Coast Castle prompted a reluctant change of policy.[1] On 13 August 1873 Sir Garnet Wolseley was appointed as Governor and Commander-in-Chief of the Gold Coast and was dispatched to the protectorate with twenty-seven special-service officers. He was instructed to raise a force from the local Fante tribes to defeat the Asante and secure a peace treaty with the _Asantehene_ (King Kofi Karikari), and only as a last resort to call for British regiments. On his arrival in October, Wolseley found that the Asante army, already weakened by hunger, dysentery and smallpox, was retiring to its own territory beyond the River Pra. Convinced that the Asante had to be punished for their aggression and British honour restored, Wolseley pressed the Fantes unsuccessfully to join a punitive expedition 'to march victorious on the Ashantee [sic] capital'. Dubbing the Fantes as 'less warlike and more peaceful than formerly', he promptly requested the dispatch of British forces. Wolseley promised to use the two months that would elapse before their arrival to build a road through the tropical rainforest to the Pra, and to employ British forces thereafter for no more than 'about six weeks, or at the most two months'.[2] On 17 November 1873 Gladstone's cabinet authorised the dispatch of three battalions. These would include the 2nd Battalion, Rifle

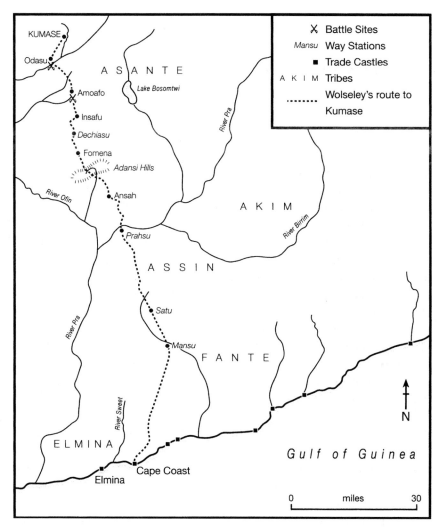

Map 1   Asante War, 1873–4

Brigade, the 23rd Fusiliers (the Royal Welch Fusiliers) and the 42nd Highlanders.

Despite the hesitations of the Liberal government, interest in the unfolding crisis grew steadily. Several newspapers, both British and American, sent their correspondents to West Africa or engaged the services of staff officers, or in the case of Reuters employed a leading merchant at Cape Coast. Winwood Reade of *The Times* possibly exaggerated when he claimed that 'Never perhaps has there been a war so fully reported for the press'[3] but the degree of interest stretched beyond the metropolis to include leading provincial papers, notably the *Manchester Guardian, Scotsman* and the *Western Morning News*. Even some smaller provincial newspapers, like the *Crieff Journal, Kinross-shire Advertiser* and the *Fifeshire Journal* – all associated with the traditional recruiting areas of the Black Watch – followed the campaign intently. They published diaries and letters from soldiers of the 42nd, first-hand accounts of their exploits, and interviews with soldiers on their return.

In fact, most accounts appeared after the end of hostilities because the campaign proved remarkably short (the 42nd left Portsmouth on 4 January and returned on 23 March) and the communications slow. As Wolseley monopolised the flow of news initially (by sending his own dispatches back on an empty steamer to Gibraltar), his early reports, commenting on the retreat of the Asante forces and the offers of peace from the *Asantehene*, led the unwary to expect that this 'little war' would come to 'a very quiet termination'.[4] Editors, who had hitherto been more concerned about the general election of February 1874 and the reports of Dr Livingstone's death, were 'startled' when the news arrived in late February of 'severely-contested' battles, involving heavy losses for Wolseley's small army. Some thought that Wolseley had suffered a 'disastrous triumph', or that the 42nd had incurred a 'deadly loss' before fuller accounts appeared, chronicling the triumph of Wolseley in capturing Kumase at minimal cost (both in men and resources).[5] If the shock aroused interest in the war, the later reports lauded the 'gallantry' of the 42nd Highlanders, especially as they had undertaken 'the heaviest part of the fighting' during the decisive battle of Amoafo.[6] None of these commentators, though, had emulated Winwood Reade and followed the Highlanders in the firing line,[7] so newspapers readily printed letters and diaries from soldiers of the 42nd describing their campaign experience.

Newspapers had already reported on the rapturous send-off of the Highlanders when they set sail from Portsmouth on the Clyde-built steamship *Sarmatian*. As the battalion had been based in Portsmouth before its departure, friends and family were among the huge crowds that cheered the 42nd from different parts of the harbour. Prince Arthur also came out in a launch to Spithead to witness the departure. The spectators were not simply cheering the 42nd, as the latter had left its bandsmen (but not its pipers) and all 'non-efficients' behind. To produce a fighting strength of nearly 700, it had accepted 130 volunteers from the 79th (Cameron) Highlanders, mainly long-service men, with two of their own officers. These volunteers, as a

Black Watch non-commissioned officer (NCO) noted in his diary, were a 'very nice body of men . . . anxious to fall into our way of doing things'.[8]

The subsequent voyage, as described by a military correspondent, was a distinctively Scottish experience. The crew was Scots, the piping pervasive, and the food included porridge, 'the staple food for breakfast, and [in subsequent meals] hotchpotch [a mutton broth with vegetables], mince collops, and other delicacies common to the country north of the Tweed'. The first Sunday service, he added, was 'not likely to be forgotten by any of us'. The Reverend G. Kirkwood, Presbyterian chaplain to the 42nd, told his congregation on the quarterdeck that 'Scotland had never been ashamed of any of her sons in their many combats in every quarter of the world, and he was sure she would not have occasion to do so now. Then he drew the picture of the good fight . . . and the everlasting reward attached to victory.' With the service barely finished, the Channel squadron of six ironclads hove in view. They advanced in two lines, allowing the *Sarmatian* to pass between them, with bands playing 'The Campbells are coming', 'The girl I left behind me' and 'Cheer boys cheer'.[9] If the voyage had the occasional incident – on 13 December, Private E. Black received twenty-five lashes for threatening to throw a sergeant overboard – the weather was generally mild, soldiers listened to lectures from Reverend Kirkwood on the Gold Coast and tried out their 'drab', grey clothing (but appreciated the right to wear a small red patch on their helmets in place of the red hackle).[10] Overall, Private Robert Ferguson described it as 'a grand voyage to the Gold Coast', but found that the 'weariest and dullest days of it' soon followed the arrival off Cape Coast (17 December), whereupon the ship remained at sea for another fortnight.[11]

Wolseley's plans had been disrupted by the dilatoriness of the Asante withdrawal and the delays in constructing a path through the tropical rainforest (over seventy-four miles from Cape Coast to Prahsu, with eight camp sites, two hospitals and 237 bridges). Both he and his officers blamed the native forces for their failure to harry the enemy effectively and the native labourers for their laziness and tendency to desert.[12] 'Even the enemy's retreat', argued Wolseley, 'cannot instil courage into these faint-hearted natives . . . they had to be driven into action, and after a success they became a panic-stricken and disorderly rabble'. The best of the tribesmen, the Hausa and Kossus, wasted ammunition, proved difficult to control and shied away from bush fighting.[13] All this had a direct bearing on the fate of the 42nd Highlanders as Wolseley had originally planned to keep them in reserve, cruising offshore but always within reach. By 18 December he decided that two British battalions, the 1st and 2nd West India Regiments, a Naval Brigade, and two regiments of native levies under Lieutenant-Colonel H. Evelyn Wood and Major Baker Russell would not suffice. He now resolved:

> when so splendid a battalion as the 42nd is ready to my hand, when I see the martial spirit which animates both officers and men, when I think of the vastly superior numbers of the enemy and see myself entirely deprived of the large force of native auxiliaries upon which I had counted, when I remember how vitally important it is that the campaign should be short and decisive, I do not think that I should be acting wisely in keeping the 42nd Regiment at sea . . .

The 1st West India Regiment would be sacrificed as the 'very nature of their material [must] be inferior to a Regiment with such traditions and in so fine a state of discipline as Her Majesty's 42nd Highlanders'.[14]

Wolseley's confidence would be matched by the eagerness of the Highlanders to get ashore and engage the enemy. H. Morton Stanley, the renowned explorer who served as war correspondent for the *New York Herald*, interviewed several of their officers as they arrived. 'They are mostly all young men of very good families', he wrote, 'with cream-coloured complexions, light hair and whiskers . . . they appear to be so very much alike'. All expressed concern about whether or not they could survive the climate and prevent the onset of fever: one had plans to deter the mosquito, another to rely on a daily intake of quinine and a third to eschew all liquors. The stewards of the *Sarmatian*, added Stanley, had complained that the officers had drunk nothing but lemonade during the voyage.[15]

Once ashore, the Highlanders received their short Snider rifles and sword bayonets and began a series of early morning marches. On 4 January they marched from Cape Coast for some seven miles along a hilly and undulating road, prompting an NCO to note in his diary:

> Very thick bush both in the hollows and on the rising ground. A great variety of trees; many I have never seen before. Many pretty birds and but- terflies. Crows are black and white. The women dress much the same as the men, and look strange with the protuberance above the hips; they wear chignons with handkerchief over it.[16]

The Highlanders were impressed, too, by the camp sites prepared by the Royal Engineers, which included large huts, each accommo- dating some eighty 'white troops', with frames of bamboo, a roof and walls of plantain leaves, and round the inside walls raised sleeping benches.[17] On the second day, as recalled by another Highlander,[18] they marched into the rainforest:

> The trees – palms, tamarinds, bamboos, gum, teak, cotton wood, etc. – are generally very tall (200 to 250 feet) meeting, in most places, overhead. Beneath is a dense growth of ferns, trailing plants, and rank vegetation. Here and there are pools of stagnant water, and occasional running streams. The atmosphere is thick and vapoury, and in many places moisture is constantly dripping from the trees. Except where the ground has been cleared for camps and villages, the sun never penetrates, and at midday, in the forest, there is only the deep gloom of twilight.
>
> On each side of the path the undergrowth is so thick that nothing can be seen beyond a few yards. There is a deathlike stillness, and only seldom is there heard a sound of life – the cry of a wild bird or animal. Here and there – generally a little off the highway – were the ruins of devastated villages, bearing silent witness to the vindictive cruelty of the Ashantees. There is a ghastly weirdness about the place, which exercises a peculiar influence on the mind.[19]

By 7 January the 42nd reached Camp Mansu, about halfway to the River Pra. Although three soldiers were already in the hospital with fever, the battalion had to remain there for nearly a week because the transport had broken down. The problem, as an NCO realised, was the 'great scarcity of carriers', and hence the inability to move sufficient stores up to the front, leaving 'several hundreds of natives' at Mansu, 'both men and women doing nothing'.[20] With the telegraph linked as far as Mansu, the 42nd knew of Wolseley's predicament at Cape Coast (where he would re-embark most of the 23rd and the Royal Artillery detachment, use men of the West India battalions as temporary bearers and later allow only a detachment of Fusiliers to accompany the expedition). Accordingly, on 11 January the 42nd called for volunteers to carry stores up to the next station for an extra shilling a day and an issue of grog. Undertaken on the following day, this movement of supplies earned a glowing tribute in a letter to *The Times* (reproduced in the Scottish press):

> 135 men of the gallant 42nd, under the command of Captain Moore, volunteered to carry stores . . . the men took the 50 lb. boxes of rice on their heads and shoulders, and with this unaccustomed burden in such a climate marched the 11 miles in good style, returning to their camp at Mansu the same evening. Every one knows how the 42nd can fight . . . but I think that they deserve as much credit for the above unpleasant and arduous labour under an African sun as for the more honourable and congenial duty of fighting.[21]

Fortunately the 42nd were spared further exertions once Wolseley overhauled the transport arrangements and managed to restore the forward movement of supplies. Apart from one officer and forty-two men retained to guard the line of communications, all of whom were reportedly 'very sorry at being left behind',[22] the Highlanders resumed their march on 18 January. They were now marching under the command of Major Duncan Macpherson as Lieutenant-Colonel John McLeod, their commanding officer whom Wolseley highly respected,[23] had been sent ahead to command the advanced guard. Soldiers struggled in the heat and humidity. By the third day the Highlanders had 'About a dozen men in hospital with fever and lots complaining. Two men [were] left sick.' Even when they reached the large camp site at Prahsu on the River Pra (21 January), which they entered at 8.15 a.m. with pipes playing to a lively reception from the Riflemen and sailors of the Naval Brigade, about forty men were 'complaining' but were 'afraid of being left behind and say they are better than they really are'. Malaria, though, had taken its toll of the advance units: the Highlanders met 'a good number of sick coming down country – mostly seamen and riflemen; many of them look very bad'.[24]

On the following day the 42nd left twenty-three men in hospital and crossed the Pra, 'a river nearly as large as the Tay at Perth', using a bridge erected by the engineers and 'set on piles of wood'. They passed several largely deserted Asante villages where 'The houses are cleaner, better built, and the roof [sic] better thatched than those on the Fantee side.' They marched along a rudimentary path north of the Pra, and used more basic camp sites (no longer resting in huts but under 'palm leaves spread on poles').[25] They crossed the Adansi Hills: 'The view from the top – 600 feet above the plain, 1,500 feet above the sea – was extensive, but monotonous – an undulating expanse of trees, surmounted by a heavy pall of mist. Here we halted for a short time to enjoy the fresh, invigorating air.'[26]

Descending from the summit they reached the large, deserted village of Dechiasu on 26 January, where they rested briefly with the headquarters and detachment of the 23rd Fusiliers. Captain Henry Brackenbury, Wolseley's assistant military secretary, observed that the 'appearance of the 42nd was most admirable; and the 23rd though not looking so strong, were reported to be in good health'.[27] Several Highlanders met the German missionary, his wife and child, whom the *Asantehene* had released as a goodwill gesture, and heard their tales of mistreatment during many years of captivity in Kumase. Motivated by these accounts, Scots were delighted to learn that the peace emissaries had failed to agree terms with Wolseley: 'I hear', wrote the NCO, 'that King Coffee [sic] is going to dispute our entry into Coomassie [sic], and of course everybody is in great glee . . . Everyone', he asserted, was 'anxious to get pushed on ahead and get the matter over.'[28]

By 28 January Wolseley, having accumulated sufficient supplies, was able to make his final plans for battle. McLeod's patrol had already skirmished with its Asante counterparts, and scouts had brought intelligence that the enemy was massing in their thousands near the village of Amoafo, with the aim of blocking the approach to Kumase. Deployed in a horseshoe formation, they manned a ridge above a mud-filled ravine into which the only path descended and then ascended on the slope beyond. Wolseley, who had 2,200 soldiers at his disposal, decided upon a frontal assault, while trying to protect his flanks and to prevent the enemy from surrounding his army. He improvised tactically (which was often a necessity in colonial warfare) and planned to advance in a hollow square, with the 42nd Highlanders forming the front face. They were to extend for 300 yards on either side of the path which would be used by the artillery, manned by Hausa gunners, under Captain A. J. Rait. The Rifles were to form the rear face while the left was to include 100 sailors and Russell's native regiment and the right face another 100 sailors and Wood's native regiment. The headquarters, medical service, ammunition limbers and the tactical reserve of Fusiliers were to march within the square. Engineers and their labourers were to hack paths parallel to the main path to open routes for the square's sides. The heavy baggage and sick were to be left at Insafu, just forward of Dechiasu, and under guard lest the Asante infiltrate the line of communications.[29]

The 42nd, under the command of Brigadier Sir Archibald Alison, a one-armed veteran of the Crimean War and Indian Mutiny, would bear the brunt of the ensuing combat. At about 7.40 a.m. on 31 January, with pipers playing 'Hey, Johnnie Cope, are ye waking yet?', five companies descended into the ravine to meet a ferocious fire from the Asantes. Private Ferguson recalled:

This was a trying way for us, young soldiers, to get under fire. The Ashantees [sic] were swarming in advance on our flanks in thousands, and I almost felt my time was up, and that I was to be potted like a rabbit in cover . . . We were fighting in sections, every man in his place, and doing his best. Seldom we got a right shot at a black fellow, they kept so well under cover, but they did keep popping at us! And so close it was too! They were generally armed with old flint firelocks, and loaded with pieces of ragged lead, rusty iron and stones. Had they been better armed more of us would have fallen . . . In such circumstances, we kept on firing and advancing as best we were able . . . most of our men were getting wounded, but only a few were going to the rear . . . When we had a moment to speak and look at each other we would glance along the files to see who were hit and if any were down. Such is the way we had to fight in the bush; it was all against us, and if a couple of big guns had not been brought to our assistance I doubt we would have fared worse.[30]

However graphic Ferguson's description (and partly on this account widely reported in local Scottish newspapers),[31] it was perforce limited in perspective. It said nothing about the disruption of Wolseley's square formation in the bush, and the friendly-fire incidents between a section of the 42nd and part of the Naval Brigade,[32] nor did it convey fully the extent of the fighting – some four hours for the 42nd to take the village of Amoafo, followed by periods of fierce fighting throughout the afternoon as Wolseley's forces repelled counter-attacks along their line of communications.[33] Of the special correspondents, only Winwood Reade of *The Times* followed the firing line and his report added to the accolades heaped on the 'gallant 42nd'. He described how they had advanced slowly 'moving from tree to tree as directed by their officers and lying down to shoot' (thereby contradicting Melton Prior's fanciful sketch of the 42nd firing erect, shoulder to shoulder, in the *Illustrated London News*).[34] Reade reckoned that the 42nd had lost two killed and nine officers and 105 men wounded, but the majority of these wounds, as Dr Troup, the regimental surgeon, confirmed, were 'slight'. After the subsequent advance through a series of ambushes, and another sharp engagement at the village of Odasu, the 42nd led the final assault on Kumase (4 February). Troup described how 'we advanced with the pipes playing, the men shooting everything before them, and cheering along the whole line'; Ferguson described how 'we entered Coomassie in the grey darking [sic], our pipers in front of the column playing the "Highland Laddie". We gave three cheers for old Scotland after all was over.'[35]

These proved the last deeds of combat as Wolseley waited in vain for the *Asantehene* to sign a treaty before burning Kumase (6 February), and then retreating to the coast as rapidly as possible (to minimise the mounting toll of sick). By 8 February they had returned to Amoafo, where Troup recalled:

We have had the brunt of the whole thing, and the regiment has behaved splendidly. I am proud to have served in the field with it, and to have earned my second medal in its company . . . I have been six days lying in the open, and two days drenched with rain; had to cross a river naked with my clothes over my head, and to sleep without a change. It is all over now and we scarcely avoid a laugh occasionally.[36]

In reflecting on the war, soldiers of the 42nd praised the 'undaunted courage and good fighting properties' of the Asante,[37] thereby confirming the impression that Wolseley's army had overcome formidable odds, both in battle and in moving through the tropical rainforest. They recalled their reception in Kumase, where local women found water for the conquering soldiers: as a sergeant affirmed, 'they could not have been kinder to us if it had been Edinburgh'.[38] Required to uphold Wolseley's ban on looting, they had little patience with their Fante auxiliaries: 'our black fellows', claimed Ferguson, 'were always stealing, and we had often to lash them for their lazy ways'.[39] If such sentiments accorded with perceptions of the 'white man's burden', the burning of Kumase seemed vindicated by the revelations of Asante practices. Like the correspondents who dispatched vivid accounts and sketches of these deeds, Dr Troup declared: 'I have seen many sickening sights. Life is nothing here. Slaves are victimised right and left, and are thrown into large pits. One of these I visited, and there were bodies in hundreds, and all along the road the same way.'[40]

All these letters amplified preconceptions expressed in many metropolitan and Scottish newspapers. If editors applauded the command and judgement of Wolseley, and recognised the value of superior military skill and equipment (both the Sniders and the 7-pounder guns employed in support), they still focused on the achievements of the 42nd. They knew that the Highlanders had suffered heavy casualties – far heavier casualties than those incurred by any other unit – and surmised that the 42nd had been 'in the thickest of the fight'.[41] They assumed, too, that the 42nd had faced 'terrible odds', and had prevailed primarily on account of their moral qualities – spirit, valour and courage, 'all their old gallantry'. As the *Stirling Observer* asserted, 'The 42nd Highlanders have anew covered themselves with glory.'[42] Hence newspapers, both at the time and subsequently, published firsthand accounts of the war and reported extensively on the return of the 42nd.

The staggered return of the ships to Portsmouth compounded this focus on a single battalion. The correspondents who flocked to the port were impressed by the immense display of flags, bunting, banners and garlands of flowers. On the pediment over the Quay Gate Arch was a garter inscribed with the motto of the 42nd, 'Nemo Me Impune Lacessit', and below which was an Anglicised version of 'Freiceadan Dubh' (Gaelic for Black Watch). Above the entrance to the George Hotel 'were the figures 42, formed with variegated lamps, and the letters B. W. formed in a similar manner . . . on either side', and in a printer's window was the sign:

> We greet ye with Welcome,
>   English, Irish and Scotch,
> But a special glad Welcome,
>   To our gallant Black Watch.[43]

Scottish correspondents were delighted by this effusive welcome for the 42nd, a welcome in numbers and excitement that far exceeded the previous welcome for the Welch Fusiliers. As the *Huntly Express* reported, this was partly because the 42nd were returning to their pre-war quarters in Clarence Barracks but partly because the bulk of the Fusiliers had been 'thwarted in their desire to engage the enemy, [while] the 42nd had been in the front of every fight, from the Prah to Coomassie'.[44] Even the units looked different: whereas the Fusiliers seemed 'dispirited by their stay on shipboard . . . and looked a squad of poor washed-out broken-down convalescents', the Black Watch appeared in 'full fighting condition' – 'brawny and bronzed and brighteyed', looking ready, as one of their officers declared , 'to start for Coomassie again tomorrow'. Their differing uniforms magnified the contrast as the 42nd, unlike the 23rd, had packed their undress uniform on board ship and so dispensed with their 'measly-looking Ashantee uniform at Spithead, and sailed into Portsmouth harbour in the bright scarlet uniform and tartan trews'.[45]

As family and friends greeted the returning soldiers on board, a sergeant of the 42nd gave a splendidly nonchalant interview to the awaiting correspondents. When asked about his injuries at Amoafo, he replied:

> I got hit twice – once in the neck here, and then in the breast, and thought it was worse than it really was when I saw blood streaming over my grey coat. Did I fall out? No, sir, I didn't. Lieutenant Mundy [sic, probably Mowbray] got a severe wound on the head close by, and as it didn't seem to occur to him that there was any need to fall I stuck by him in the front.[46]

There was extensive coverage of the subsequent parade when the 42nd, preceded by their kilted band and the five pipers from the war, marched through the streets of Portsmouth to the Governor's Green for a reception by Lord Templetown (commanding-in-chief, southern

Figure 2 'Highlanders March Past the Queen' (Illustrated London News, 11 April 1874)

district) and the municipal authorities. 'If the Fusiliers', opined the *Scotsman*, 'had their thousands of spectators, the Black Watch had their tens of thousands, and it was generally agreed that never even in the days of the Crimean War had Portsmouth presented such a sight as to-day.'[47] Further reviews followed: on the next day by the Duke of Cambridge, the commander-in-chief, and, on 30 March, by Queen Victoria when she reviewed all the military forces from the Asante War at Windsor Park (where it was announced that Lance-Sergeant Samuel McGraw, who was on the sick list of the 42nd, would receive the Victoria Cross). The *Illustrated London News* depicted both the return of soldiers in Portsmouth and the Windsor review by focusing on the 42nd, first in their trews and later in their kilts as they marched past the queen.[48]

The royal patronage, following the ecstatic welcome in Portsmouth, capped the public acclaim for the 42nd Highlanders. Their achievements were seen as emblematic of Scotland in several respects. As one of the older Scottish regiments, and in the view of some writers, 'the most popular of the Scottish regiments', they had not only added to their roll of distinguished service but had done so identifying with their 'dear old land, whose name was on their lips when they marched in triumph' into Kumase.[49] Despite the absence of the kilt, they had remained culturally distinctive, with their pipers playing throughout the war and in the post-war parades. Notwithstanding reports that the pipes had barely been heard during battle in the forest, the *Huntly Express* insisted that the five pipers, 'marching with swinging gait at the head of their companies in the African jungle . . . scared the Ashantees with the unwonted sound of the bagpipe'.[50]

As important, at least in some quarters, was the role of the 42nd in bringing about the success of a campaign launched by the previous Liberal government. After the electoral victory of the Conservatives, some Scottish Liberals found solace in Wolseley's triumph. While the *Scotsman* repudiated criticism of the campaign and rejected sneers about the quality of the Asantes as military foes, the *Stirling Observer* reaffirmed that if peace could be secured with the *Asantehene*, trade with the hinterland could follow and then it would be 'our duty' to try to 'induce the Ashantees to give up their slave-holding and human-sacrificing habits'.[51] In short, hopes invested in this short campaign were consistent with an emerging Liberal-imperial credo, and certainly the reception accorded the 42nd was a harbinger of the passions that future campaigns would arouse.

For many Scots, though, the achievements of the 42nd were simply a matter of national pride. As a letter-writer to the *Falkirk Herald* asked, 'breathes there a Scotchman whose pulse does not beat full and strong when he reads of the doings of our gallant 42D?'[52] Whether the writer realised it or not, the reference to 'reading' was highly perceptive. Although Melton Prior of the *Illustrated London News* composed sketches of the campaign reflecting the 42nd prominently, and Wolseley allowed these sketches to be sent with the official dispatches,[53] the Asante War, fought in a tropical undergrowth with men dressed in a drab grey kit, hardly lent itself to memorable paintings and prints. Nor were many artifacts brought home: gold and valuables were gathered by prize agents before Kumase was burned, and looting occurred despite the ban, but there were limits on what could be carried and loot had to be smuggled past guards on the River Pra.[54] So the printed medium predominated and, despite a spate of histories written later in the year by special correspondents and Wolseley's staff officers, interest in the war waned fairly quickly. The conflict had ended with a draft treaty and partial indemnity but without composing relations between the Asante state and its coastal neighbours.[55]

Nevertheless, the 42nd had earned further renown at home, south of the border, and wherever accounts of the war were read. In an unusually small army, it had proved all too conspicuous, prompting Stanley's invidious comparison in the *New York Herald* (reprinted in the Scottish press) that 'the conduct of all other white regiments . . . pales before that of the 42d'.[56] Like other units, the 42nd had adapted to tropical conditions, but had seized the opportunity of serving in the firing line to bear the brunt of a frontal assault and fight with distinction within the depths of the bush, a profoundly alien environment. In these circumstances eyewitness testimony had an immediate appeal, whether correspondents praising the achievements of the 42nd or soldiers chronicling their impressions of an exotic land and recounting their arduous experiences. Scots could take pride not only in the success of the 42nd but also in the recognition of that success by the exuberant crowds in Portsmouth and the royal review. Finally, they knew that these achievements derived from the confidence of Wolseley in the fighting capacity of the 42nd. Soon to be known as 'our only general', Wolseley observed that 'Nothing could have exceeded the admirable conduct of the 42nd Highlanders [during the battle of Amoafo], on whom fell the hardest share of the work.'[57] The triumph of the 42nd was all too clear.

Notes

1 W. D. McIntyre, 'British Policy in West Africa: The Ashanti Expedition of 1873–4', *Historical Journal*, V, no. 1 (1962), pp. 19–46.

2 The National Archives (TNA), Public Record Office (PRO), WO 33/26, Major-General Sir G. J. Wolseley to War Office, 13 October 1873; see also A. Lloyd, *The Drums of Kumasi* (London: Longmans, 1964), pp. 67–8, 79–81, and McIntyre, 'British Policy in West Africa', p. 35.

3 Winwood Reade, *Story of the Ashantee Campaign*, p. 134. Several journalists accompanied the Abyssinian campaign of 1868, D. Bates, *The Abyssinian Difficulty* (Oxford: Oxford University Press, 1979), pp. 102–3.

4 'The Ashantee War', *Aberdeen Journal*, 25 February 1874, p. 8; on Wolseley's use of the communications, see Wilkinson-Latham, *From Our Special Correspondent*, p. 126.

5 *Stirling Observer and Midland Counties Express*, 5 March 1874, p. 4; *Falkirk Herald*, 28 February 1874, p. 2; *Perthshire Advertiser*, 4 March 1874, p. 2; *Glasgow Herald*, 26 and 27 February 1874, pp. 4 and 4.

6 *[Dundee] Weekly News*, 7 March 1874, p. 4. The Scottish newspapers reprinted reports from the metropolitan newspapers, particularly the *Daily News*, 'The Battle of Amoaful', *Scotsman*, 28 February 1874, p. 7, and 'The Ashantee War. Interesting Account of the Battle of Amoaful. Gallant Conduct of the 42D Highlanders', *Montrose, Arbroath and Brechin Review*, 6 March 1874, p. 2. For another report in the English

press, see 'Burning of Coomassie', *Western Morning News*, 9 March 1874, p. 3.

7 While the correspondent of the *Daily News* admitted that he could only comment on 'the result' of the battle, the *Scotsman*'s correspondent conceded that he had 'witnessed but a limited part of what I have attempted to describe', *Scotsman*, 28 February and 5 March 1874, pp. 7 and 5; Reade, *Story of the Ashantee Campaign*, p. 306.

8 'The Ashantee War. Diary of a Non-Commissioned Officer of the 42D Regiment', *Kinross-shire Advertiser*, 28 March 1874, p. 2; see also 'The Black Watch. Twenty-Two Years' Experience in the 42nd Highlanders', ch. 2, *[York] Evening Press*, 7 November 1895, p. 2.

9 'At Sea with the Forty-Second Regiment', *Fifeshire Journal*, 29 January 1874, p. 7.

10 'The Ashantee War. Diary of a Non-Commissioned Officer', p. 2.

11 'A Stirlingshire Soldier's Account of the War', *Stirling Observer*, 2 April 1874, p. 6.

12 TNA, PRO, WO 33/26, Wolseley to War Office, 15 December 1873; see also 'Ashantee War. Extract From A Letter From Lieut. H. Jekyll, R. E.', *The Royal Engineers Journal [REJ]*, 4 (2 March 1874), pp. 15–16.

13 Parliamentary Papers (PP), Wolseley to the Secretary of State for War, 9 November 1873, *Further Correspondence respecting the Ashantee Invasion*, No. 4, C. 893 (1874), XLVI, p. 20; see also I. Harvie, 'The Raid on Essaman, 14 October 1873: An Account by Lieutenant Edward Woodgate of an Operation during Wolseley's Ashanti Expedition', *Journal of the Society for Army Historical Research [JSAHR]*, 77 (1999), pp. 19–27.

14 TNA, PRO, WO 33/26, Wolseley to War Office, 18 December 1873; see also H. Kochanski, *Sir Garnet Wolseley: Victorian Hero* (London: The Hambledon Press, 1999), p. 65.

15 H. M. Stanley, *Coomassie and Magdala: The Story of Two British Campaigns in Africa* (London: Sampson Low, 1874), pp. 103–4.

16 'The Ashantee War. Diary of a Non-Commissioned Officer of the 42D Regiment', *Kinross-shire Advertiser*, 4 April 1874, pp. 2–3.

17 Ibid., p. 2; 'The Black Watch. Twenty-Two Years' Experience in the 42D Highlanders', ch. 4, *[York] Evening Press*, 11 November 1895, p. 2.

18 The author gives his name as 'C.M. Archibald' but this is almost certainly a pseudonym as there was no such name listed in the regiment's medal book for this campaign or the campaigns of the 1880s. Nevertheless, his memoir which is printed in twenty-five issues of the York *Evening Press* seems authentic in many particulars, and at the very least adds to the perception of the local newspaper-reading public about the trials, tribulations and triumphs of the Black Watch in Africa.

19 'The Black Watch. Twenty-Two Years' Experience in the 42D Highlanders', ch. 3, *[York] Evening Press*, 8 November 1895, p. 2. Although

this quotation retains the original text, the paragraphs have been realigned.

20 'The Ashantee War. Diary', 4 April 1874, p. 2.

21 Ibid.; 'The 42d Regiment', *The Times*, 9 March 1874, p. 7; 'Pluck of the 42D Highlanders', *The Edinburgh Evening News*, 11 March 1874, p. 3; A. Lloyd, *Drums of Kumasi*, pp. 95–6.

22 'The Ashantee War. Diary', 4 April 1874, p. 2.

23 Field Marshal Viscount Wolseley, *The Story of a Soldier's Life*, 2 vols (London: Constable, 1903), 2, p. 313.

24 'The Ashantee War. Diary', 4 April 1874, p. 2; 'The Black Watch: Twenty-Two Years' Experience', ch. 4.

25 'The Ashantee War. Diary', 4 April 1874, p. 2.

26 'The Black Watch. Twenty-Two Years' Experience', ch. 5, *[York] Evening Press*, 12 November 1895, p. 2.

27 Captain H. Brackenbury, *The Ashanti War: A Narrative*, 2 vols (Edinburgh: Blackwood, 1874), 2, p. 146.

28 'The Ashantee War. Diary', 4 April 1874, p. 2.

29 *Morning Advertiser*, 28 February 1874, p. 5; see also J. Keegan, 'The Ashanti Campaign', in B. Bond (ed.), *Victorian Military Campaigns* (London: Hutchinson, 1967), pp. 163–98.

30 'A Stirlingshire Soldier's Account of the War', p. 6; see also 'The Black Watch. Twenty-Two Years' Experience', ch. 5.

31 Printed in the *Stirling Observer*, it was twice reprinted in the *Falkirk Herald*, 4 and 9 April 1874, pp. 3 and 4.

32 'The Services of the Naval Brigade', *Hampshire Telegraph and Sussex Chronicle*, 28 March 1874, p. 8; Brackenbury, *Ashanti War*, 2, pp. 171–2.

33 'A Stirlingshire Soldier's Account of the War', p. 6; TNA, PRO, WO 33/26, Wolseley to War Office, 1 February 1874; Brackenbury, *Ashanti War*, 2, p. 179.

34 'The Ashantee War', *The Times*, 17 March 1874, p. 11; 'The Ashantee War: The 42nd Highlanders in the Front', *Illustrated London News*, 21 March 1874, p. 268; Reade, *Story of the Ashantee Campaign*, pp. 312–13, 317–19; Brackenbury, *Ashanti War*, 2, p. 183.

35 'The Ashantee War', p. 11; 'Letter from a Surgeon of the 42nd', *Yorkshire Telegraph*, 28 March 1874, p. 3; 'A Stirlingshire Soldier's Account of the War', p. 6; see also BWRA, 0080, Sir A. Alison in 'Record of Service of the 42nd Royal Highland Regiment', p. 14.

36 'Letter from a Surgeon of the 42nd', p. 3.

37 'The Ashantee War – Letters from Officers', *Grimsby News*, 13 March 1874, p. 3.

38 'Reception of the 42nd Highlanders', *Crieff Journal*, 27 March 1874, p. 4.

39 'A Stirlingshire Soldier's Account of the War', p. 6.

40 'Letter from a Surgeon of the 42nd', p. 3; see also Melton Prior, 'Sketches from Coomassie: the King's slaughtering place', *Illustrated London News*, 25 April 1874, pp. 388–9.

41 *Stirling Observer*, 5 and 12 March 1874, pp. 4 and 4; *Falkirk Herald*, 28 February 1874, p. 2; and *Glasgow Herald*, 11 March 1874, p. 4. See also 'The Ashantee War', *Aberdeen Journal*, 18 March 1874, p. 8, and Brackenbury, *The Ashanti War*, 2, p. 183.

42 *Falkirk Herald*, 28 February 1874, p. 2; *Stirling Observer*, 12 March 1874, p. 4.

43 'Reception of Troops from the Gold Coast', *Hampshire Telegraph and Sussex Chronicle*, 21 March 1874, p. 7.

44 'Arrival of the Black Watch', *Huntly Express*, 28 March 1874, p. 7.

45 Ibid.; 'The Ashantee Expedition. Reception of 42D Highlanders', *Scotsman*, 24 March 1874, p. 5.

46 'The Ashantee Expedition. Reception of the 42D Highlanders', p. 5.

47 Ibid.

48 'Reception of the 42nd Highlanders', p. 4; 'Review of the Ashantee Troops by the Queen', *Montrose, Arbroath and Brechin Review*, 3 April 1874, p. 2; 'The Return of the Troops from Ashantee: The Black Watch', 'The Review at Windsor' and 'Review at Windsor of the Troops from the Ashantee War: the 42nd Highlanders Marching Past the Queen', *Illustrated London News*, 4 and 11 April 1874, pp. 317, 335, 337.

49 *Stirling Observer*, 12 March 1874, p. 4, and *Falkirk Herald*, 28 February 1874, p. 2.

50 'Arrival of the Black Watch', p. 7; on doubts about the audibility of the pipes, see 'The return from Coomassie', *Western Morning News*, 24 March 1874, p. 3, and Reade, *Story of the Ashantee Campaign*, p. 311.

51 *Scotsman*, 27 February and 7 March 1874, pp. 4 and 5; *Stirling Observer*, 12 March 1874, p. 4.

52 *Falkirk Herald*, 12 March 1874, p. 5.

53 Prior, *Campaigns of a War Correspondent*, p. 27.

54 Ibid., pp. 24–5, 28–9; Wolseley, *Story of a Soldier's Life*, 2, p. 363; 'Coffee Calcalee's Umbrella', *Illustrated London News*, 21 March 1874, p. 278.

55 Keegan, 'The Ashanti Campaign 1873–4', in Bond (ed.), *Victorian Military Campaigns*, pp. 195–6.

56 'H. M. Stanley's Testimony to the Valour of the 42D', *Montrose, Arbroath and Brechin Review*, 10 April 1874, p. 2.

57 TNA, PRO, WO 33/26, Wolseley to the War Office, 1 February 1874.

3

IMPERIAL TESTS: ZULUS, AFGHANS AND BOERS

ᴄᴧ

From November 1878 over the next twenty-eight months British forces fought three major colonial campaigns against the Zulus, Afghans
and Boers, suffering serious defeats in each conflict (at Isandlwana,
Maiwand and Majuba). The wars derived from the 'forward' imperial
policies of the Conservative government of Benjamin Disraeli, later the
Earl of Beaconsfield – policies intended to stifle the indirect threat to
India from Russian influence in Afghanistan, and to compose the ten-
sions between the Boer republics, the British colonies and the independent native states in southern Africa. Lord Carnarvon, the Colonial
Secretary, had sought to bring all the African regimes together under a
British confederation: Natal agreed reluctantly in 1875 and the bank-
rupt Transvaal succumbed in April 1877 but, with this annexation,
Britain became embroiled in the border dispute between the Transvaal
and the Zulus. Impulsive 'men on the spot', Lord Lytton, the Viceroy
in India, and Sir Bartle Frere, the High Commissioner for southern
Africa, then precipitated the Afghan and Zulu wars. Lytton, alarmed
by reports of a Russian mission to Kabul, gained the approval of a
divided cabinet before sending Sher Ali, the Amir of Afghanistan, an
ultimatum on 2 November 1878. Frere acted on his own initiative at a
meeting with the envoys of the Zulu king Cetshwayo (11 December
1878) when he demanded that the Zulus disband their military system
within thirty days or take the consequences.[1] The ensuing wars, like the
Anglo-Transvaal War (1880–1), proved immensely controversial, not
least in Scotland where Liberalism held sway (in forty-one of the sixty
seats after the 1874 elections) and jingoism was purportedly less preva-
lent than south of the border.[2] The Scottish press, nonetheless, chronicled the exploits of the Scottish regiments in all three campaigns and
reprinted letters from soldiers at the front. The latter described the
rigours of campaigning across inhospitable terrain and in extremes of
climate, the feelings of serving on the line of march, in camps and
battles, and their impressions of native peoples, who either assisted or
contested their imperial missions.

THE ANGLO-ZULU WAR (1879)

Although the Afghan and Zulu wars erupted within two months of each other, the conflict with the Zulus attracted far less interest initially. This reflected partly the relative importance attached to the defence of Britain's imperial rights on the North-West Frontier, partly the matter of timing (as the metropolitan press had already sent special correspondents to India), but partly the overconfidence born of an easy victory in the Ninth Cape Frontier War (1877–8). Melton Prior of the *Illustrated London News* and his rival artist, Charles E. Fripp of the *Graphic*, had accompanied the 90th (Perthshire) Light Infantry when it was sent to reinforce the forces already fighting the Xhosa. They arrived after the two significant actions of the war had occurred – both defeats for the Xhosa – and had little to report beyond skirmishing and 'desultory warfare against widely-scattered bands of troublesome foes'.[3] Accordingly, when Frere's ultimatum expired on 11 January 1879 and three British columns crossed into Zululand, only Charles L. Norris-Newman of the *Standard* and the *Natal Times* accompanied the invading force. He attached himself to the Central Column under Colonel Richard Glyn, with the overall commander of the British forces, Lord Chelmsford, in attendance. As a consequence, the first reports of the annihilation of the 1st Battalion, 24th Foot at Isandlwana (22 January) and the heroic defence of Rorke's Drift (22/23 January) arrived in London via Chelmsford's dispatch and the report of Norris-Newman on 11 February 1879.[4]

These reports prompted the cabinet to send reinforcements and galvanised interest in the war. Despite the many criticisms of Chelmsford and Frere, there was widespread acceptance that British prestige had to be retrieved after so many soldiers had fought and died 'with desperate courage and bravery . . . We must carry [the war] through', intoned the *Glasgow News*, but even this standard bearer of Conservatism in Scotland expressed only grudging support for a war being fought 'for territory' which was never likely 'to be of much use', and on behalf of 'peculiarly ungrateful' colonists in Natal.[5] Just as the metropolitan newspapers now sent special correspondents and artists to the front, Scottish newspapers followed suit, with the *Ayr Advertiser*, *Glasgow News* and the *Bridge of Allan Reporter* commissioning reports from officers in the 2nd Battalion, 21st (Royal Scots) Fusiliers and the 91st Argyllshire Highlanders respectively. In fact, both the *Glasgow News* and the *Bridge of Allan Reporter* published lengthy extracts from the letters and diaries of Captain W.

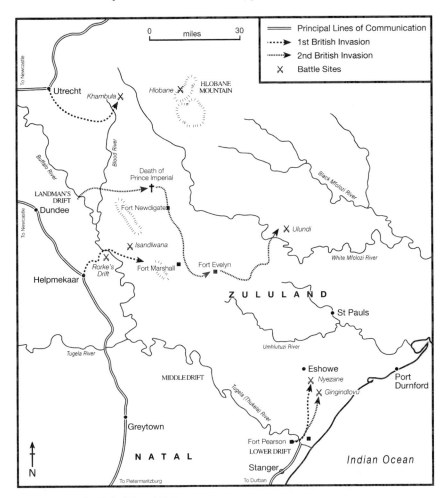

Map 2 *Anglo-Zulu War, 1879*

Prevost (91st).[6] Although Scottish units had not fought in the first battles, and the testimony of individual Scots who survived Isandlwana or fought at Rorke's Drift only appeared later,[7] the Scottish press reported the enthusiastic scenes at Southampton, with huge crowds urging the 91st, as it boarded the *Pretoria* on 19 February, to 'Avenge the 24th'. Local observers praised the appearance of the 91st – 900-strong without a single deserter – when it left Aldershot, and the *Illustrated London News* included two major illustrations of their departure (one on the front page), whereupon Prior, following the tartan, sent sketches of their arrival at Durban and their departure for the front.[8]

Notwithstanding the hopes invested in these reinforcements, Chelmsford's predicament remained acute. Having lost wagons, tents, rifles, guns, ammunition and considerable equipment at Isandlwana, he had withdrawn his depleted column to the other side of the Natal border. Another column under Colonel C. K. Pearson had also encountered stiff resistance in the south of Zululand; it had occupied an abandoned mission at Eshowe, which it fortified and held under siege for a couple of months. Only the third column under Colonel H. Evelyn Wood, VC, remained active in the north, mounting a series of aggressive patrols to harry the Zulus. Of the two infantry regiments under Wood's command, one was his own 90th Light Infantry. The regiment, as a Crieff soldier claimed, 'were in good fighting trim . . . we are old warriors (for this is our second war) and are used to fighting darkies'. Having skirmished with the enemy on several occasions 'and beat them every time', he was not dismayed by the news of Isandlwana.[9] Such bravado was soon put to the test when a patrol of mounted infantry found themselves trapped on Hlobane mountain top, and, in a desperate retreat, fifteen officers and seventy-nine men were killed. On the following morning (29 March) Private John Graham from Ayr recalled that we were 'all lamenting our loss', when word came that an entire Zulu army was approaching their camp at Khambula. Unlike Isandlwana this camp, holding 2,086 officers and men, was well located on a ridge with a redoubt and wagon laagers protecting the men and oxen. As the 'three black masses' approached, possibly in excess of 20,000 Zulus, Graham described how 'We let them come pretty close, and then every man opened fire on them, and six big guns sent shell amongst them, which made them scatter.' For four hours the battle raged, with some Zulus briefly penetrating the cattle kraal before they were driven off by two companies of the 90th under Major Robert Hackett (who would be blinded in the battle). Disciplined, concentrated fire power prevailed, whereupon the Zulus began to retire, pursued by mounted infantry and artillery salvoes. 'They were clean done up', wrote Graham, 'and some of them threw down their arms and cried for mercy; but I don't think there was any shown on our side.'[10]

Wood, like the defenders of Rorke's Drift, had followed traditional Boer tactics in countering the Zulus when the latter enjoyed numerical superiority and manoeuvred adroitly on the battlefield. Wood's forces killed some 3,000 warriors while losing eighteen NCOs and men killed outright and a further ten from the eight officers and fifty-seven NCOs and men wounded.[11] Another utterly lop-sided result followed at Gingindlovu (2 April 1879), when some 12,000 Zulus attacked the Eshowe relief force (3,390 whites and 2,280 blacks), then encamped in another wagon laager with an entrenchment and parapet. The 91st comprised part of this force, commanded by Lord Chelmsford. Once again the disciplined fire power of the Martini Henry rifles, supported by Gatling machine guns and rockets, took their toll (473 bodies, according to Prevost, were found within 1,000 yards radius of the laager).[12] Within an hour and a half, the Zulus withdrew, pursued by mounted infantry and native auxiliaries (leaving the corpses of several hundred Zulus along the line of retreat). It was another crushing victory, with Chelmsford losing only two officers and eleven men killed and four officers and forty-four men wounded. 'Our men stood it well', wrote a colour-sergeant of the 91st, but 'Nothing in the world could stand our fire. Really the fight was splendid in one way; yet very hard to see our fellow-creatures sent to eternity.'[13] The Highlanders praised their enemy; Prevost acknowledged 'some fine men' among the dead, and Lieutenant (later Captain) William R. H. Crauford commended the bravery and skirmishing of the Zulus: 'we all admire very much the way they advanced to the attack . . .'[14]

Although Chelmsford's column relieved Eshowe, the Scots had had scant opportunity to distinguish themselves. The 91st had served alongside the 57th, six companies of the 3rd Battalion, 60th Rifles, five companies of the 99th and two companies of the Buffs, a Naval Brigade including 'as cheery a lot of men – some very young – as anyone would care to command' and two battalions of the Natal Native Contingent, who were 'wonderfully gifted in field movements'.[15] But the Highlanders, as Crauford complained, had 'done hardly anything in the way of fighting in the open . . .'[16] Nor did the fighting from laagers and entrenchments lend itself to memorable depiction. There were sketches of Gingindlovu in the *Illustrated London News*, but these were based on originals from army and naval officers as Melton Prior never witnessed the battle. Having had a premonition of impending death, he sent a private artist, named Porter, in his place, and Porter was one of the first to be killed. The great paintings of war would focus on the heroism of Rorke's Drift and the 'last stand' at Isandlwana, notably the two paintings of *Rorke's Drift* by Alphonse de Neuville in 1879 and by Elizabeth Butler in 1880 and *The Battle of Isandhlwana* (1885) by Charles Fripp.[17] Scottish newspapers accepted that massive fire power, exploiting the defensive advantages of square formations, had thwarted the bravery of the Zulus: 'At Ginghilovo [sic]', wrote the *Perthshire Advertiser*, 'our Martini-Henrys swept away the Zulus like a broom.'[18]

Frustration with the later course and character of the war persisted. When two divisions undertook the second invasion of Zululand, the 91st served under Major-General Henry H. Crealock in the 1st Division, while the 21st served under Chelmsford in the 2nd Division, which would be joined by Wood's renamed 'Flying Column' (containing the 90th Light Infantry). From both divisions Scottish officers bemoaned the difficulties and slowness of the ox-drawn transportation moving across the trackless hills of Zululand to the north and the muddy coastal route to the south. According to one Fusilier, Chelmsford's division had about 480 wagons (actually over 600 wagons) on the line of march, occupying eight miles in length. 'These wagons', he explained, 'contain our only means of existence, and must be defended to the death.'[19] Compounding the delays was the labour of building small forts along the line of communications, cutting wood, 'a scarce commodity out here' and sometimes several miles distant, and then leaving companies behind to occupy the posts.[20] Once united with Wood's column, there were 'seven thousand fighting men' in the 2nd Division, requiring 'nine hundred waggons [sic] and drawn by fifteen thousand oxen', hence the claim of a Fusilier: 'that a British army is a terribly cumbrous machine, and quite incapable of rapid movement'.[21] If these descriptions alarmed Scottish readers concerned about the mounting costs and purpose of the campaign, the Fusilier's bleak descriptions of Zululand cannot have afforded much comfort:

> The features of the surrounding country are the same as heretofore – the same everlasting table-topped and round-topped hills, the same deep dongas, the same treeless expanse of parched grass . . .
>
> This is Zululand, a land admirably suited to the wild pastoral tribes who inhabit it, who herd cattle, grow Indian corn, and shift their places of abode from year to year, who live in wickerwork huts or in caves, and who acknowledge only one law, one religion, one faith – that of their King. I can see nothing in the people or their country to indicate that the Zulus are ground down under a cruel despotism, nor do I believe they are.[22]

Nor were the descriptions of soldiering in Zululand likely to satisfy those who expected accounts of major battles with deeds of heroism and personal sacrifice. Soldiers laboured in 'bitterly cold' mornings and during days that were 'blazing hot and windy' with the dust 'blinding and distracting'. 'If you were to see the Fusiliers nowadays as they parade in their shirt sleeves', with

> arms and seventy rounds of ammunition round their waist, bronzed, bearded, and travel stained, you would scarcely recognise the smart lads who, within the last few years, have proudly donned for the first time the busby and grenade far away on the banks of the bonnie Doon. The men look every inch soldiers.[23]

These writers also commented on the great controversies of the second invasion, particularly the killing of the Prince Imperial, Louis Napoleon, a favourite of the queen, at the very outset of the campaign (1 June 1879). Soldiers deplored not merely the killing of the prince, reportedly with 'eighteen assegai wounds', and another two soldiers, but also the escape of the remainder of the party, including the accompanying staff officer, Lieutenant J. B. Carey, who 'saved his own life, but lost, or at least failed to try and save, the life of the young Prince'. If soldiers in the 2nd Division were particularly distraught at the spectacle of the body being brought back to camp on the following day on 'an ambulance wagon accompanied by the whole cavalry brigade',[24] Captain Crauford reported the shock felt in the other division when it heard the news and realised that this 'would create a sensation in England', as it did.[25] The Fusiliers later visited the battlefield at Isandlwana where men of the 24th were belatedly burying the bodies of their fallen comrades (and the act of leaving corpses unburied for six months had been another source of anguish at home). They found a battlefield strewn with carcasses of cattle and horses still 'festering in the sun' and collected relics from the site, in one case 'a Zulu shield, battered and crumpled, a cricketing pad, half of Wolseley's pocket book, and a song, "Do they miss me at Home?" '. They retrieved the diary of Lieutenant Pope, updated on the day of the battle, after the apparent withdrawal of the Zulus before the advance of Colonel Durnford's native horsemen. The last entry reportedly stated: 'Enemy retreat – men fall out for dinners' before the right horn of the Zulu *impi* swung round to attack the camp.[26]

What Scots could not do, or at least not do with credibility, was claim any distinctive role in the final defeat of the Zulus. Only two companies of Scots Fusiliers and eight companies of the 90th, some 936 men, participated in the advance on Ulundi. They struggled through dense bush, covering barely four miles and five miles a day respectively in the last two marches, before Chelmsford brought his force of 4,166 whites and 958 blacks to the bank of the White Mfolozi River on 2 July 1879. After Colonel Redvers Buller and his mounted infantry had conducted a daring reconnaissance on the following day, and identified suitable ground for the forthcoming battle, Chelmsford left 529 whites and ninety-three black soldiers to defend the entrenched camp and launched his final advance on 4 July. His army proceeded in a large hollow square formation towards their chosen site of rising ground, from which there were excellent fields of fire. With the infantry arranged four deep, supported by twelve pieces of artillery and two Gatling machine guns, the attacking Zulus, possibly 20,000 in number, faced overwhelming fire power. The volleys of Martini Henrys and artillery salvoes, as described by a corporal of the 90th, 'played great havoc with them. It also kept them at a respectful distance.'[27] Although the Zulus swept round to assault the rear face where the Scots Fusiliers were deployed alongside two companies of the 94th, it was somewhat implausible of an officer to claim that the Scots 'bore the brunt of the battle', and that the steadiness of their fire repulsed the enemy.[28] The Zulus may have come closer to the rear face than any other but they never engaged in hand-to-hand combat and the battle lasted a mere forty minutes. Chelmsford's casualties were derisory (two officers and ten men killed, one officer wounded, who later died, and sixty-nine men wounded) whereas the Zulus, routed by the pursuing cavalry and mounted horsemen, probably lost 1,500 men.[29] More reasonably, the same officer asserted that friends and relatives of the Fusiliers, whose ranks were 'chiefly filled from Ayrshire', would derive 'no small pride and gratification' from hearing how 'manfully and nobly they conducted themselves under such trying circumstances . . .'[30]

The Scottish press never claimed this victory as a national triumph. Although the Dundee *Weekly News* at least mentioned the presence of the 21st, their editorial, like so many others, focused upon the effects of the 'deadly hail' of Martini Henry bullets and 'volleys of canister', while the *Scotsman* commended another victory, as at Gingindlovu, that was 'short, sharp, and decisive' but this time fought in the open without entrenchments.[31] As the victory had been followed up by the destruction of Cetshwayo's kraal (and the capture of the king on 27 August 1879), it proved conclusive. It had also been earned at a 'trifling cost', thereby apparently redeeming Chelmsford's professional reputation.[32]

Scottish Liberals, nonetheless, soon focused on the prodigious costs of the campaign which hardly redounded to the credit of

Chelmsford, Frere or Disraeli. The more extreme critics even described the war as 'an eternal blot on our national greatness and the less said about it the better'.[33] The war ended without any victorious homecomings: the 21st, 91st and the 99th remained in Africa, while the 90th moved on to India. Nor did the outcome of the war (a British withdrawal and Wolseley's abandonment of Frere's confederation in favour of dividing Zululand into thirteen kingdoms – an unstable arrangement that led to civil war) vindicate the aims of 'forward' imperialism. Scots could derive little satisfaction from this conflict.

THE SECOND ANGLO-AFGHAN WAR (1878–81)

In many respects the outbreak of the Second Anglo-Afghan War overshadowed the events in Zululand. It began earlier with the expiry of the British ultimatum on 20 November 1878, whereupon three separate columns invaded Afghanistan. Initially, the campaign was conducted with considerable skill and success, and in a blaze of publicity. The column of Sir Donald Stewart marched unopposed from Quetta to Kandahar; the Peshawar Field Force under Sir Sam Browne overcame resistance at the fort of Ali Masjid and proceeded through the Khyber Pass towards Jalalabad; while the Kurram Field Force under Major-General Frederick Roberts, VC, passed through the Kurram Valley and turned the Afghan regulars from their strongly held position at Peiwar Kotal (1 December). Scottish units only served under Roberts, with the right wing of the 72nd Highlanders in their red, Royal Stuart tartan trews engaged in the flanking movement at Peiwar Kotal. This wing served alongside the 5th Gurkhas in an Anglo-Indian force, with a mountain battery and four guns on elephants. Some 2,300 men undertook a night march up a difficult track, clambering over huge boulders and crossing icy streams. By early morning they surprised the Afghan regulars and drove them from their formidable position on the kotal. The *Illustrated London News* claimed that this 'smart, clean and well-behaved Highland regiment' had demonstrated its 'prowess' at Peiwar 'by the smartest bit of fighting yet seen in this Afghan War'. Among its many sketches from the front were one of the Gurkhas storming Peiwar through the dense pine woods, supported by Highlanders, and another of Highlanders dancing the 'Tullochgorum reel before a camp bonfire' which 'must delight the heart of every Scotchman'.[34] By 28 December 1878 the *Glasgow News* contended that 'the Afghan war is very near its end'.[35]

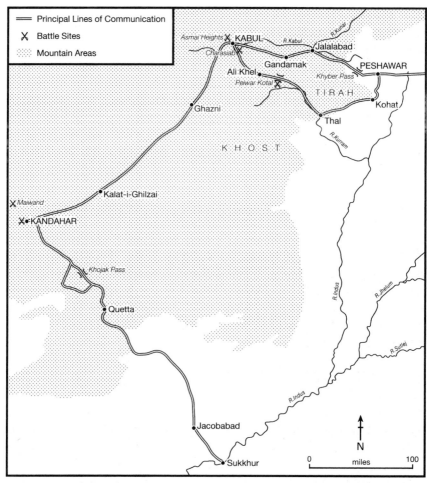

Map 3   Second Anglo-Afghan War, 1878–81

Apart from minor attacks on their lines of communication, the columns avoided major engagements thereafter: Stewart's column occupied Kandahar, Browne's Jalalabad, and Roberts's settled in Ali Khel for the winter, where the other wing of the 72nd and the 92nd Highlanders in their Gordon kilts arrived in the spring of 1879. Hopes of marching on Kabul, some eighty miles distant,[36] were soon dashed by the willingness of the new Amir, Yakub Khan, to make peace at Gandamak (26 May 1879) and allow a British envoy, Major Sir Louis N. Cavagnari, to enter Kabul. Most British forces (and correspondents) then withdrew from Afghanistan, but the subsequent massacre of the envoy and his escort in Kabul on 3 September 1879

Figure 3 *'Execution at Kabul' (Graphic, 14 February 1880)*

aroused demands for retribution and the occupation of Kabul. Roberts's Kabul Field Force, including the 72nd and 92nd, advanced on Kabul, defeating enemy forces on the hills of Charasiab (6 October). Thereafter it entered Kabul and began executing alleged assassins of Cavagnari, some of whom were depicted in the *Graphic* under escort by 92nd Highlanders.[37] In the absence of any political settlement, Roberts's force remained in the nearby cantonments of Sherpur and came under attack from Mohammed Jan's army. It fought a bloody battle on the Asmai Heights (14 December) and withstood a siege until 23 December 1879, whereupon it repulsed a massed attack and consolidated its hold over the Afghan capital.

The reporting of these actions in which both Scottish units were prominent was hardly extensive. Roberts had had a major row with the press in January 1879 and demanded the removal of Hector Macpherson of the *Standard* over the inaccuracy of his reporting and his altering of a telegram that Roberts had approved. Thereafter the Indian government banned 'noncombatant correspondents' from the next phase of the war, only allowing the more compliant Howard Hensman of the *Pioneer* (Allahabad) and the *Daily News* to report events.[38] Nor were many letters sent to family and friends in Scotland as both the 72nd and 92nd were long-service battalions that had served in India since the early 1870s. However, the *Falkirk Herald* had a former employee, Sergeant James Aitken,[39] serving in the 72nd and he sent five informative letters to the paper.

The war had become highly controversial in Scotland, with the two parties split deeply over the rectitude, costs and implications of the invasion, especially after the murder of Cavagnari. While the Conservative *Glasgow News* maintained that this was a war 'for our existence as an Imperial Power', a mission that was 'in every way worthy of a great and high-spirited nation', William E. Gladstone, in his Midlothian speeches of November 1879 and March 1880, denounced the disasters of Beaconsfieldism and advocated a foreign policy that avoided 'needless and mischievous engagements'. Speaking before vast crowds, he extolled 'the rights of the savage . . . the happiness of his humble home [and] the sanctity of life in the hill villages of Afghanistan, among the winter snows . . . as sacred in the eyes of Almighty God as are your own'. He later likened the attack on the 'high-spirited and warlike people' of Afghanistan to the attack on 'the mountain clans' of Scotland, an act of folly that risked 'making ourselves odious and detested'.[40] In this fiercely partisan atmosphere, the Scottish Liberal press took military victories for granted and continued to denounce the underlying policy: 'Everybody', wrote the *Scotsman*, 'is rightly proud of the courage and skill of our soldiers, but it will be strange if the country condones the evil done by a Ministry that made war without excuse . . .'[41]

Nevertheless, the *Scotsman* like other newspapers resented the lack of news during the siege of Kabul and relied on the reports of Hensman in the *Daily News*. Hensman, who later wrote a book based on these reports, was fulsome in his reporting of the Highlanders (and his book was dedicated to the 72nd and 92nd for all their hospitality during the war). In describing the battle of Charasiab, where Roberts had barely 3,800 men, including sick, available for his uphill attack against a strongly defended position held by superior numbers, Hensman claimed that the 72nd 'bore the brunt of the fighting', leading the attack on the centre and right of the Afghan position: 'They had on several occasions to cross open ground, and in spite of the exposure they pushed forward with an *élan* that could not be surpassed.' Meanwhile, the 92nd attacked the enemy's left in 'one of the most gallant feats of the day', with Major George S. White leading fifty Highlanders against a hill, later dubbed 'White's hill', held by several hundred Afghans. The Highlanders not only dispersed the defenders but then took two further hills and seized twelve guns in an action for which White would be awarded the Victoria Cross.[42] When Roberts entered Kabul, Hensman maintained that the two 'Highland regiments, forming two living walls stretching far away towards the city, were the great representative of British Infantry'. As he added, 'Nothing could exceed the splendid form in which these regiments turned out, the bronzed and bearded faces of the soldiers, showing that but few "six-year men" were in their ranks.'[43] In subsequent reports on the Afghan assault, he described counterattacks against tribesmen on nearby peaks as conducted in 'gallant style' by the 92nd. He wrote of heroic deaths in battle (notably Lieutenant Forbes of the 92nd trying to save the body of Colour-Sergeant Drummond 'from mutilation') and the extraordinary courage of Lance-Corporal George Sellar of the 72nd, who was severely wounded after reaching an enemy position well ahead of the attacking party (for which he would be awarded a VC). During the subsequent siege, Hensman praised the stoicism of the 72nd in their snow-filled bastions: 'The sentries in their greatcoats were simply white figures standing rigidly up like ghosts, the snow-flakes softly covering them from head to foot, and freezing as they fell.'[44]

Sergeant Aitken was less florid in his descriptions. He had already expressed his frustration that the Treaty of Gandamak had 'dispelled any lingering hopes of further glory' but evinced pride and pleasure that a fellow NCO, Sergeant Greer, had been promoted to a second lieutenancy for his gallantry at Peiwar Kotal. Greer had assumed command of a company of 5th Gurkhas after their captain had been killed and led them on to victory. 'These gallant little fellows', wrote Aitken, 'declare that they too are Highlanders, and fraternise with our men in a most amicable manner.'[45] Aitken also described how the Kabul Field Force commemorated the anniversary of this 'brilliant engagement', with Roberts awarding four distinguished conduct medals and commending the 72nd for its part in the Afghan operations. Within six days the battalion was 'hotly engaged . . . in driving large swarms of Afghans off the Asmai heights, about a mile from barracks'. Daily attacks followed by an enemy whom Aitken reckoned to number 'at least 40,000' (some estimates are much larger)[46] but, in the final mass assault on the 23rd, they 'were repulsed with immense loss'. The battalion, conceded Aitken, had paid a heavy price: two officers and sixteen men killed and twenty wounded on the 14th, with Captain Spens slain with 'innumerable sword-cuts'. On the other hand, the enemy had suffered huge losses, particularly in their final attack, and had dispersed. The Highlanders were now able to celebrate Hogmanay with liberal supplies of grog (although forty-seven received silver bars for remaining teetotallers throughout the campaign) and the band played Scottish airs.[47] Colonel (later Brigadier-General) Charles MacGregor, though normally well-disposed towards his fellow countrymen, recalled that they 'made a hideous row on New Years night for two hours . . .'[48]

Over the next six months reports from Afghanistan aroused much less interest. Aitken wrote mundane letters on picquet duty during the winter months and a month-long expedition into the hinterland in the summer. Despite all the rigours of marching, fully accoutred and carrying seventy rounds of ammunition, over stony and dusty tracks, barely covering ten miles per day, the experience 'was unmarked by excitement'. Of more importance for the 72nd was the arrival of some 150 young soldiers from Stirling Castle, replacing the losses of seven officers and 186 men, most of whom had either died from disease or been invalided back to India or England. This 'infusion of young blood', opined Sergeant Aitken, was 'highly desirable'; they were soon 'hard at drill, getting knocked into form under Sergeant Pickard'.[49]

The value of this training was soon put to the test. By 28 April the Conservative government had fallen from office (and Conservative representation in Scotland had plummeted to seven seats out of sixty). Gladstone, the new Prime Minister, had replaced Lord Lytton by Lord Ripon, and resolved to withdraw from Afghanistan as soon as Abdur Rahman, a nephew of Sher Ali, could be installed as the new amir (22 July 1880). Just as the garrison in Kabul was packing up to leave, news arrived that an Anglo-Indian force had been annihilated at the battle of Maiwand (27 July 1880), and that Kandahar was now besieged by forces under Ayub Kahn, a brother of Yakub Kahn. Both the shock of the defeat and the scale of the losses (twenty-one officers and 948 men killed, eight officers and 169 men wounded)[50] prompted demands for retribution and the relief of the beleaguered garrison. Roberts responded rapidly; on 8 August he marched out of Kabul, commanding 10,148 fighting men, including the 72nd and the 92nd, with 8,173 followers and 11,224 baggage animals to relieve Kandahar, some 300 miles away. Completing the epic march on 31 August, Roberts planned an attack on the enemy and routed them on the following day. The dramatic arrival of the relief force after a virtual absence of news during the march itself, and the suddenness of the decisive victory, earned paeans of praise for Roberts and caught the public imagination as no other episode in the war had done.[51]

The Scottish press, though in many cases still critical of the origins, costs and consequences of the war,[52] lauded the crowning victory of Roberts: in the *Scotsman*'s opinion, it surpassed 'any incident of Eastern warfare since the deeds of Havelock, Outram, Rose, and Lord Clyde during the Sepoy war'.[53] Roberts, who had won the so-called 'race for the peerage' by reaching Kandahar before the relief force from Quetta under Major-General Robert Phayre, was now praised as a military 'genius' and a 'dashing general' in Scotland. His victory had restored the prestige of British arms after the 'blunder' of Maiwand.[54] As more news filtered home, Scottish newspapers seized upon reports that the Highlanders had led the two assaults on the Afghan positions. The *Aberdeen Journal* claimed that the 92nd had suffered more casualties than any other unit in undertaking 'the most serious, the most arduous and . . . the most essential operation of the day'.[55] But the 72nd had suffered too, losing two officers and eleven men killed, including their commanding officer, Lieutenant-Colonel F. Brownlow. The Scottish press reported the final accolades of Roberts as he presented medals to the 72nd and 92nd on the eve of their return to India:

No Afghans could stand against such a steady, bold attack. You beat them at Cabul [sic], you have beaten them at Candahar [sic], and you can now leave the country, feeling assured that the very last troops the Afghans wish to meet in the field are Highlanders and Goorkhas [sic]. You have made a name for yourselves in Afghanistan.[56]

Like Wolseley's praise of the Black Watch in the Asante War, these plaudits from Roberts testified to the recognition of the distinctive contributions of the 72nd and the 92nd, that were fully in accordance with the traditional images of Highland soldiery. Scots duly celebrated these achievements in song, painting and memorials. At an immense gathering of Highlanders in Glasgow, a Gaelic song in praise of the 92nd's achievements was received with tremendous applause. Vereker Hamilton, the brother of Lieutenant Ian Hamilton of the 92nd, composed a painting of the 92nd Highlanders in action at Kandahar (two versions of which were hung in the Royal Academy, although it was less successful than the earlier version by R. Caton Woodville). All ranks of the 72nd subscribed to a memorial, erected on the esplanade of Edinburgh Castle, that commemorated the service of their fallen comrades in Afghanistan.[57]

Ironically, the last letter of Sergeant Aitken, published long after the initial euphoria, added a welcome note of realism to some of the commentaries on the march and battle. He admitted that the unopposed march had been a grim affair 'with improper food, scarcity of water, and marching some days twenty-four miles across a barren desert' (this was a slight exaggeration as the longest day's march was twenty-one miles and the daily average some 13.7 miles).[58] Yet his description of the 'great' strain upon the men, with many falling out along the line of march and one 72nd man committing suicide, was accurate; it accorded with MacGregor's description of the march, confined to his diary, as a 'disorganised rabble' and hardly on a par with the previous march of Sir Donald Stewart's column from Kandahar to Kabul (27 March to 2 May 1880) in the face of stiff Afghan opposition.[59] Aitken, nonetheless, confirmed popular impressions of the battle, especially 'the resolute advance' of the Kabul army, the deep sense of loss felt about the deaths in the 72nd, including the 'irreparable loss' of their 'gallant' commanding officer, and the camaraderie that had sustained them in Afghanistan, not least with the 5th Gurkhas:

We parted with our old friends the 5th Goorkhas [sic] on the morning of the 1st October. The two regiments have been inseparable since the commencement of the campaign, having fought side by side in every engagement. When they marched away on the morning of the 1st the 72nd turned out and cheered them lustily.[60]

THE ANGLO-TRANSVAAL WAR (1880–1)

Scots were unable to welcome their heroes home from Afghanistan as the 72nd (soon to become the 1st Battalion, Seaforth Highlanders) would serve in Egypt in 1882, while the 92nd (soon the 2nd Battalion, Gordon Highlanders), though under orders to return home, found themselves diverted to Natal in 1881. Within the Transvaal the Boers, who had never reconciled themselves to British rule, had their hopes dashed by the inability of Gladstone's divided cabinet to grant them independence. Resenting both the revenue-raising activities of Sir Owen Lanyon, the Governor of the Transvaal, and alleged incidents of indiscipline by British soldiers, the Boers proclaimed a republic on 16 December 1880. Within four days the Boers ambushed a British column at Bronkhorstspruit and invested the seven small garrisons in the Transvaal. Sir George Pomeroy Colley tried to relieve these garrisons by leading a column from Natal through the Drakensberg Mountains at Laing's Nek. On 28 January 1881 he was defeated in a frontal assault at Laing's Nek and on 8 February suffered another reverse at Schuinshoogte hill. Finally, he sought to outflank the Boer position by seizing Majuba hill, an extinct volcano rising 2,500 feet above the Boer camp.

For this operation, launched on the evening of 26 February 1881, he had some fresh soldiers, namely the 92nd Highlanders. As the first kilted regiment to be seen in Natal, they received a warm reception in Durban and marched ahead as the vanguard of a much larger force arriving in the colony and en route from Britain (with many of the war correspondents). Colley now chose to seize Majuba with a composite force of seven companies (three of the 92nd (180 men), two of the 58th, two of the 3rd 60th Rifles and a small Naval Brigade), without any artillery or Gatling guns. Leaving three companies to guard the line of communications, Colley occupied the summit with 405 officers and men. On the following day some 450 Boers climbed the hill under a hail of covering fire and then overwhelmed the defending force, killing Colley and routing the British from the summit. Of the British forces engaged, six officers and ninety men were killed, seven officers and 125 men wounded, and seven officers and forty-nine men captured, with nearly half of the casualties occurring after they had fled the summit.[61]

With only three correspondents (Carter of the *Natal Mercury*, Hay of the *Daily News* and Cameron of the *Standard*) accompanying Colley's force, their reports of the disaster were reproduced widely,

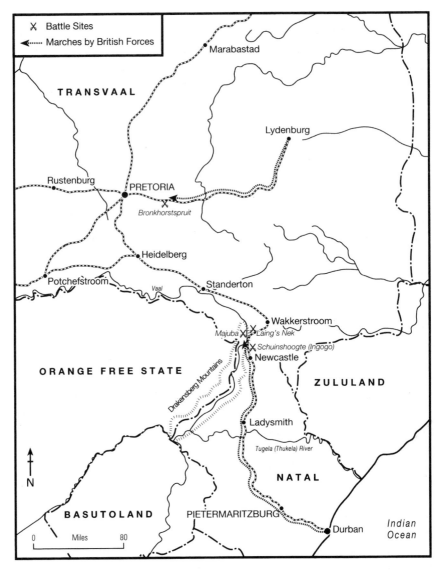

Map 4   *Anglo-Transvaal War, 1880–1*

not least in Scotland.[62] Despite Cameron's remarks about the 'steadiness' of the Highlanders on the exposed forward kopje (they were the first to be overrun), and a resolute final stand led by Lieutenant Hector Macdonald, 'Fighting-Mac', who with 'revolver in hand' threatened 'to shoot any man who passed him', Scottish newspapers tried desperately to explain the debacle. Some editors claimed that the ammunition supply had run out and/or the Boers had attacked in overwhelming numbers (neither of which was true).[63] So desperate was the *Scotsman* to find some redeeming feature from this disaster that it claimed: 'Few more impressive stories are to be found in the records of British valour than that of the gallant 92d Gordon Highlanders, who, when their ammunition failed, hurled stones on their advancing foes . . .' (a myth soon dispelled by press correspondents who witnessed the battle).[64]

More perceptively, editors claimed that the 92nd could not be blamed for the blunders of Colley, his underestimation of the enemy or his faulty tactics.[65] There was scant public correspondence from the 92nd itself, which had suffered 125 casualties, the largest number of any unit,[66] although several officers wrote privately to Sir George White.[67] Nevertheless Hamilton, who was severely wounded in the battle, later wrote an account for General Dillon that was shown to the queen. After the terrible climb on the previous night, he claimed that the men were 'too excited to feel fatigue, and I saw no signs of it' (a critical point, as Colley had reportedly ordered his men to rest rather than construct redoubts after the strain of the climb). The small force had to deploy at intervals of twelve paces to cover the extensive perimeter and Hamilton, in command of eighteen Gordons on the forward knoll, soon found his exposed position coming under 'a most accurate fire'. Any hope that the twenty soldiers under Lieutenant Macdonald on a kopje to the left could have enfiladed the Boer advance was soon dashed. As these men found themselves exposed and shot in the back crawling to the narrow top of the hill, Hamilton ran back to Colley repeatedly to press for reinforcements and later to request a bayonet charge, which the general denied: 'It is my firm belief that had a charge been ordered at this moment we should have cleared the hill . . . [Instead] Bullets from an enemy we could not see, and were not permitted to assault, came in amongst us from every direction.'[68]

Hamilton's account merely confirmed impressions in Scotland that the 92nd had responded gallantly under fire, as it had done in Afghanistan (an issue glorified in Highland poetry),[69] and that the battle had been bungled by Colley. In Aberdeen, where the 92nd was to be based under the system of territorial localisation, citizens raised a regimental benevolent fund for the widows and dependants of the fallen soldiers (including the families of those who had married 'off the strength'). The fund had prestigious support, including the Duke of Gordon and Richmond, the Marquis of Huntly, the Earls of Crawford, Fife and Kintore, as well as Aberdeen's Lord Provost and the three local

Liberal Members of Parliament. On 23 March 1881 a large cross-party public meeting convened under the auspices of the Earl of Aberdeen, Lord Lieutenant of the county, to launch the fund. The gathering of the local peerage, gentry, city officials, ministers, advocates, professors, doctors, businessmen and merchants heard numerous expressions of sympathy for the 'great losses' sustained by the 92nd, claims that they had shown the 'same spirit of heroism and unshakeable discipline' on Majuba that had distinguished 'the grand old regiment', and an insistence by Lord Saltoun that the reverse had occurred 'not through their fault for they fought with all the gallantry that men could do'.[70] Nearly one month after this meeting the *Illustrated London News* published a famous sketch of the Majuba battle, showing kilted Highlanders scrambling down the hillside in headlong retreat pursued by Boers.[71]

In the interim, Sir Evelyn Wood had signed a peace agreement with the Boers, despite protests from the queen among others that the national honour had to be redeemed. Gladstone was now adamant that Britain should disengage from the Transvaal (other than in foreign affairs) and gained support for this policy from the cabinet and the House of Commons.[72] Compounding this ignominious end to the war was the capitulation of the Potchefstroom garrison – the only garrison forced to do so. As the garrison was largely composed of the 21st Royal Scots Fusiliers, the *Ayr Advertiser* deprecated those Boers who had broken the terms of the truce and failed to let a relief convoy through, but, like many Scottish Liberals, hoped that the anguished feelings over the war would soon 'calm down'.[73]

The unsatisfactory outcome hardly dampened the affection for the Gordon Highlanders. When the battalion returned to Scotland, its reappearance in the capital after a passage of eighteen years was eagerly anticipated.[74] On 9 October 1882, the battalion marched from Granton to Edinburgh Castle past 'ever-increasing crowds' who had waited for one or two hours along the route. Although few had any relatives in the the 92nd, some of whom were returning after fourteen years' foreign service, there was huge interest in the 'thoroughly seasoned soldiers', many wearing Afghan medals, who marched behind their pipers:

> The long straight hill of Pitt Street and Hanover Street presented one long vista of faces, looking from every window and other coign of vantage, the top of the hill at George Street appearing to be barricaded by a mass of human beings. There was little or no cheering – Edinburgians are not prone to that sort of demonstration – but there was a good deal of waving of handkerchiefs by the fair portion of the onlookers . . .

An 'alarming weight of people' pressed on the railings erected at the head of the Mound and when the Gordons wheeled into the Lawnmarket they received 'the most enthusiastic ovation they had yet encountered' from the 'denizens of the Lawnmarket and Castlehill'. Formal receptions and dinners would follow as the local press published yet more eulogies to the historic achievements of the 92nd Highlanders.[75]

Notes

1 M. Cowling, 'Lytton, the Cabinet, and the Russians, August to November 1878', *English Historical Review*, LXXVI (1961), pp. 60–79; B. Robson, *The Road to Kabul: The Second Afghan War 1878–1881* (London: Arms and Armour Press, 1986), pp. 49–52; D. R. Morris, *The Washing of the Spears* (London: Sphere, 1968), pp. 289–94.

2 M. Fry, *Patronage and Principle: A Political History of Modern Scotland* (Aberdeen: Aberdeen University Press, 1987), pp. 88–9; I. G. C. Hutchison, *A Political History of Scotland 1832–1924* (Edinburgh: John Donald, 1986), p. 119.

3 'The Kaffir War', 'South Africa and the Kaffir War' and 'The Kaffir War', *Illustrated London News*, 9 March, 13 April and 27 April 1878, pp. 230, 332 and 379.

4 'The Zulu War', *The Times*, 11 February 1879, p. 5; Wilkinson-Latham, *From Our Special Correspondent*, pp. 137–8, 145–50; I. Knight, *The Sun Turned Black:Isandlwana and Rorke's Drift – 1879* (Rivonia: William Waterman Publications, 1995), p. 203.

5 'The Disaster at the Cape', *Glasgow News*, 12 February 1879, p. 4; see also 'The South African Disaster', *Aberdeen Journal*, 12 February 1879, p. 4; 'The Situation at the Cape', *Dundee Courier & Argus*, 3 May 1879, p. 2.

6 Although the writer remains anonymous in the newspapers, his identity is revealed in ASH Museum, N-C91.1, Crauford Mss, Captain W. R. H. Crauford to Carry, 2 June 1879.

7 'The Disaster at Rorke's Drift. Narrative of a Dundee Soldier', *[Dundee] Weekly News*, 8 March 1879, p. 5; TNA, PRO, WO 33/34, p. 280, Statement by 665 Private H. Grant enclosed in Lord Chelmsford to the Secretary of State for War, 4 April 1879 and reproduced in N. Holme, *The Noble 24th* (London: Savannah, 1979), p. 193.

8 'Reinforcements for the Cape', *Bridge of Allan Reporter*, 8 March 1879, p. 2; 'The Zulu War', *Aberdeen Journal*, 20 February 1879, p. 3; 'The Departure of the 91st Regiment', *The Times*, 20 February 1879, p. 10; 'The Zulu War: Embarkation of the 91st Highlanders at Southampton', 'The Zulu War: The 91st Regiment Leaving The Pretoria at Durban' and 'The Zulu War: The 91st Regiment Leaving Camp at Durban for the

Front', *Illustrated London News*, 1 March, 26 April and 3 May 1879, pp. 189, 401 and 413.

9 'The Zulu War', *Strathearn Herald*, 5 April 1879, p. 2.

10 'Letter from Zululand', *Ayr Advertiser*, 26 June 1879, p. 5; for similar accounts of the battle by 90th soldiers, see 'Letter from Zululand', *Dover Express*, 5 September 1879, p. 2; 'A Manchester Soldier's Account of Col. Wood's Victory', *Manchester Courier*, 14 May 1879, p. 6; 'A Sheffield Soldier at Khambula', *Sheffield Daily Telegraph*, 8 May 1879, p. 3.

11 I. Knight and I. Castle, *Zulu War 1879* (London: Osprey, Campaign Series 14, 1994), p. 84; on the comparison with Rorke's Drift, see 'Relief of Colonel Pearson', *Dundee Courier & Argus*, 23 April 1879, p. 2.

12 'The 91st Highlanders at Gingihlovo', *Glasgow News*, 22 May 1879, p. 3. There were other claims of almost 700 bodies, Morris, *Washing of the Spears*, p. 465.

13 'The 91st at the Cape', *Bridge of Allan Reporter*, 10 May 1879, p. 3; see also 'With the 91st at the Cape', *Bridge of Allan Reporter*, 5 July 1879, p. 3; 'Letter from Lieut. Cookson of Worksop', *Sheffield Daily Telegraph*, 13 May 1879, p. 3; and I. Knight, *Brave Men's Blood: The Epic of the Zulu War, 1879* (London: Guild Publishing, 1990), pp. 104–7.

14 'The War at Natal', *Bridge of Allan Reporter*, 24 May 1879, p. 3; ASH Museum, N-C91.1, Crauford Mss, Crauford to his father, 4 April 1879 and to Carry, 2 June 1879.

15 'The 91st Highlanders in Natal', *Glasgow News*, 25 April 1879, p. 3, and 'The 91st Highlanders in Zululand', *Glasgow News*, 8 May 1879, p. 5.

16 ASH Museum, N-C91.1, Crauford Mss, Crauford to Carry, 28 April 1879.

17 Wilkinson-Latham, *From Our Special Correspondent*, p. 152; Usherwood and Spencer-Smith, *Lady Butler*, pp. 77–80, 166, 173–4; see also the sketches in the *Illustrated London News*, 24 May 1879, pp. 477, 481–2, 484–5.

18 'Breechloaders and Sabres at Ginghilovo', *Perthshire Advertiser*, 28 April 1879, p. 4; see also the *Falkirk Herald*, 26 April 1879, p. 2; *[Dundee] Weekly News*, 26 April 1879, p. 4; and *Bridge of Allan Reporter*, 26 April 1879, p. 2.

19 'The 21st Fusiliers in South Africa' and 'The 21st Royal Scots Fusiliers in Zululand', *Ayr Advertiser*, 24 July 1879, p. 4 and 14 August 1879, p. 5; ASH Museum, N-C91.1, Crauford Mss, Crauford to his father, 22 May 1879; on transport, see Morris, *Washing of the Spears*, pp. 551–2; Knight, *Brave Men's Blood*, p. 152.

20 Both the 21st and the 91st were split up along their respective lines of communication, 'The 21st Scots Fusiliers in Zululand', *Ayr Advertiser*, 26 June 1879, p. 5, and ASH Museum, N-C91.1, Crauford Mss, Crauford to his father, 19 May 1879 and to Carry, 3 August 1879.

21 'The 21st Royal Scots Fusiliers in Zululand', p. 5.

22 Ibid.

23 'The 21st Scots Fusiliers in Zululand', p. 5.

24 'The 21st Fusiliers in South Africa', p. 4.

25 ASH Museum, N-C91.1, Crauford Mss, Crauford to his father, 10 June 1879 and to Carry, 3 August 1879.

26 'A Long Ride in Zululand – A Visit to the Field of Isandula [sic]', *Ayr Advertiser*, 21 August 1879, p. 5.

27 'The Battle of Ulundi', *Manchester Courier*, 10 September 1879, p. 3; see also J. Laband, *The battle of Ulundi* (Pietermaritzburg: Shuter & Shooter, 1988), pp. 21–4; 'The 21st Royal Scots Fusiliers at the battle of Ulundi', *Ayr Advertiser*, 28 August 1879, p. 4; 'Letter from Zululand', *Dover Express*, 12 September 1879, p. 2.

28 'The 21st Royal Scots Fusiliers at the battle of Ulundi', p. 4.

29 Laband, *The battle of Ulundi*, pp. 22, 35–6, 44–5.

30 'The 21st Royal Scots Fusiliers at the battle of Ulundi', p. 4.

31 'The Zulu War', *[Dundee] Weekly News*, 26 July 1879, p. 7, and *Scotsman*, 24 July 1879, p. 4.

32 *Scotsman*, 24 July 1879, p. 4; 'The Anticipated Close of the Zulu War', *Falkirk Herald*, 24 July 1879, p. 4; 'The Zulu Defeat', *Glasgow News*, 24 July 1879, p. 4; *Bridge of Allan Reporter*, 26 July 1879, p. 2, and *Ayr Advertiser*, 24 July 1879, p. 4.

33 *Strathearn Herald*, 26 July 1879, p. 2; see also *Ayr Advertiser*, 28 August 1879, p. 4.

34 'The Afghan War', *Illustrated London News*, 18 January 1879, pp. 54 and 56; see also Robson, *Road to Kabul*, pp. 84–6; M. Barthorp, *Afghan Wars and the North-West Frontier 1839–1947* (London: Cassell, 1982), pp. 68–9.

35 *Glasgow News*, 28 December 1878, p. 4.

36 'A Soldier's Life in the East', *Falkirk Herald*, 19 July 1879, p. 4; GHM, PB 75, 'Extracts from Arbuthnott S. Dunbar's letters during the Afghan Campaign 1879', 14 April 1879, p. 13.

37 'Afghans escorted to the gallows in the ruins of the Residency by troops from the Highland regiments and the Rev. J. Adams', *Graphic*, 14 February 1880, p. 149.

38 Wilkinson-Latham, *From Our Special Correspondent*, pp. 141–2: Robson, *Road to Kabul*, pp. 93–4; Trousdale (ed.), *War in Afghanistan*, p. 103.

39 His first letter which reveals his past connection with the *Herald* office is signed 'J. A.' but his final letter reveals his full name and rank. 'A Soldier's Life in the East' and 'The 72nd Highlanders in Afghanistan', *Falkirk Herald*, 19 July 1879, p. 4, and 6 November 1880, p. 2.

40 'The Disaster at the Cape', *Glasgow News*, 12 February 1879, p. 4; 'Mr Gladstone's Visit to Mid-Lothian', *Scotsman*, 27 November 1879,

p. 5; 'The General Election', *Scotsman*, 18 March 1880, p. 5; R. Kelley, 'Midlothian: A Study in Politics and Ideas', *Victorian Studies*, 4, no. 2 (1960), pp. 119–40.

41 *Scotsman*, 9 October 1879, p. 4.

42 *Scotsman*, 29 December 1879, p. 4; H. Hensman, *The Afghan War of 1879–80* (London: W. H. Allen & Co., 1881), pp. 32–6; see also Trousdale (ed.), *War in Afghanistan*, p. 99.

43 Hensman, *Afghan War*, p. 58.

44 Ibid., pp. 202, 209, 238.

45 'A Soldier's Life in the East', p. 4.

46 Even an estimate of 100,000 in Barthorp, *Afghan Wars*, p. 84.

47 'The 72D Highlanders in Afghanistan', *Falkirk Herald*, 26 February 1880, p. 3.

48 Trousdale (ed.), *War in Afghanistan*, p. 142.

49 'The 72nd Highlanders in Afghanistan' and 'The 72D Highlanders in Afghanistan', *Falkirk Herald*, 22 April 1880, p. 2, and 24 July 1880, p. 4.

50 Robson, *Road to Kabul*, pp. 203, 239; see also L. Maxwell, *My God! – Maiwand* (London: Leo Cooper, 1979).

51 Robson, *Road to Kabul*, pp. 250–1; D. Murray, 'Kabul to Kandahar', *Soldiers of the Queen*, 102 (2000), pp. 13–23; I. F. W. Beckett, *The Victorians at War* (London: Hambledon, 2003), ch. 5.

52 *Strathearn Herald*, 8 September 1880, p. 2; *Huntly Express*, 11 September 1880, p. 4; *Scotsman*, 6 September 1880, p. 4. On the race for the peerage, see Beckett, *Victorians at War*, ch. 5.

53 *Scotsman*, 6 September 1880, p. 4; see also *Nairnshire Telegraph*, 8 September 1880, p. 2.

54 *Elgin Courant*, 7 September 1880, p. 2; *Ross-shire Journal*, 10 September 1880, p. 2; *Aberdeen Journal*, 7 and 13 September 1880, pp. 4 and 4.

55 *Aberdeen Journal*, 6 and 13 September 1880, pp. 5 and 4; see also *Stirling Observer*, 9 September 1880, p. 4.

56 'General Roberts and the 72nd Highlanders', *Huntly Express*, 9 October 1880, p. 8; see also Trousdale (ed.), *War in Afghanistan*, p. 240.

57 Lieutenant-Colonel C. Greenhill Gardyne, *The Life of a Regiment: The History of the Gordon Highlanders*, 3 vols (London: The Medici Society, 1903–29), 2, p. 157; V. M. Hamilton, *Things That Happened* (London: Edward Arnold, 1925), pp. 269–70; Murray, 'Kabul to Kandahar', p. 22.

58 Compare 'The 72D Highlanders in Afghanistan', *Falkirk Herald*, 6 November 1880, p. 2, with Beckett, *Victorians at War*, p. 47.

59 Compare 'The 72D Highlanders in Afghanistan', p. 2, with Trousdale (ed.), *War in Afghanistan*, p. 236.

60 Aitken's views in 'The 72D Highlanders in Afghanistan', p. 2, are confirmed in P. Mason, *A Matter of Honour: An account of the Indian Army, its officers & men* (London: Jonathan Cape, 1974), p. 382.

61 J. Lehman, *The Boer War* (London: Buchan & Endright, 1985), pp. 228, 236–8, 242, 260; I. Castle, *Majuba 1881: The Hill of Destiny* (London: Osprey, 1988), p. 82.

62 'The Disaster in the Transvaal', *Scottish Standard*, 5 March 1881, p. 3; 'Graphic Account of the Battle', *Huntly Express*, 5 March 1881, p. 6; 'The Disaster in the Transvaal', *Glasgow Herald*, 1 March 1881, p. 5; 'Account of the Battle', *Nairnshire Telegraph*, 2 March 1881, p. 3.

63 Compare TNA, PRO, WO 33/38, Lieutenant-Colonel H. Stewart to GOC, Natal, 4 April 1881, p. 219; 'The Majuba Hill Disaster', *Standard*, 1 March 1881, p. 5; *Western Morning News*, 31 March 1881, p. 3; with *Falkirk Herald*, 3 March 1881, p. 4; *[Dundee] Weekly News*, 5 March 1881, p. 4; *Glasgow Herald*, 2 March 1881, p. 6.

64 Compare *Scotsman*, 1 March 1881, p. 4, with *Ayr Advertiser*, 3 March 1881, p. 4.

65 *Aberdeen Journal*, 1 March 1881, p. 4; *[Dundee] Weekly News*, 5 March 1881, p. 4; *Falkirk Herald*, 3 March 1881, p. 4.

66 Lehman, *Boer War*, p. 260.

67 British Library (BL), Asia, Pacific and Africa Collections, White Mss, MSS Eur F108/91, Douglas to White, 5 April 1881; Macdonald to White 20 April 1881; Macgregor to White, 6 May 1882; Hay to White, 12 May 1882.

68 General Sir I. Hamilton, *Listening for the Drums* (London: Faber and Faber, 1944), pp. 133–9; whether a bayonet charge would have worked is a moot point but it was the one tactic that the Boers feared, see Major G. Tylden [translation], 'Majuba, 27th February, 1881: A Contemporary Boer Account', *JSAHR*, 17 (1938), pp. 9–12.

69 'To the 92nd (GORDON) Highlanders', *Ross-shire Journal*, 11 March 1881, p. 4.

70 'The 92nd Highlanders', *Aberdeen Journal*, 24 March 1881, p. 6; 'Honour to the 92nd Highlanders', *[Dundee] Weekly News*, 26 March 1881, p. 4; on marriages 'off the strength', see M. Trustram, *Women of the regiment: Marriage and the Victorian army* (Cambridge: Cambridge University Press, 1984), pp. 30–2, 187–9.

71 'The 92nd Highlanders', p. 6; 'The Transvaal War: Sketches by Our Special Artist', *Illustrated London News*, 23 April 1881, p. 413.

72 R. Shannon, *Gladstone: Heroic Minister 1865–1898* (London: Allen Lane, 1999), p. 273.

73 *Ayr Advertiser*, 31 March 1881, p. 4; I. Bennett, *A Rain of Lead: The Siege and Surrender of the British at Potchefstroom 1880–1881* (London: Greenhill Books, 2001).

74 *Edinburgh Courant*, 30 September 1882, p. 4.

75 'Arrival of the Gordon Highlanders in Edinburgh', *Scotsman*, 10 October 1882, p. 5.

4

HIGHLANDERS IN EGYPT

⌒

After the controversies surrounding the origins and conduct of the Zulu and Afghan Wars, followed by the defeats of the Anglo-Transvaal War, the intervention in Egypt, authorised by a Liberal cabinet, represented a major imperial initiative. Once approved by a vote of credit in the House of Commons on 27 July 1882, it involved the dispatch of the largest expeditionary force from Britain since the Crimean War, with regiments leaving Britain, the Mediterranean garrisons, Aden and India. The campaign culminated in the battle of Tel-el-Kebir on 13 September 1882, enabling Sir Garnet Wolseley to enter Cairo two days later. For Scottish Liberals, who were imbued with the Midlothian ethos and had possibly overlooked the fine print of Gladstone's speeches (about avoiding only 'needless and entangling' engagements) or had forgotten his bellicose record (a military expedition had been authorised by every cabinet in which he had served since 1843),[1]there were three consolations: the war proved mercifully short, it was overwhelmingly decisive without any disasters, and its aim was supposedly a 'temporary' occupation of Egypt.[2] In fact, the occupation proved anything but temporary; it produced several subsequent expeditions into the Sudan (Chapters 5 and 7) and required a British military presence in Egypt that lasted until 1953. If Disraeli's purchase of shares in the Suez Canal (1875), followed by the assumption of Anglo-French control over Egyptian finances in 1878, had laid the foundations of the British involvement in Egypt, the intervention of 1882 committed successive Liberal and Conservative governments to an imperial role in Egypt.

Egyptian resentment of the foreign presence underpinned the nationalist agitation led by the minister of war, Colonel Arabi Pasha. When Khedive Tewfik, acting under French pressure, tried to dismiss him, riots erupted in Alexandria (11 and 12 June 1882), leading to the deaths of over fifty Europeans and lurid reporting from British officials in Cairo.[3] Gladstone's cabinet resolved to intervene to restore order and maintain 'all established rights in Egypt, whether they be those of the Sultan, those of the Khedive, those of the people of Egypt, or those of the foreign bondholders' (of whom Gladstone was one).[4] The *Scotsman*, a prominent champion of Liberalism, agreed that the anarchy had to be suppressed, even if 'the actual massacres have been exaggerated'. In reporting the debate over the vote of credit, it claimed that the government had 'the support of the great majority in Parliament and in the country'.[5] The main Conservative newspapers in Scotland, the *Edinburgh Courant* and the *Glasgow News*, agreed that Britain had to protect her strategic and financial interests in Egypt, while more 'advanced' Liberal newspapers, like Glasgow's *North British Daily Mail* and the *Kilmarnock Standard*, accepted that the cause of restoring order in Egypt was just and so dissociated themselves from the 'peace-at-any-price party'.[6]

Testifying to the popular appeal of the war was the rapidity with which the metropolitan press and the large provincial newspapers sent their correspondents to the front. There were at least ten of them able to report on the naval bombardment of Arabi's defences at Alexandria (11 July), and the occupation of the city by sailors and marines two days later, armed with Gatling machine guns.[7] As military units from Malta reinforced the British positions at Alexandria and the suburb of Ramleh, the expeditionary force began to leave the United Kingdom. On 7 August the 1st Battalion, Black Watch marched out of Edinburgh Castle and encountered surging, cheering crowds all along the route from the esplanade to Waverley station. Although veterans had left the capital to hearty send-offs before, they could not remember such a display of emotion, and Bandsman A. V. Barwood, on his first campaign, recalled huge crowds greeting the Black Watch at every station from Edinburgh to London.[8] Officers and other ranks responded to this outpouring of emotion by writing numerous letters during their 'delightful' voyage on the *Nepaul*; George Miller, who was a scripture reader with the Highland Brigade, claimed that once the ship reached Gibraltar, 'over a thousand letters had been sent by the good old Black Watch, cheering the hearts of wives and mothers in auld Scotland'.[9] If true, it was a foretaste of the letter-writing from the front where soldiers would utilise the services of the newly instituted Army Post Office Corps, composed of volunteers from the 24th Middlesex (Post Office) Rifle Volunteers, and six post offices (two of which accompanied the 1st and 2nd Divisions on the line of march).[10]

When the Black Watch and the 2nd Battalion, Highland Light Infantry (HLI) reached Egypt, they joined the Queen's Own Cameron Highlanders (from Gibraltar) and the 1st Battalion, Gordon

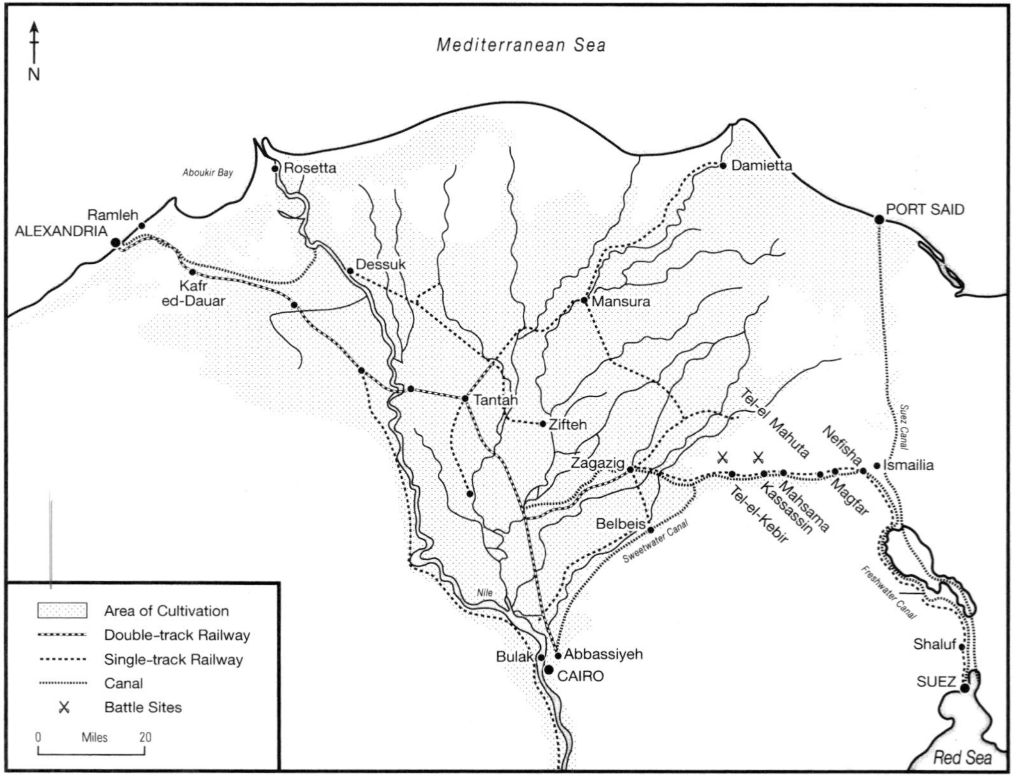

Map 5 *Intervention in Egypt, 1882*

Highlanders (from Malta) to form the Highland Brigade, part of the 2nd Division. Acclimatisation proved particularly difficult for soldiers coming from Britain, with Private Lachlan McLean (Black Watch) finding the heat in Alexandria 'something fearful, the sand about six inches deep, and the dust so thick that we could not see three paces in front of us'.[11] Even more irritating for all soldiers and marines were the ants, mosquitos and, above all, the flies: as Lieutenant H. W. Denne (Gordon Highlanders) observed, the flies settled on individuals not 'one at a time but in hundreds'. Bathing regularly at Ramleh afforded immense, if temporary, relief.[12]

Of the early correspondents from Egypt, several soldiers reported genuine hostility towards Arabi, reflecting both the animus of local Europeans towards him as the purported instigator of the 'massacres' and their own indignation about the ransacking of properties by his supporters.[13] Soldiers and marines, though, were even more eager to describe their baptisms of fire and their skirmishing with the enemy. They participated in regular reconnaissance patrols from Ramleh, engaging at long range with Arabi's forces deployed in defensive positions at Kafr ed-Dauar. A Stirlingshire marine, who had formerly worked in the office of the *Stirling Observer*, reassured his parents that 'The Arabs are very poor marksmen, or else they could have killed every man in my company', as it advanced across an exposed, open plain.[14] A Black Watch officer, engaged as a military correspondent for the *Scotsman*, agreed that the accuracy of the enemy's fire was 'very bad', and that the Highland Brigade, commanded by the Asante veteran Sir Archibald Alison, looked forward to action under the overall command of Sir Garnet Wolseley.[15]

On 30 August the brigade embarked at Alexandria to sail towards Port Said, passing through the Suez Canal, en route to Ismailia. Wolseley had sought to outflank Arabi by switching his point of attack to the east and launching a direct assault on Cairo along the Sweetwater Canal and its accompanying railway. Arabi responded by reinforcing his defences at Tel-el-Kebir, by building dams across the canal (the only source of fresh water to Ismailia) and by opening the locks on the southern branch of the canal, which carried fresh water to the port of Suez. To conserve the precious supply of water at Suez, the 1st Battalion, Seaforth Highlanders, which included two companies of the 2nd Battalion and had arrived from Aden on 8 August, were sent down the canal in a gunboat to engage the enemy at Shaluf (20 August). They disembarked and, in the words of a Crieff soldier, 'found what kind of stuff they [the enemy] were made of'. Reports soon reached Scotland of the heroic efforts of Lieutenant Lang in leading a party of sailors and Seaforths across the canal under enemy fire to turn the Egyptian flank.[16] By dispersing the enemy, the Seaforths managed to close the lock gates and preserve the supply of drinking water for Suez.

With his southern flank secured, Wolseley ordered several units forward to disperse the enemy, repair sections of railway track and clear the dams. Although the Highland Brigade was not involved in the skirmishing and artillery duels, some Scots were involved and wrote of their achievements. Among the many descriptions of the famous cavalry charge on the night of 28 August near Kassassin Lock were a somewhat garbled account by Lieutenant-Colonel David Milne-Home, the Conservative MP for Berwick-upon-Tweed, who was seriously injured in the charge, and a more accurate version from a trooper of the 2nd Life Guards from Edinburgh. He recalled that

> We had covered some ten miles distance – intending, as I understood, to charge the enemy's guns – and were trotting along, when a line of his infantry, about 200 hundred yards off, opened fire right across our front. We at once charged, and literally cut the enemy to pieces.

Unhorsed in the charge, he fought in the mêlée, found another mount and joined in the capture of the Egyptian camp, where tons of ammunition and some 1,000 rifles were seized.[17]

Capturing enemy supplies was all too important, as the leading units outran their commissariat and the railway did not function on a regular basis until early September. As Dr Alex S. Rose explained in a letter to his father in Brechin, all units, including the medical support, undertook arduous duties at this time amid the searing heat and deep sand. They lacked double-lined tents and endured appalling food, as well as water whose 'smell and taste are more easily . . . imagined than described'. The shortage of horses hindered the movement of hospital stores, left his staff exhausted after moving camps, and impaired the care of the mounting toll of sick. 'The transport service', he claimed, 'had somehow broken down, the result being that we were much hampered in all our movements, and sometimes were left quite helpless.' Once encamped at Kassassin, the British encountered an Egyptian counter-attack on 9 September, and, in Rose's opinion, were extremely fortunate that so many of the shells burrowed into the sand instead of exploding on impact.[18]

This letter, like so many others, arrived after the news of the victory at Tel-el-Kebir and the capture of Cairo reached Britain. Scottish newspapers immediately assumed that the Highland Brigade must have been prominent in the battle but the initial, and somewhat cryptic, report from Wolseley merely claimed that all were brave but that the Irish had distinguished themselves in the fighting.[19] As notification of the casualty returns soon followed, it dawned on editors north of the border that this commentary was far from adequate. The *Scotsman* asserted that the Highland Brigade and the Seaforth Highlanders (who served with the Indian contingent) had assumed a 'conspicuous part in the capture of Tel-el-Kebir. No portion of the British force bore themselves more splendidly, or, it is understood, suffered more heavily on that day . . .' Although the Highland Brigade amounted to about one-sixth of the force, it had suffered 74 per cent of the killed and 46 per cent of the wounded (according to the initial casualty returns).[20] As the returns became more detailed, the *Dundee Courier & Argus* protested that 'the Royal Irish had two men killed' while 'the Highland Brigade had forty-five killed', and that even if 'Wolseley's praise of the Irish troops was well deserved, as their bravery is well known', the Highland Brigade had not received the praise 'it deserved'.[21] Compounding this indignation was the absence of any reference to Major-General Alison in the dispatch (despite a mention of the Duke of Connaught, who had commanded the Guards, a unit held in reserve throughout the battle). In deprecating this oversight, Glasgow's *North British Daily Mail* maintained that 'The burden of the fray fell where the men fell thickest, and that was at the point where the Highlanders fought.' It insisted that the doubt cast upon their prowess by Sir Garnet Wolseley's dispatch should be removed and their gallantry vindicated.[22]

The letters of soldiers and the reports of war correspondents now assumed an even greater significance than normally. The honour of Scottish regiments seemed at issue and a profusion of letters from Egypt was published. Even 'a hurried account' from a Black Watch officer, claiming that the old 42nd entered the trenches 'first', was not only published in the *Scotsman* but reprinted in several newspapers.[23] Effusive tributes in the metropolitan press were reproduced in Scotland, including Cameron's account in the *Standard* which described the charge and identified Private Donald Cameron (Cameron Highlanders) as the first man to mount the parapet and the second to fall, an event confirmed by his comrade in arms, Private W. Wood. Cameron was immediately hailed as a local hero in Perthshire.[24] The Dundee *Weekly News* reprinted another report from the *Daily Telegraph*, lauding the advance of the 'gallant Seaforths' south of the canal. Despite a barrage of badly aimed fire, they charged the enemy trenches, seizing four guns, and made for the battery beyond. A young lieutenant had led the assault 'with conspicuous bravery, straight at a piece which was just ready to fire', leaving the gunners 'aghast at his audacity'.[25]

As impressions of Highland heroism were now taking root, the first major letter from the front – a letter of about 3,000 words from a Black Watch NCO – was published on 5 October in the Edinburgh *Daily Review*. The first of several evocative, first-hand accounts, it described the twenty-five-mile march from Ismailia, the preparations for the battle, and the storming of the entrenchments. The author described how the Highland Brigade had struggled across the desert under the 'blistering sun' over three days from Ismailia to Wolseley's camp at Kassassin. A couple of days' rest followed while they waited for supplies to be brought up by boat and trains, whereupon the brigade assembled for the night march on Tel-el-Kebir. After marching into the night, they stopped for a brief sleep and then, in preparation for the assault, were

> told not a shot was to be fired, to rush over the ditches and earthworks and bayonet them . . . The 42d was on the right in two lines, 50 yards apart; then on our left came the other Highland regiments. The Guards etc., were – I don't know where; anyhow they did nothing.

The dawn was just rising when the brigade came within about a hundred yards (probably over 200 yards but accounts of the distance varied) of the 'redoubtable fortress'. After the enemy opened fire, the men fell to the ground and then

> charged by no word of command, for none could be heard. The cheer that was given was terrific . . . Not a man flinched at the charge. The pipes struck up, while all the time, as far as we could see to the front – right and left – was a sheet of flame from the enemy's rifles and cannon.

The men plunged into a ditch about six feet wide by eight feet deep and so had to climb a wall about fourteen feet high. The Highlanders responded 'by driving our bayonets into the soil, and climbing up against a terrific storm of bullets, the din being terrific'. Officers and NCOs led the onslaught, 'bayoneting and shooting every man'. Sergeant-Major John McNeil, sword in hand, killed six in succession before falling mortally wounded with three shots in the stomach and groin. As the enemy fled from the first trench, some reassembled in the second and began firing shot and shell into the Highland Brigade:

> 'This will never do', said Lord Kennedy, who was with me: 'C Company, follow me', and off we went. It was now daylight . . . Not a shot was fired, not a word spoken, while we opened up in loose order, brought our bay-

Figure 4 *'The Battle of Tel-el-Kebir: First in the Fray' (*Illustrated London News, 7 October 1882)*

onets to the charge, gave a Highland cheer, and at them we went. While their fire was blinding us we bayoneted 60 men there, and reversed their cannon and fired on themselves.

British cavalry and artillery followed, filling in part of the trench and galloping into the fort: 'We gave them a deafening cheer, which they returned, galloped in front of us, wheeled about the guns, and poured grape, shot, and shell after the now retreating army.'[26]

It was a measure of the letter's significance that it was reprinted two days later in *The Times*, where it was compared with a second 'somewhat bald' dispatch from Wolseley. The letter was commended as giving 'an excellent picture of what happened', and showing how men like Lieutenant Kennedy, acting in the 'presence of great danger,' can achieve 'high deeds'. The impact of the letter was magnified by its appearance in *The Times* on the same day as the *Illustrated London News* carried Prior's graphic depiction of Highlanders storming the trenches on its front page, entitled 'First in the Fray'.[27] The NCO's letter or extracts from it were reprinted in numerous English and Irish newspapers.[28]

Wolseley's second and much fuller dispatch aroused even more indignation than the first. In view of the testimony from correspondents, war-artists and the soldiers themselves, another bland report seemed incomprehensible. Once again Wolseley referred initially to the exploits of the 2nd Brigade (in which the Royal Irish and the Royal Irish Fusiliers served), 'well supported' by the Guards under the Duke of Connaught, before acknowledging that the Highland Brigade under Alison reached the enemy's defences first. Thereafter, as the *Scotsman* summarised, Wolseley only mentioned that the Highlanders stormed the fortifications in a 'dashing manner', while south of the canal the 'most gallant' Seaforths stormed the enemy line in an 'impetuous onslaught'. What the Scottish editors did not know was that the dispatch, in which Wolseley also praised the discipline and endurance of the young soldier (implicitly endorsing the government's army reforms) and commended the medical arrangements and support services (so concealing the main deficiencies of the campaign), was a carefully crafted document.[29] Wolseley wanted a peerage and a pension desperately. As he informed his wife, 'The government owe me a great deal . . . The battle of Tel el Kebir has been worth millions to Gladstone's administration and if they behave shabbily towards me I shall show them up.' He feared resistance at Court and so praised the Duke of Connaught and 'that useless fellow Fitz George' (the son of the Duke of Cambridge), insisting that 'the Queen's only sympathies & solicitude are for Her own selfish self and Her family'.[30]

Wolseley's praise of the Irish soldier was particularly important and adroitly timed. Ever since the Fenian penetration of army units in the 1860s and the abortive Fenian rising of 1867, the loyalty of the Irish soldier had been a concern, not least in 1882 when Gladstone was trying to suppress the agrarian agitation in Ireland by a mixture of coercion and land reform. His efforts to reach an accommodation with the imprisoned Charles Stuart Parnell in the so-called Kilmainham 'treaty' (April 1882) had just been thwarted by the Phoenix Park murders (6 May 1882).[31] So positive reports on Irish soldiery were bound to be welcome in London.

Unaware of Wolseley's quest for a peerage and a pension (both of which he would receive), many Scottish newspapers fulminated. 'The press and public opinion of the United Kingdom are putting things to rights', claimed the *Dundee Courier & Argus*.[32] At Fort William a public gathering passed a resolution protesting about Wolseley's dispatch and condemning the slight done to the 'brave Highlanders'.[33] Edinburgh's *Daily Review* reproduced a report in the *Liverpool Post* claiming that 'Scotch national sentiment' felt affronted, and that 'the British Empire at large will regard with grateful satisfaction the splendid services rendered by Sir Archibald and his brave Highlanders'.[34]

Scottish newspapers reported that many soldiers serving in non-Highland units praised the Highlanders and recognised their sacrifices. They printed several letters from Scots Guardsmen confirming that the Highlanders entered the Egyptian lines first, driving the enemy before them and inflicting terrible carnage at the point of the bayonet. The *Strathearn Herald* printed a letter from a Crieff sergeant serving in the York and Lancaster regiment, who admitted that his regiment had been very lucky in the battle, unlike the Highland Brigade which had 'lost pretty heavily – more especially the 74th and 79th'.[35] The Scottish press also reported that the Highlanders resented the 'scant justice' done to their services and those of their fallen comrades. 'The Highlanders are somewhat piqued', wrote a Black Watch officer, ' that no special mention was made of them. Men could not possibly have behaved better.'[36] Lieutenant Henry Denne (Gordons) assured his father that 'Our brigade did all the work . . . The Guards came in at 7 o'clock after all the firing was over.' Writing on 20 September, he had heard already 'that the Irish Brigade have got all the credit. If this is true I don't know how it can be as here we got it all.'[37]

The Royal Marines, who had fought in the front line of the 2nd Brigade alongside the two Irish units and the York and Lancaster, also felt overlooked and shared the resentment of the Highlanders. A Dundonian Marine protested that the services of the marines had been ignored while 'upon regiments to their right and left and in the distant rear compliments were showered'. He sympathised with the Highlanders as they had 'behaved splendidly', confirming that 'Everyone here gives the Highlanders great praise.' He regarded the services of the Marines, the two Irish regiments and the Highlanders as on a par: 'it would be difficult to give one a greater share of honour than another'.[38] The *Aberdeen Journal*, nonetheless, suspected that the partiality of Wolseley towards the Irish troops reflected political sensitivity or 'good diplomacy', that is, praising 'the Irish troops' at a time 'when conciliatory and healing measures are the order of the day'.[39]

Another group who testified to the prowess of the Highlanders were Englishmen serving in Highland battalions. They confirmed the arduous experience of marching through the deep sand from Ismailia: 'I never felt so tired in all my life', admitted Private James Judson (Black Watch).[40] They wrote of the pre-battle preparations, including the briefing to attack 'in the old style with the bayonets, and on no account to fire until within the entrenchments': as a Wakefield soldier added, 'It is to be an old-fashioned fight such as was fought by the Highlanders of old.'[41] The subsequent night march, recalled Private George Bedson (Black Watch) from Stafford, 'was a grand sight', with 'the two lines advancing in the night; they looked like walls moving'.[42] In the final charge, the officers led from the front: 'I shouted "Charge"', wrote Lieutenant-Colonel Abel Straghan (HLI) to his mother in Hereford. 'There was no time to think of dismounting or of the absurdity of charging a redoubt on horseback. The great thing was to get the men on.'[43] The men responded with 'a right good British cheer', wrote Judson, and began bayoneting the enemy: 'Heartrending was the sight of the dead and dying, who lay all around us – an old man here, a young lad there, or a riderless horse galloping madly on in confusion.'[44]

This outpouring of concern and indignation merely ensured that letters from the front found a ready outlet in the Scottish press. Although most soldiers concentrated on the battle itself, an event that lasted barely an hour from the charge of the Highland Brigade at 4.55 a.m., there were some important differences. First, there were fewer letters from the Gordon Highlanders than from the other Scottish units because the regiment had fewer connections with Scotland. Prior to its amalgamation with the 92nd in 1881, the old 75th had not been in Scotland since 1820 and had drawn the overwhelming majority of its recruits from England and Ireland.[45] Secondly, the Seaforths, operating south of the canal, had a different battle experience. Following their officers, they had charged the Egyptian guns and ignored the firing over their heads. In losing only one man killed (shot through his Afghan medal) and three wounded, they had dispersed the Egyptians rapidly, shooting them over 'like rabbits' and capturing their guns. A Seaforth from Crieff described it as 'about the shortest fight that ever I had, and as cheap a medal that any army got'.[46] For these veterans of the march from Kabul to Kandahar, their great achievement was following on from the victory and marching through the heat of the day to seize the vital railway junction of Zagazig before nightfall. As an Arbroath soldier asserted, the Seaforths had done 'what I believe no other English regiment could do – fight for five hours [that is, including the preparatory march], and march thirty miles before night'.[47]

Pride in their marching prowess was not the exclusive preserve of the Seaforth Highlanders: all soldiers whether Scots, English or Irish recognised that marching involved tests of fitness, endurance and discipline. The Highland Brigade, though, had certainly suffered in its march from Ismailia. After spending over a week on board ship, they had marched through the soft sand of the desert, often 'a foot to eighteen inches in depth', over a period of fifty-two hours.[48] Soldiers recalled the dismal ordeal, marching at night and resting under the glare of the sun, eating only a 'few hard, broken biscuits' and drinking polluted canal water, in which Arabi had floated down his dead. They admitted that hundreds fell out on the line of march, particularly on the first march, and some recalled the appalling stench at the sites of recent skirmishes, notably at Tel-el-Mahuta.[49]

Following rest and recuperation at Kassassin camp, many described the preparation for the night march on Tel-el-Kebir and the *frisson* of excitement that rippled through the ranks following Alison's order 'to fight in the good old Highland fashion. Never mind firing at them. Press on and let them feel the cold steel.'[50] Approximately halfway through the seven-mile march, the men paused to rest and drink rum, whereupon the captains of companies reminded their men that they would charge in the early morning 'in the good old fashion of Scottish warfare, the way our forefathers used to fight'.[51] Having distributed the rum, Quartermaster John Ainslie (Cameron Highlanders) followed the two lines which at one stage lost their bearings and the two wings almost marched into each other. He was mightily impressed by the silent tramp through the night (punctuated only by a drunken soldier of the HLI): 'this slow funeral-like march impressed me more than even the battle itself, for every minute I expected the enemy to open fire on us . . .'[52]

The Highlanders had marched ahead of the other brigade and were closer to the entrenchments when the first shots were fired. They responded, as a Cameron Highlander described, with 'a wild Highland cheer, regardless of the bullets whistling around our heads' and charged ahead with bayonets ready.[53] If few reflected on the confusion experienced as they crossed the ditch and clambered into the trenches, still less on the falling back of some Gordons and Camerons when fighting the Sudanese soldiers manning part of the Egyptian defences, they dwelt upon the feelings experienced. While Corporal Robertson reckoned that their cheer 'fairly frightened the wits out of the Arabs', Daniel Campbell, a fellow Black Watch soldier, recollected that 'some of our men were half-mad to see their comrades falling before they were able to strike a blow; and whenever they got within reach of the enemy they fought like lions'.[54] A Cameron NCO claimed that the charge 'was the finest sight I ever saw in my life. We were like a lot of mad dogs let loose. We charged right up to the trench, into it, and right into their own ground without firing. I tell you the Egyptians will not be in a hurry again to stand before the Highlanders.'[55] 'The bayonet', wrote Private Lachlan McLean (Black Watch),

> was the only thing we used, and we used it right well. It was horrible work, and a horrible sight when it was done. The gunners were lying in tens and twenties under their guns; they were the only ones that seemed to make a stand . . . A French reporter was telling a few of us that our charge was more like a rush of demons than a charge of men.[56]

Although the battle proved short and overwhelmingly lop-sided, Scots wrote of their narrow escapes. Many appreciated that the casualties would have been even higher had the enemy been able to reduce the elevation of their artillery.[57] The HLI took the heaviest casualties (seventeen killed and fifty-seven wounded); they attacked a peculiarly daunting redoubt, protected by a ditch that was 'exceptionally wide, deep and steep, and unlike other portions of the enemy's lines, composed of hard compact sand and gravel'. A Glasgow Highlander regarded these entrenchments as 'the strongest of the kind I have ever seen, and in possession of British soldiers would have been deemed impregnable'.[58] Yet the victory came at a terrible price. Juxtaposed with stories of valour, spirit and courage under fire were accounts of honourable deaths in battle, fully in accord with warrior-hero tradition. Both the Egyptian gunners and the Sudanese soldiers proffered staunch resistance: the latter, as Captain R. C. Coveny (Black Watch) recalled, 'died very game', as did young Scottish officers, often sons of well-connected families. Among those killed at the head of their men were Lieutenants Louis Somervell (HLI) and Graham Stirling of Strowan, Perthshire, who fell, according to one of his sergeants, 'as a Black Watch man should'.[59] Many recounted the daring exploits of

Sergeant-Major McNeil, a very tall man who was conspicuous in the fighting and fell mortally wounded 'while bravely leading on our men. He has gone', added Drummer W. Bogle, 'with the universal regret of every man in his regiment.'[60]

McNeil received his last drink of water from James Mathers, one of two scripture readers, who wrote an account of the harrowing scenes in the aftermath of the battle. The readers moved about the mounds of dead, dying and wounded, giving water and peaches where they could to the wounded, including the 'poor wounded Arabs'. They found examples of spiritual grace among the wounded 'Christian soldiers', one of whom urged his doctor to attend the others first 'for they are not ready to die, and I am'. As Mathers and Miller added: 'Such is the power of the gospel.'[61] Quartermaster Ainslie was equally solicitous, dispensing rum to injured soldiers in a field tent, an offering that may have been more beneficial than the water. A Black Watch sergeant, having described the wounded as 'burying their heads in the sand to cool them and all who were able crying for water', could only find canal water 'that you would not wash the door-step with, as it was thick with blood and mud . . .'[62]

While some Scots remained with the burial detail, 'where it was almost impossible to draw a breath of fresh air' after four days but at least lived off the provisions in Arabi's camp,[63] others moved on to occupy key sites along the railway (the Gordons at Tantah, the Black Watch at Belbeis). Lacking proper supplies due to the inadequate transport arrangements, the Black Watch languished for eight days without tents, eating hard biscuits and preserved meat and drinking muddy canal water. 'Our luxuries', wrote Corporal Robertson, 'were the mosquitoes and sandflies who did not forget to take it out of our bare legs at night.'[64] As the forces were now stationery, often quartered in verminous and insanitary conditions, diarrhoea, dysentery and ophthalmia took an increasing toll. At Tantah where the Gordons remained for twelve days, five officers and 140 men fell sick and were sent away for treatment. Even in Cairo, where soldiers initially occupied spacious barracks, a Scottish sapper reported that 'There's a lot of sickness here amongst our troops, and I am sorry to say we are all more or less sick.' Despite the local 'stench', he still regarded Cairo as 'a beautiful city' and relished living in a room 'that a laird would be proud of in Scotland . . .'[65] Private Geddes, a Scots Guardsman from Bannockburn, was equally impressed with Cairo as a city, especially the 'magnificent' mosque of Mehemet Ali. Geddes had entered the city as early as 15 September, part of the escort for Wolseley, and had seen the tumultuous reception for the general from the Europeans and native Christians.[66]

Once Highland and other units reached Cairo, or tented quarters nearby at Ghezirah, and the Khedive returned, a grand review of 18,000 British troops was held at Abdin Palace on 30 September. After the march past the Khedive, Private Campbell described him as 'a very pleasant-looking, big, stout man, and he appeared to be well pleased with our warlike appearance'.[67] The crowd, as reported in the metropolitan press, greeted Sir Archibald Alison warmly: the 'one-armed general, conspicuous by his inability to salute otherwise than by a graceful bow . . . The General, who wore a sprig of native heather in his helmet, enjoys much popularity, and so do the Highlanders.' *The Times* alluded to the impression that the Highlanders had been 'rather ungenerously ignored in official dispatches', and observed that the crowd 'seemed disposed to grant unofficial honours', cheering loudly when the Black Watch appeared leading the Highland Brigade. When the Indian Division followed, the Seaforths appeared particularly smart, with most men wearing the Afghan medal and the Kandahar Cross.[68]

After all the controversy over the official dispatches, several Scottish newspapers reproduced the final address of Alison to the brigade when he laid down his command on 21 October 1882. Commanding a Highland Brigade, he declared, had fulfilled a dream of his youth, and he had most admired not their 'fiery valour' in rushing over the entrenchments but 'the disciplined restraint of the long night march over the desert . . .' When the battle was over, he added, his first thought was

> had my older chief Sir Colin Campbell risen from his grave, he would have been proud of you. He would have thought that you had well maintained the reputation of the Highland regiments, and the honour of the Scottish name; he would have deemed you worthy successors of that now historic brigade which he led up the green slopes of Alma![69]

An NCO of the Cameron Highlanders, who had served in the Indian Mutiny, reciprocated these sentiments, claiming that 'Since the days of old Sir Colin Campbell . . . I have never known of an officer so much beloved as our present chief, Sir A. Alison.'[70] This linkage between the exploits of the Highland Brigade in Egypt and those of its predecessors would be reproduced in popular histories, notably James Cromb's *The Highland Brigade: Its Battles and Heroes*.[71]

The veteran status of the Cameron NCO testified to another controversy associated with the campaign, namely the purported vindication of the army reforms of Cardwell and Childers. Victory, in the opinion of Childers, fully justified the introduction of short-service enlistments, the creation of an Army Reserve and the abolition of flogging on active service. His assertions, supported by Gladstone in his parliamentary vote of thanks, and by Wolseley in his dispatches, were endorsed by Liberal politicians and newspapers in Scotland. As the *Inverness Courier* asserted: 'Our experience in Egypt seems to show that we have obtained the right sort of men.' [72] Several Scottish newspapers responded by reproducing an analysis of the Highland Brigade in the *Standard*, which showed that men in the HLI had an average service of eight years, that the Cameron Highlanders had 460 men over twenty-four years old and none under twenty, and the Gordons 370 men over twenty-four years service and none under twenty-one. The Black Watch had the highest proportion of younger men but it had replaced all its men under twenty years' of age by Reservists and had 300 men of over six years' service. 'These regiments', it concluded, 'cannot be considered as young. They have a strong nucleus of steady old soldiers in the ranks, and differ very widely from regiments composed of short-service men.'[73]

Scotland had little opportunity to praise these soldiers, whether young or old, as the Highland Brigade remained in Egypt as part of the army of occupation. If there was scant evidence of jingoistic displays north of the border (until the South African War), this may reflect not only the continuing prominence of religious and other domestic political issues[74] but also the rarity of Scots being able to welcome home returning regiments after major engagements. Just as Scottish units failed to return immediately after the Zulu, Afghan or Boer wars (the 92nd took six months to do so), only the 1st Seaforth returned to England after the Egyptian campaign. Having served abroad since 1871, they now returned after the Afghan and Egyptian campaigns to receive a heroes' welcome at Cowes and occupy a new station at Parkhurst, Isle of Wight.[75] On 18 November the battalion participated in the great review of 8,000 troops by the queen, watched by a 'countless multitude' along the entire route to St James's Park. Wearing their Royal Stuart tartan trews for the last time, their 'physique and bearing', claimed the *Standard*, 'excited universal admiration'. Their 'war-torn frames' and 'sunburnt, almost swarthy complexions' testified to long service in the East.[76]

The campaign had a lasting appeal, prompting numerous paintings and prints of the major battles of Kassassin and Tel-el-Kebir. Quite apart from the sketches in the *Illustrated London News* and the

Graphic (including a coloured supplement in the latter's edition of 3 March 1883 entitled 'The Highland Brigade at Tel-el-Kebir'), there were several paintings of the Seaforths and Camerons in action. These included the depiction of the Camerons charging by F. Claridge Turner, known only in chromolithograph, and *The Charge of the Seaforth Highlanders at the Battle of Tel-el-Kebir* (July 1883) painted by Frederick Cowie for the Prince of Wales.[77] Alphonse Marie de Neuville's highly acclaimed, all-action painting of the Black Watch in *Tel-el-Kebir* (1883) contrasted with Elizabeth Butler's *After the Battle* (1885), a somewhat ill-proportioned representation of Wolseley riding towards a drawbridge past files of cheering Highlanders. Although Butler found 'crowds of Highlanders to represent, and went in for the minutest rendering of the equipment then in use', she knew that her husband disapproved of the painting, since beating 'those poor fellaheen [sic] soldiers was not a matter for exultation'. So, after the painting's eventual appearance at the Royal Academy in 1885, and only 'moderate success', she had it cut up.[78]

Her husband, Lieutenant-Colonel William Butler, acknowledged that the army now enjoyed 'a good deal of public and private adulation' after its return from Egypt.[79] If this was evident in the massive displays of public enthusiasm in London when the Household Cavalry returned, and at the great review in November, causing excitement 'among all classes',[80] Glasgow was at least able to bestow belated recognition on the services of Sir Archibald Alison. When he returned from Egypt in 1883, the Lord Provost presented Alison with a sword of honour before a large gathering in the City Hall and Lady Alison with a diamond tiara. In a ceremony reported in the metropolitan as well as the Scottish press, with a sketch on the front page of the *Illustrated London News*, Alison accepted the honour on behalf of the Highland Brigade and recounted its exploits without overlooking the difficulties of the night march to Tel-el-Kebir or the resistance encountered in the entrenchments. He praised the 'great principle of nationality', not least as Wolseley had recently spoken in Dublin, urging the Irish to emulate the Scots and form an Irish Brigade. Alison declared that

> I am very certain that as each nation has its own distinctive character, so these men will be best understood and best handled by those of their own blood (Cheers) . . . There are two sentiments, gentlemen, to which you can always appeal in the British soldier and never appeal in vain – one is memory of his country, and the other is the reputation of his corps (Cheers). Once try them, and you have no idea of the power it presents.[81]

The *Glasgow News* described the occasion as a 'red-letter day in the history of the city'; Glasgow had honoured one of its own, Sir Archibald, and his regiments, and had done so without any 'evanescent' sense of 'triumph and victory'.[82]

Notes

1 H. C. G. Matthew, *Gladstone 1875–1898* (Oxford: Clarendon Press, 1995), p. 123; Shannon, *Gladstone: Heroic Minister*, pp. 305–6.

2 *Dunfermline Journal*, 16 September 1882, p. 2; *Kilmarnock Standard*, 23 September 1882, p. 2.

3 A. Schölch, 'The "Men on the Spot" and the English Occupation of Egypt in 1882', *Historical Journal*, 19, no. 3 (1976), pp. 773–85; I. F. W. Beckett, *Victoria's Wars* (Aylesbury: Shire Publications, 1974), p. 55.

4 *Parl[iamentary] Deb[ates]*, third series, 270 (14 June 1882), col. 1146; Shannon, *Gladstone: Heroic Minister*, pp. 306–7.

5 *Scotsman*, 25 and 27 July 1882, pp. 4 and 4.

6 *Edinburgh Courant*, 31 July 1882, p. 4; *Glasgow News*, 14 September 1882, p. 4; *Kilmarnock Standard*, 15 and 29 July 1882, pp. 2 and 2; and *North British Daily Mail*, 13 and 17 July 1882, pp. 6 and 4.

7 Wilkinson-Latham, *From Our Special Correspondent*, p. 171.

8 'The Black Watch', ch. 12, *[York] Evening Press*, 21 November 1895, p. 2; BWRA, 0203/1, A. V. Barwood, diary, 1 December 1882, p. 1.

9 'Letter from an Invergordon Young Man in Egypt', *Invergordon Times*, 13 September 1882, p. 3; 'An Army Scripture Reader's Account of the Highland Brigade at Egypt', *Nairnshire Telegraph*, 31 January 1883, p. 3.

10 P. B. Boyden, *Tommy Atkins' Letters: The History of the British Army Postal Service from 1795* (London: National Army Museum, 1990), p. 21.

11 'Letter from an Invergordon Young Man in Egypt', p. 3.

12 GH Museum, PB 228, Lieutenant H. W. Seton-Karr, diary, 19–20 August 1882; PB 64/1, Lieutenant H. W. Denne to his father, 22 August 1882; 'The Marines on Shore', *Scotsman*, 23 September 1882, p. 7.

13 'A Journey to Egypt', *Scotsman*, 4 September 1882, p. 5; 'Letter from an Invergordon Young Man in Egypt', p. 3; see also BWRA, 0203/1, Barwood, diary, 1 December 1882, p. 5.

14 'The War in Egypt', *Stirling Observer*, 28 September 1882, p. 4; see also GH Museum, PB 64/1, Denne Mss, Denne to his father, 22 August 1882.

15 'The Black Watch at Ramleh', *Scotsman*, 8 September 1882, p. 5.

16 'The Engagement at Shaluf', *Scotsman*, 4 September 1882, p. 5; 'The Battle of Tel-el-Kebir', *Strathearn Herald*, 21 October 1882, p. 2.

17 'Letter from a Life Guardsman Belonging to Edinburgh', *Edinburgh Courant*, 16 September 1882, p. 5; 'Colonel Milne-Home's War Experiences', *Edinburgh Evening News*, 22 September 1882, p. 4.

18 'Letter from a Townsman in Egypt', *Brechin Advertiser*, 10 October 1882, p. 3; see also Lieutenant-Colonel E. W. C. Sandes, *The Royal Engineers in Egypt and the Sudan* (Chatham: The Institution of Royal Engineers, 1937), pp. 42–4.

19 'The War', *The Times*, 14 September 1882, p. 6; *Edinburgh Courant*, 14 and 15 September 1882, pp. 4 and 4; *Ross-shire Journal*, 15 September 1882, p. 2; *North British Daily Mail*, 14 September 1882, p. 4.

20 *Scotsman*, 18 and 21 September 1882, pp. 4 and 4.

21 'The Highlanders in Egypt', *Dundee Courier & Argus*, 30 September 1882, p. 2; on final casualties, see M. J. Williams, 'The Egyptian Campaign of 1882' in Bond (ed.), *Victorian Military Campaigns*, pp. 243–78, especially p. 274, and D. Featherstone, *Tel El-Kebir* (London: Osprey, 1993), p. 86.

22 'Who bore the brunt of Battle?', *North British Daily Mail*, 22 September 1882, p. 4.

23 'The Black Watch', *Strathearn Herald*, 30 September 1882, p. 2; *[Dundee] Weekly News*, 30 September 1882, p. 7.

24 'A Perthshire Hero at Tel-el-Kebir', *Kinross-shire Advertiser*, 7 October 1882, p. 3; 'A Local Hero Killed at Tel-el-Kebir', *Blairgowrie Advertiser*, 7 October 1882, p. 4; 'A Local Hero of Tel-el-Kebir', *[Dundee] Weekly News*, 7 October 1882, p. 7.

25 'Gallantry of the Seaforth Highlanders at Tel-El-Kebir', *[Dundee] Weekly News*, 30 September 1882, p. 7.

26 'The Battle of Tel-El-Kebir', *[Edinburgh] Daily Review*, 5 October 1882, p. 5.

27 *The Times*, 7 October 1882, pp. 5 and 7; 'The Battle of Tel-El-Kebir: First in the Fray', *Illustrated London News*, 7 October 1882, p. 1.

28 *Irish Times*, 9 October 1882, p. 5; *Westcott's Local Press*, 12 October 1882, p. 6; *Cornish Times*, 14 October 1882, p. 3; *Portsmouth Times*, 18 October 1882, p. 7; *Isle of Wight Journal*, 21 October 1882, p. 6; *Reading Mercury*, 28 October 1882, p. 7.

29 *Scotsman*, 7 October 1882, p. 6; see also 'Battle of Tel-El-Kebir. Written Despatch from Sir Garnet Wolseley', *Derby Mercury*, 11 October 1882, p. 3.

30 Royal Pavilions Libraries and Museums (RPLM), Brighton and Hove City Council, Hove Library, Wolseley Collection, W/P.11, Sir G. Wolseley to Lady Wolseley, 21 and 28 September 1882, ff. 21 and 23.

31 Both Lord Frederick Cavendish, the new Chief Secretary of Ireland, and his Under-Secretary, T. H. Burke, were murdered. On Fenian infiltration, see E. M. Spiers, 'Army organisation and society in the nineteenth century', in T. Bartlett and K. Jeffery (eds), *A Military History of Ireland* (Cambridge: Cambridge University Press, 1996), pp. 335–57.

32 'Honour to Whom Honour is Due', *Dundee Courier & Argus*, 13 October 1882, p. 4; see also 'The Situation in Egypt', *Argyllshire Herald*, 14 October 1882, p. 2.

33 'The Highland Brigade', *Strathearn Herald*, 14 October 1882, p. 2.

34 'Sir Archibald Alison and the Highlanders', *[Edinburgh] Daily Review*, 13 October 1882, p. 5.

35 'Letter from a Crieff Soldier', *Strathearn Herald*, 14 October 1882, p. 2; 'A Dundee Soldier at Tel-El-Kebir', *Dundee Courier & Argus*, 6 October 1882, p. 5; 'The Scots Guards at Tel-El-Kebir', *Edinburgh Courant*, 13 October 1882, p. 2.

36 'The Highland Brigade', p. 2; 'Tel-El-Kebir', *Scotsman*, 19 October 1882, p. 5.'The Highlanders and Sir Garnet Wolseley, Indignation at Cairo', *Aberdeen Weekly Journal*, 14 October 1882, p. 3.

37 GH Museum, PB 64/3, Denne Mss, Denne to his father, 20 September 1882.

38 'Slight to the Marines', *[Dundee] Weekly News*, 21 October 1882, p. 7.

39 *Aberdeen Journal*, 2 October 1882, p. 2; there may have been some truth in this as Wolseley evinced little favouritism for the Irish, whom he once described as 'savages', RPLM, Wolseley Collection, W/P.13, Wolseley to Lady Wolseley, 13 October 1884, f. 25.

40 'A Soldier's Account of Tel-El-Kebir', *[York] Evening Press*, 16 October 1882, p. 3 (reprinted in the *York Herald*, 17 October 1882, p. 5).

41 Ibid. and 'A Yorkshireman's Account of the Capture of Tel-El-Kebir, *[Batley] Reporter*, 7 October 1882, p. 3.

42 'A Private Soldier's Description of the Battle of Tel-El-Kebir', *Staffordshire Advertiser*, 30 September 1882, p. 6.

43 'More About Tel-El-Kebir. Interesting Letter to Herefordshire People', *Hereford Times*, 21 October 1882, p. 2.

44 'A Soldier's Account of Tel-El-Kebir', p. 3.

45 Greenhill Gardyne, *The Life of a Regiment*, 2, p. 241.

46 'Letter from Another Crieff Soldier', *Strathearn Herald*, 21 October 1882, p. 2; see also 'A Soldier's Experiences at Tel-El-Kebir', *Banffshire Journal*, 10 October 1882, p. 3, and 'The 72D Highlanders at Tel-El-Kebir and Zagazig', *Edinburgh Courant*, 13 October 1882, p. 5.

47 'Letter from an Arbroath Man', *Dundee Courier & Argus*, 11 October 1882, p. 3; see also 'Letter from Another Crieff Soldier', p. 2; 'The Indian Contingent at Zagazig', *[Dundee] Weekly News*, 14 October 1882, p. 7; Fairrie, 'Cuidich 'N Righ', p. 42.

48 'The Black Watch at Tel-El-Kebir', *Stirling Observer*, 12 October 1882, p. 2; 'March of the Highland Brigade from Ismailia to the Front', *Edinburgh Courant*, 27 September 1882, p. 5; 'Another Officer's Letter', *Nairnshire Telegraph*, 4 October 1882, p. 4 (reprinted in the *Broad Arrow*, 7 October 1882, p. 502).

49 'Another Officer's letter', p. 4; 'A Montrosian's Account of the Battle of Tel-El-Kebir', *Dundee Courier & Argus*, 13 October 1882, p. 5; 'Extracts from the Diary of Lieut. H. H. L. Malcolm, 79th Q. O. Cameron Highrs, during the Egyptian War, 1882', *The 79th News*, no. 202 (April 1933), p. 151.

50 'A Glasgow Highlander's Description of Tel-El-Kebir', *Glasgow News*, 10 October 1882, p. 5; see also 'The Black Watch at Tel-El-Kebir', p. 2; 'A Soldier's Letter', *Scotsman*, 13 October 1882, p. 5.

51 'A Montrosian's Account of the Battle of Tel-El-Kebir', p. 5.

52 'Soldiers' Letters', *Scotsman*, 6 October 1882, p. 5; Williams, 'The Egyptian Campaign of 1882', in Bond (ed.), *Victorian Military Campaigns*, p. 272; Lieutenant-Colonel L. B. Oatts, *Proud Heritage: The Story of the Highland Light Infantry*, 4 vols (London: Thomas Nelson, 1959), 2, pp. 362–3.

53 'Soldiers' Letters', p. 5; 'An Aberdonian Diary', *Aberdeen Journal*, 19 October 1882, p. 3; 'The Black Watch at Tel-El-Kebir', p. 2.

54 'Corporal Robertson at Tel-El-Kebir', *Fife Herald*, 26 October 1882, p. 6; 'A Rothesay Man at the Charge at Tel-El-Kebir', *Rothesay Express*, 18 October 1882, p. 3; Williams, 'The Egyptian Campaign of 1882', in Bond (ed.), *Victorian Military Campaigns*, p. 273.

55 'The Charge at Tel-El-Kebir', *Elgin Courant and Courier*, 6 October 1882, p. 3.

56 'The Battle of Tel-El-Kebir – Letter from an Invergordon Young Man', *Invergordon Times*, 11 October 1882, p. 2; 'Letter from an Auchterarder Soldier', *Perthshire Advertiser*, 11 October 1882, p. 4.

57 'The Storming of Tel-El-Kebir' and 'The Late Lieutenant G. Stirling', *Strathearn Herald*, 7 and 21 October 1882, pp. 2 and 2; 'A Dundee Highlander at Tel-El-Kebir', *Dundee Courier & Argus*, 11 October 1882, p. 3; 'Letter from an Arbroath Man', p. 3; 'A Soldier's Experience at Tel-El-Kebir', p. 3.

58 'The Highland Brigade', *Scotsman*, 11 October 1882, p. 7; 'A Glasgow Highlander's Description of Tel-El-Kebir', p. 5; 'The Late Major Colville', *Bridge of Allan Reporter*, 14 October 1882, p. 2; Featherstone, *Tel El-Kebir*, p. 86.

59 BWRA, 0204, Lieutenant-Colonel Coveny, 'Letters from Egypt and the Soudan', p. 8; 'The Late Lieutenant Somervell', *Glasgow News*, 21 October 1882, p. 4; 'The Storming of Tel-El-Kebir', p. 2.

60 'The Black Watch at Tel-El-Kebir', p. 2; see also 'A Black Watch Sergeant at Tel-El-Kebir', 19 October 1882, p. 3; 'The Late Lieutenant G. Stirling', p. 2; 'The War in Egypt', *Bridge of Allan Reporter*, 21 October 1882, p. 2.

61 'Army Scripture Readers with the Highland Brigade in Egypt', *[Edinburgh] Daily Review*, 28 September 1882, p. 5.

62 'Soldiers' Letters', p. 6; 'The Storming of Tel-El-Kebir', p. 2.

63 'The Marines at Tel-El-Kebir. Letter from a Dundee Man', *[Dundee] Weekly News*, 14 October 1882, p. 7.

64 'A 42D Man at Tel-El-Kebir', *Kinross-shire Advertiser*, 28 October 1882, p. 3; 'Affairs in Egypt', *North British Daily Mail*, 16 October 1882, p. 5; see also BWRA, 0203/1, Barwood diaries, 2 December 1882, pp. 14–15.

65 'Letter by a Soldier to his Crieff Friends', *Strathearn Herald*, 14 October 1882, p. 2; see also GH Museum, PB 64/4 Denne Mss, Denne to his father, 15 October 1882.

66 'The War in Egypt', *Bridge of Allan Reporter*, 14 October 1882, p. 2.

67 'A Rothesay Man at the Charge at Tel-El-Kebir', p. 3.

68 'Egypt', *The Times*, 2 October 1882, p. 3; 'Review of the British Army at Cairo' and 'The Grand Review at Cairo', *Illustrated London News*, 7 and 21 October 1882, pp. 370 and 418; GH Museum, PB 64/4, Denne Mss, Denne to his father, 15 October 1882.

69 'Sir Archibald Alison and the Highland Brigade', *Huntly Express*, 18 November 1882, p. 6; 'The Highland Brigade', *Stirling Observer*, 9 November 1882, p. 2.

70 'The Highland Brigade', *Stirling Observer*, 9 November 1882, p. 2.

71 Cromb, *The Highland Brigade*, ch. 28.

72 *Inverness Courier*, 10 October 1882, p. 2; see also 'Mr Childers and the Army', *Cornubian and Redruth Times*, 27 October 1882, p. 3; *Parl. Deb.*, third series, 274 (26 October 1882), cols 182, 194; and Andrew Grant, MP, quoted in the *Edinburgh Courant*, 9 October 1882, p. 4.

73 'The State of Egypt', *Standard*, 11 October 1882, p. 5; 'Egypt', *Glasgow Herald*, 11 October 1882, p. 7; ' "Young" and "Formed" Soldiers in the Campaign', *Fife Herald*, 12 October 1882, p. 6.

74 Hutchison, *A Political History of Scotland 1832–1924*, pp. 119–20.

75 'Public Reception of the Seaforth Highlanders', *Portsmouth Times*, 1 November 1882, p. 8.

76 'The Royal Review', *Standard*, 20 November 1882, pp. 5–6.

77 Harrington, *British Artists and War*, p. 216.

78 Butler, *An Autobiography*, p. 194; Usherwood and Spencer-Smith, *Lady Butler*, pp. 85–8; 'Fine Arts', *Illustrated London News*, 28 April 1883, p. 425.

79 Butler, *An Autobiography*, p. 249.

80 *The Times*, 20 November 1882, p. 9.

81 'Presentation to Sir A. Alison', *The Times*, 19 October 1883, p. 6; 'Presentation of a Sword of Honour to Sir Archibald Alison in the City Hall, Glasgow', *Illustrated London News*, 27 October 1883, p. 393.

82 'Honour for Honour', *Glasgow News*, 19 October 1883; see also 'Sir Archibald Alison', *North British Daily Mail*, 19 October 1883, p. 4.

5

ENTERING THE SUDAN

❧

Occupying Egypt, even on a 'temporary' basis, may have preserved internal order and secured the Suez Canal, but it ensured that Britain would have to confront an evolving crisis in the Sudan (where internal order was the responsibility of the Khedive acting on behalf of the Sultan). When Mohammad Ahmed, the self-styled Mahdi, or 'Expected One', launched a rebellion to reform Islam and destroy the infidels, Egypt tried to crush the revolt through its provincial governors. After a series of failures, the Khedive dispatched an army of 11,000 men under the command of Colonel William Hicks, a retired Indian Army officer, but it was annihilated on the plain of Shaykan, near El Obeid (5 November 1883), leaving only a few hundred survivors. As the Mahdists now threatened further towns, including Khartoum, and potentially Egypt itself, they posed a challenge that Britain could not ignore. In the ensuing conflicts Scottish battalions served in two of the three campaigns, earning further plaudits and some controversy. Their military prominence reflected a series of ministerial initiatives that aroused profound debate between the parties and even more acutely among Scottish Liberals about the priorities and practice of Liberal imperialism.

Gladstone's cabinet resolved initially to evacuate the remaining garrisons in the Sudan, an immense undertaking involving the withdrawal of thousands of civilians and pockets of Egyptian troops scattered across the country. As ministers pondered the implications, they encountered a public outcry, fanned by the influential *Pall Mall Gazette*, that it should send Major-General Charles 'Chinese' Gordon to Khartoum. Bowing before public pressure, four members of the cabinet met Gordon on 18 January 1884 and agreed to send him up the Nile to 'consider and report' on the situation.[1] This fateful decision earned approval across the political spectrum in Scotland. If Conservatives like the Earl of Seafield complained about the tardiness of the appointment, they expressed the 'utmost confidence' in Gordon himself because of his 'long experience' and 'local knowledge' of the country, where he had served as governor of Equatoria (1874–6) and governor-general of the Sudan (1877–80). 'If any man is capable of pacifying the Soudan', asserted the *Edinburgh Courant*, 'General Gordon is he', a view endorsed by many newspapers, whether Conservative or Liberal.[2] Several editors reminded their readers that Gordon had resigned his private commission with the King of the Belgians to serve his country; that he had earned his 'Chinese' sobriquet by virtue of brilliant military achievements in the Second Opium War; and that he had previously suppressed the slave trade in the Sudan. Respected in Scotland as a 'Christian soldier', Gordon was also recognised by the Dundee *Weekly News* as 'a man of extraordinary energy and ample resources': many Scots had every confidence in him.[3]

Nor was this merely a passing matter in the editorial columns. Like the metropolitan press, Scottish newspapers acknowledged that the Sudan had become 'an absorbing topic of discussion'.[4] They followed the unfolding drama of Gordon's mission, sustained by his bulletins, proclamations and the reports of an accompanying correspondent, Frank Power of *The Times*, until the telegraph-line from Khartoum was cut on 12 March, and then by messages smuggled out of the city and later reports from the relief column.[5] Although news appeared intermittently, sometimes with gaps of several weeks, the Scottish press, like its English counterpart, remained fascinated by the religious appeal of the Mahdi. They reported his uncompromising declarations and those of Osman Digna, his able commander in the eastern Sudan, notably a letter from Osman Digna to Rear-Admiral Sir William Hewett at Suakin, stating that the Mahdi 'will not accept bribes from you, and also will not leave you in your infidelity, so there is nothing for you but the sword, so that there will not remain one of you on the face of the earth'.[6] Conservative and Liberal editors shared the widespread perception that the followers of the Mahdi were inspired by religious fanaticism and so were 'a hundred times more warlike than the Egyptians'.[7]

Compounding such concerns were the worsening events in the Sudan, particularly in the eastern region, where Britain sought to defend Suakin and the nearby ports on the Red Sea. After another rout of an English-led Egyptian army under Colonel Valentine Baker at El Teb (4 February 1884), and the massacre of the garrison of Sinkat when it tried to conduct a fighting withdrawal four days later, public clamour mounted, not least over the fate of the women and children and the reported 'weeping and wailing' of women in Suakin. Sir Edward W.

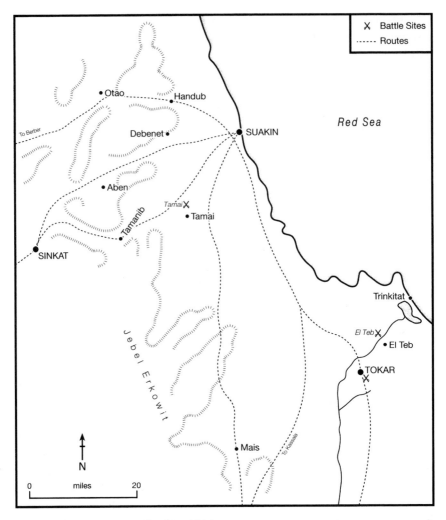

Map 6   Operations near Suakin, 1884

Hamilton, Gladstone's private secretary, detected 'a very strong and universal feeling that something must be done . . . a mixture of Jingoism and sentiment', endorsed by the queen and Horse Guards. Gladstone again bowed before public pressure and dispatched a relief force to save the garrison at nearby Tokar.[8] The *Glasgow News* welcomed this belated recognition of Britain's responsibilities following her 'humiliation' and 'disgrace' over Sinkat, while more radical commentators feared lest the recrudescence of jingoism would drive the government towards adopting a more aggressive foreign policy.[9]

The ensuing campaign proved extremely short, controversial

and inconclusive. The relief force under Major-General Sir Gerald Graham, VC, assembled at Fork Baker, near the Red Sea port of Trinkitat, on 28 February. It fought two bloody battles at El Teb (29 February) and Tamai (13 March) before burning Osman Digna's camp and withdrawing from the region on 3 April 1884 (leaving a small force to guard Suakin). The only Scottish units involved came from the army of occupation, namely the 1st Battalions, the Black Watch and the Gordon Highlanders, part of a well-balanced force of some 3,000 infantry, 750 cavalry and mounted infantry, two batteries of light artillery, engineers, and a Naval Brigade operating six machine guns.[10] Accompanying the relief force were the leading correspondents and artists of the metropolitan and provincial press, who had already reported on the debacle of Baker Pasha's column. As they had access to rapid lines of communication from Suakin, their reports reached Britain within days of the major battles[11] and many were reprinted in the Scottish press. The correspondents established the parameters of the campaign debates, eclipsing the impact of letters from soldiers which arrived several weeks later and, in most cases, after the campaign was over.

Controversy stalked the campaign from the outset as Tokar fell to the Mahdists while Graham was assembling his force. He still resolved to advance, purportedly to bury the dead at El Teb and protect any fugitives, and so marched out of Fort Baker with his men in a large square formation, with the Gordons in front, the Black Watch in the rear. Neither along the line of march nor in their accounts of the ensuing battle with 6,000 Mahdists would the correspondents make any invidious comparisons between the units (including the 2nd Battalion, Royal Irish Fusiliers). Burleigh and Cameron both referred to the inspirational music of the bagpipes on the line of march, and Burleigh claimed that a Gordon was the first to fall and that the F and G companies of Gordons captured the final earthwork after three to four hours of intensive fighting.[12] Yet the dominant theme in all accounts, and reflected fully in the Scottish commentary, was the 'reckless bravery' of the Beja tribesmen, their offensive zeal whether in groups or singly, their 'indifference to the cavalry' and their resolve to continue fighting even if wounded. 'Fanaticism', wrote Cameron, 'no doubt has something to do with the extraordinary valour which was displayed; still, the race is undoubtedly a fine one.'[13]

British fire power prevailed, killing over 1,500 Mahdists while the British lost thirty-five killed and 155 wounded.[14] Any satisfaction with the outcome was quickly doused by the revelation that Tokar had fallen without resistance, and that most of the garrison had gone over to the enemy. Graham, nonetheless, occupied the town and evacuated some 600 Egyptian men, women and children. He withdrew his force to Trinkitat, redeployed by ship to Suakin and thence marched on Osman Digna's camp at Tamai. Coming under fire on 12 March, Graham deployed his brigades in two separate squares for the decisive assault on the following day. He accompanied the 2nd Brigade composed of the Black Watch, York and Lancaster, Royal Marine Light Infantry and a naval machine gun detachment. Encountering the enemy on the edge of a ravine, he ordered the Black Watch to charge, which opened a gap in the square that tribesmen exploited with alacrity. The whole square was thrown into confusion, machine guns were lost temporarily, and the Highlanders and their comrades were forced to retire about 800 yards 'like lions at bay'.[15] Fortunately the 1st Brigade on their right and the cavalry and mounted infantry on their left held firm and allowed the 2nd Brigade to rally, whereupon the attack was pressed home, scattering Osman Digna's forces and burning his village. Once again about 2,000 of the enemy were killed and possibly a similar number wounded, but British casualties in the hand-to-hand fighting were relatively heavy with 105 killed and about the same number wounded. The Black Watch bore the brunt with sixty-one killed and thirty-three wounded. Apart from the defeats of Isandlwana, Maiwand and Majuba, Tamai had been Britain's bloodiest battle in the past ten years.[16]

Even before the receipt of official dispatches, the press interpreted the 'lessons' of Tamai. Eyewitnesses reckoned that 'Highland heroism' had prevailed: Prior recalled the sight of 'those brave Highlanders trying to force back a mass of savages', while Burleigh, who fought alongside the Black Watch, described how 'big' Jamie Adams, one of the 'finest and strongest men in the Black Watch', and Colour-Sergeant Donald Fraser fought the 'swarthy savages' with 'rifles (buts as well as bayonets)' and then with their fists before dying from loss of blood.[17] Unlike those correspondents, Cameron of the *Standard* had fled the scene, riding off to Suakin to report the collapsing square. Many newspapers, unaware of Cameron's funk, reprinted his description of how the 'savages, animated alike by natural courage and religious fanaticism', had attacked the square with ferocity and 'lightning' speed. Such tactics, he added, required 'the greatest prudence and caution, and that unskilfulness in handling and unsteadiness in movement, may possibly bring on a disaster'.[18] The *Scotsman* developed this implicit criticism: 'it must have been a "bad quarter of an hour" for General Graham and the officers under him'. It also embellished Cameron's reference to the wavering of the York and Lancaster men by claiming that they had yielded before the 'sheer weight and impetuosity of the enemy'.[19] However, Sir Archibald Alison, speaking before the Highland Society of London on 22 March, provided a salutary corrective, paying tribute to all the infantry involved. In a widely reported speech, he described the recent hand-to-hand fighting as 'by far the hardest . . . he could recollect since he joined the army', and that 'the rallying from that attack must appear one of the finest things in the history of British arms'.[20]

In writing from the front, soldiers appreciated that friends and family would already have read of their exploits in the press.[21] Nevertheless, they provided interesting anecdotes about their journey, acclimatisation, and rapid engagement with an unknown enemy. Private Peter McRae (Gordons) recounted the discomfort of marching out of Fort Baker 'up to the knees in mud' (as it had rained initially at Trinkitat), marching through prickly bush that scratched their knees terribly and then fighting a tenacious foe.[22] Private W. G. Martin, a Welsh Gordon Highlander, agreed that 'The rebels are a lot of brave men', and Major Robert Coveny (Black Watch), a veteran of African warfare, affirmed that 'I never saw such fellows fight as those Hadendowa Arabs: they know not what fear is in most cases . . .'[23] Black Watch soldiers recounted their near-escapes, especially in the hand-to-hand fighting at Tamai, and admitted that they had been caught in an ambush when their view was obscured by the cloud of gunpowder.[24] Yet their most serious allegation, one which elicited sympathy from officers and men in other regiments,[25] was that they had been ordered to charge by Graham, and that this advance had opened a gap in the square. Had this allegation been made solely by ordinary soldiers, like Private James Hope or Bandsman A. V. Barwood,[26] it might have aroused less controversy, but confirmation in a graphic letter from Captain Andrew Scott-Stevenson ensured widespread coverage north and south of the border.[27]

A photocopy of this letter remains in the Black Watch Archive[28] but only extracts were published at the time, partly on account of its length and partly on account of its withering critique of Graham and Gladstone. The published extracts included diagrams of the battle, explaining how the square was broken, and described how officers reacted in the heat of battle:

Old Charlie Eden as cool as if he was partridge shooting; little Brophy, lame, but pretending to be sound; Sandy Kennedy, with his eyeglasses in his eye and his wife's watch round his neck; Bald, my gigantic subaltern, sweating, and with a bluejacket's hat on – he lost his helmet. Sir John [McLeod]'s son, Duncan, wounded swearing he was all right; old Bob Coveny, smiling with confidence and Norman McLeod, with his firm lips, thirsting for more blood. Speid, looking as calm as a judge, and young Macrae, an Argyleshire lad, who only joined us the day before the battle in his trews, & armed with a spear-head, crying to be at the niggers again.

If editors published extracts that confirmed popular notions of the heroic-warrior in battle, bolstered by assumptions of racial superiority, they were more discreet about (or were not shown) the charge that Graham had berated the Black Watch after El Teb (where he considered it 'out of hand') and had reassigned the battalion to lead the advance on Tamai (with all the labour of constructing zarebas – protective perimeters made of mimosa thorn bushes – for each camp site). Accordingly, the battalion responded eagerly when ordered to charge, opening up a gap that the enemy exploited. Forced to defend their front and rear, Scott-Stevenson like his fellow officers 'fought like a demon & only wanted to kill, kill, kill these awful plucky demons'. He was all too aware of the battalion's heavy losses, particularly in sergeants, and had no doubt who was to blame: 'I wish old Gladstone had been in that square'.[29]

Denne shared much of this scepticism. He deprecated the earlier relief of Tokar after the battle of El Teb: 'The General made an ass of himself by having a sort of triumphal march with some cavalry round the town . . . It's just the sort of bunkum I should expect of him. The relief of Tokar was in fact all humbug, we were too late, the place had fallen.' He knew that the Black Watch had been considered 'unsteady' at El Teb (and thought that they had been assigned the thoroughly unpleasant burial detail as a consequence),[30] but blamed Graham for his handling of the two squares at Tamai. He claimed that 'everyone is heartily sick of this useless waste of life to bolster up government'.[31]

Although the breaking of 'a British square', as immortalised by Rudyard Kipling in his poem 'Fuzzy-Wuzzy',[32] continued to vex the Black Watch, the issue had less impact outside military circles in Scotland. As Graham admitted responsibility for ordering 'the gallant rush' of the battalion at Tamai, and Wolseley formally commended the Black Watch, this was not a lingering source of controversy.[33] Of more immediate concern was the futility of the expedition, namely a British withdrawal leaving Suakin secure but Sinkat, Tokar and the route to Berber in enemy hands, as well as Gordon besieged. Whereas some Scottish Liberals supported the government's policy, hoping that

Gordon could 'hold out' as the 'fighting Arab clans' dispersed, others hoped that the 'dignified retreat' from the Sudan would be followed by a reversion to Midlothian principles. Jingoism, as these writers feared, had been boosted by the campaign, with the *Dunfermline Journal* deeming it 'grotesque' that the National Anthem should have been sung in churches after the victory of El Teb.[34] However scant the evidence of imperialist passion in Scotland in the 1870s, it was clearly apparent by the mid-1880s (or at least at particular moments during the campaign) and these sentiments underpinned demands within the Conservative press to 'crush' the Mahdi. In making such demands, the *Glasgow News* disdained any desire for 'an African Empire' but insisted that a relief force must be sent to rescue Gordon.[35]

Faced with criticism on both sides, and with debates among the military about the best route for any relief force,[36] Gladstone sought refuge in delay and obfuscation. He tried to reassure supporters that Gordon was safe (and had not requested a relief force), and characterised the Sudanese as a 'people struggling to be free, and they are struggling rightly to be free'.[37] As the Mahdists pursued their freedom by seizing Berber in May, and by tightening the siege around Khartoum while Gordon refused to leave, Gladstone eventually bowed before pressures to send an expedition. On 5 August 1884, Parliament approved a vote of credit 'in case it might be necessary' to undertake operations in relief of Gordon.

The ensuing campaign would be commanded by Wolseley, who had gained the support of the government for an expedition up the Nile in preference to the much shorter desert crossing from Suakin to Berber. Convinced that soldiers, assisted by native boatmen, could be transported rapidly and cheaply by river (largely on the basis of his successful Red River expedition of 1870), Wolseley envisaged transporting the relief force (including the 1st Battalions, the Black Watch and the Gordon Highlanders) and all their stores nearly 1,650 miles up river from Cairo. This massive logistical exercise involved the construction of 800 whale-boats, each capable of carrying twelve men and supplies for a hundred days (the last of which would not leave England until 3 October), the recruitment of 386 Canadian voyageurs and the assistance of 300 Kroomen from West Africa to carry stores around the cataracts. Wolseley planned to transport his force by train over 229 miles to Assiout, and thence by steamer and barge to Wadi Halfa. The boats would then have to be hauled round the second cataract near Sarras and sail on to Korti, accompanied by mounted troops and transport on the banks. He later resolved to send a

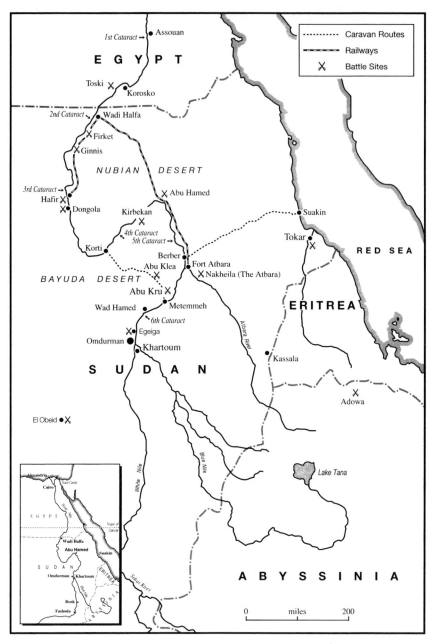

Map 7   Egypt and the Sudan, 1884–98

column, mounted on camels, across the Bayuda Desert to Metemmeh to make contact with Gordon's steamers while a river column pressed up the Nile to link up with the other column at Metemmeh.[38]

Although a large number of correspondents accompanied the campaign, including some 'specials' contracted to report for Scottish newspapers, Denne, writing in mid-January 1885, was dismayed by the limited reportage in the press.[39] This reflected a dearth of news from Gordon, the absence of fighting before the end of the year, and a lack of anxiety about Gordon himself. His last cryptic message, dated 14 December and published in London on 2 January 1885, indicated that Khartoum was 'all right' (but this was probably intended to deceive any interceptors as an accompanying warning urged the relief force to make haste).[40] Reporting proved even more desultory once the two columns embarked on their separate missions (with the Highland battalions serving in the river column). The smaller desert column encountered the fiercest resistance, fighting two costly, if successful, battles at Abu Klea and Abu Kru. However, the 'dread silence' from this front was not broken until the end of January as the correspondents, two of whom were killed, struggled to dispatch their reports.[41]

Scottish soldiers kept diaries and sent letters chronicling their labours on the Nile, but only a few appeared in the press.[42] Postal delays may have been partially responsible, but the letters may have lacked appeal as they were bereft of deeds of heroism and valour in the face of the enemy. Bandsman Barwood wrote a candid and comprehensive series of letters, which were later preserved as his diary in the Black Watch Archive. He admitted that the regiment had left Cairo in a 'disgraceful state', with some men too drunk to stand in the ranks and another twenty so 'riotous' that they swore at bystanders and had to be detained in the guard room. The regiment, nonetheless, enjoyed the leisurely journey up to Wadi Halfa (twelve days by steamer and barge), if not the unchanging diet of hard biscuits and preserved meat. Barwood described the banter with the natives ashore, the exotic scenery, a morale-boosting visit from Wolseley and the historic monuments at Luxor, Thebes and on the island of Philae. Work became much slower, more laborious and dangerous as the men had to row or pull their boats over the rapids, try to keep the boats of each company together, and periodically unload, carry and then reload their cargo of seventy boxes (some of which weighed as much as sixty-five pounds). Barwood recalled how he was at times 'quite exhausted, my hands cut and blistered, wet through all day, scarcely any clothes whole, and my feet and legs also cut'. As boats foundered occasionally on the rocks or capsized or broke their rudders, Barwood found himself 'up to the waist in water every day and at all times of the day. Tugging the boats with all our might, sometimes only to see the rope break or the nose of the boat give way and then several men go into the rapids, never to be found'.[43]

In fact, remarkably few men drowned (although Major Nicholas Brophy (Black Watch) was one of them) and most boats proved repairable,[44] enabling the soldiers to reach Korti, albeit in many cases lice-ridden and suffering from scurvy. The Scots had not prospered in the boat race to Debbeh, where Wolseley had offered £100 for the fastest regiment. Not only did the 1st Battalion, the Royal Irish win the prize but the Gordons learned that they had come a very close second, failing on account of their last few boats: as Denne reflected, this was 'very provoking'.[45] Rivalry with the Irish resurfaced later in the campaign (as Ian Hamilton recalled over fifty years later) when the Royal Irish were chosen to march across the desert under Buller's command to relieve the depleted desert column. The Irish gained accolades for an outward march over 152 miles in eleven days (with a four-day halt at Gakdul wells) and a return march over the same route in only sixty-seven marching hours.[46] None of this boosted the triumphant and heroic-warrior image of the Scottish soldier but this rivalry, like the earlier relief over the news from Abu Klea and Abu Kru, was swept aside by the controversy over the 'sudden' and 'very unexpected' fall of Khartoum on 26 January 1885.[47]

Scotland shared the national anguish expressed within a tidal wave of literary, poetic and newspaper commentary.[48] The 'disastrous news' (*Elgin Courant*) was 'a sad blow to the whole United Kingdom' (*Kinross-shire Advertiser*) and 'a personal grief to every man of British race' (*Glasgow News*). 'The crisis in the Soudan', asserted the *Falkirk Herald*, had become 'the all-engrossing topic of the day'.[49] On the great imperial issue of the moment, Scots shared the widespread anxiety about the fate of Gordon (which would not be resolved for another six days) and accepted the early rumours that the garrison had fallen through treachery (whereas the Mahdists had stormed the city). Scottish Liberals later defended the government over the delay in sending the relief column by claiming that the timing was irrelevant since treachery could have occurred at any time.[50]

When news arrived of Gordon's death, Scots lauded the 'fallen hero', the 'gallant defender of Khartoum' and the soldier who had died a noble death, following the 'path of honour, self-sacrifice and splendid achievement'. Even the *Dundee Advertiser*, a critic of Gordon for exceeding his orders, admitted that the nation would mourn the loss of 'a brave and intrepid servant'.[51] Many newspapers recognised the significance of Gordon's religious symbolism and his potential for martyrdom. The *Scotsman* hailed the 'great Puritan soldier', the *Kilmarnock Standard* commended the 'piety of this hero', while the *Highland News* reflected upon the 'simple faith and gallant heart' of this 'brave Christian soldier':

> When we contemplate the terrible fate which has overtaken him, alone and unfriended among savage hordes fired with a fanatical zeal and frenzied with a mad thirst for Christian blood, our hearts are filled with a bitter and regretful sorrow . . . Truly General Gordon, of all men, deserves the martyr's crown.[52]

In the midst of all this grief and emotion, not least in Aberdeenshire where the Gordon name had particular appeal, there was a sense of national humiliation, anger, and a belief, by no means confined to Scottish Conservatives, that the government had to restore the nation's honour and secure Egypt from the Mahdist threat.[53] Robert Louis Stevenson wrote of 'these dark days of public dishonour'.[54] The *Glasgow News* demanded vengeance by 'breaking the Mahdi's power' and retaking Khartoum: 'The task of creating a new and better order where tyranny and force have reigned supreme since time immemorial has again fallen to the people of this little island in the Western seas.'[55] Few Liberals wanted to acquire a 'treeless, waterless, desolate land', and some favoured a reversion to Midlothian principles without any military commitment in the Sudan, but others supported the government in ordering Wolseley to crush Mahdism and in launching another expeditionary force (without Scottish units) under Graham's command in the eastern Sudan.[56]

Whatever their views on policy, many Scots were elated by news of the first and only victory of the river column at Kirbekan (10 February 1885). Such news, as the *Dundee Courier* remarked, was 'much needed' after the fall of Khartoum, especially as it involved six companies of the Black Watch fighting alongside a similar force of the South Staffordshire regiment.[57] This was also the first attack by British forces on the Mahdists, armed with Remington rifles, holding fixed positions on the bank of the Nile. The Scottish press praised the tactics adopted, namely the pinioning of the enemy by two guns and two companies of Staffords in the front while the other companies assaulted their rear; they also recognised the strength of the enemy's position: 'rocky and broken ground, strengthened

Figure 5   *'The War in the Soudan – The Battle of Kerbekan'* (Illustrated London
News, *21 March 1885)*

by loopholed walls, from behind which they kept up a heavy and well-
directed fusillade'. Ultimately the assault required the use of the
bayonet to storm the eminence.[58]

Doubtless there was an element of over-reaction in the descriptions
of the battle after the news of Gordon's death. The Scottish press, like
the 'specials' writing from the front, exulted in the triumph of the Black
Watch. 'The Highlanders', claimed the *Glasgow News*, 'swept on as
the music of the pipes mingled with the whistle of the bullets; and once

more the fanaticism of the East quailed before the hardier courage of the resolute North'.[59] 'Never was victory more complete or more gallantly won', claimed the *Scotsman*; 'we cannot but feel a flush of pride at the victory of our brave countrymen', added the *Elgin Courant*: 'It was no square pouring a hailstorm of bullets upon advancing hordes, it was man to man and steel to steel. Inch by inch the Soudanese were beaten back and, as reports say, all but exterminated.'[60]

In paying tribute to the heroism of the Black Watch, Scottish editors acknowledged that the 'Stafford lads' had displayed similar qualities, fighting with 'equal bravery and courage' (in seizing the highest ridge in the Mahdist position).[61] R. Caton Woodville depicted the combined assault in the *Illustrated London News* with a double-page illustration of both regiments in action, based on a sketch from a South Staffordshire officer.[62] If Scots hoped that this timely victory would dishearten the enemy, and inhibit any forward movement after the capture of Khartoum, they recognised that a heavy price had been paid in the loss of senior officers: Major-General William Earle and lieutenant-colonels from each regiment, Philip H. Eyre and Robert Coveny, were all killed. Otherwise the casualties for both regiments were remarkably similar and relatively light, with the Black Watch losing four men killed and twenty-three officers and men wounded.[63]

An officer of the Black Watch confirmed many of these details, albeit in less florid prose, for the *Daily Telegraph*. He explained how the various Black Watch companies, 'dressed in the kilt', manoeuvred round the Mahdist position and made sure that there could be no escape along the bank of the Nile. Companies A, C and E, half of the Black Watch, engaged then advanced in 'line over 300 yards of open ground, the three companies marching as steadily as if on parade, notwithstanding the heavy fire directed on us'. Several men were lost at this stage before they began to storm the enemy positions, repulse an enemy counterattack, and then enfilade the enemy as they scampered 'from rock to rock', trying to escape to the river. Once the position was carried, the general was killed in entering a loopholed stone house (a detail confirmed by Sergeant Watts, who accompanied him). Meanwhile, the South Staffordshire men pressed on to seize the high hill, completing the rout of the enemy over some five hours. The officer counted 105 enemy corpses among the rocks in his area and claimed that 'The 42nd fought with coolness and gallantry throughout the severe action'.[64]

Any solace provided by the victory, whether at home or in the Sudan, proved short-lived as the river column was recalled after

Buller's withdrawal of the desert column. On 13 March 1885, Private Robertson (Black Watch) wrote to his father that

> This has been an awful sickener of a job . . . It is a great pity General Gordon being killed, and so many fine officers. I suppose it would cause a great consternation at home. I don't see what benefit is to be derived from this country. We all wish they would withdraw the troops from it altogether, for it has been a heartbreak ever since we came to it . . .[65]

He got his wish as the Liberal government grasped the opportunity of a Russian incursion into Afghanistan to begin a phased withdrawal from the Sudan. After a decision of cabinet on 7 May, both Wolseley and Graham had to terminate their operations, with the policy of evacuating the Sudan sustained by the incoming Conservative government in June 1885.[66]

Despite the sudden death of the Mahdi, possibly from typhus in June 1885, resurgent Mahdism still posed a threat to Egypt's southern frontier and Suakin. As the Egyptian Army required further training before it could mount a defence, British forces had to be involved. For about a year the Cameron Highlanders served on the frontier force. The Camerons had joined Wolseley's relief force in November 1884 and, based at Korosko, were intended to sustain a line of communications across the desert to support the river column when it reached Abu Hamed. Denied this task by the withdrawal, the Camerons remained in Korosko for about ten months, building mud huts, playing sports and enjoying cordial relations with the natives who enjoyed the bagpipes.[67] In October 1885 the battalion left Korosko to garrison the small fort at Kosheh, the most southerly frontier post guarding the eighty-seven mile railway from Wadi Halfa to Akasheh.

In early December 1885 they came under attack from a Mahdist army of possibly 6,000 men sent north by Khalifa 'Abdullahi, who had succeeded the Mahdi. The Camerons conducted a vigorous defence of the fort, patrolled the Nile on a stern wheeler, the *Lotus*, and periodically assisted their black Sudanese allies in a zareba on the other side of the river. Diaries of their exploits were published in the Scottish press as the Camerons bought time for General Sir Frederick Stephenson to come from Cairo and organise a counter-attack with two brigades and mounted support. Having lost four killed and twenty-four wounded by 29 December,[68] the Cameron Highlanders relished the opportunity to join in the pre-dawn advance on 30 December. A soldier described how it felt to get 'our legs a bit stretched. Upon my word, it was like getting out for a holiday, so glad were we to have a chance of putting an end to our imprisonment.' Six companies (about 450 men) took part, extending right and left in 'a thin red line' (this was the last battle the British fought wearing red):

> When the order was given to fix bayonets, the ready click and the fierce, determined look of the men unmistakably told of pent-up revengeful passion about to find an outburst. The thought of comrades killed and wounded like rabbits in a warren during all those harassing days in the fort worked with revengeful fierceness in the mind of each.

He wrote of how they cleared the houses in the village of Kosheh: 'It was nasty work. There were a good many inside, and it was a desperation stand with them.' He praised, too, the 150 Sudanese blacks who cleared the riverbank: 'Gordon was right, They are real good fellows . . . When we met in the rear of the houses, and had captured the enemy's guns, we gave them a cheer, to which they lustily responded.' The combined Anglo-Egyptian forces drove on to the village of Ginnis until the *ansar* were in full retreat, leaving some 500 dead and 300 wounded compared with British casualties of seven killed and thirty wounded.[69]

This victory, though skilfully conducted, failed to arouse much interest at home as the Mahdists abandoned their planned invasion and the British withdrew from their exposed defences, sacrificed the railway and retreated to a more defensible position at Wadi Halfa. The Scots had relatively little to celebrate; they could neither extol any triumph achieved specifically or exclusively by Highlanders nor welcome home battle-scarred veterans from the Sudan (the three Highland regiments returned to duties in Egypt or the Mediterranean, with the Camerons only returning home in 1887). They knew that their soldiers had fought a tenacious enemy, whose bravery was thought to have been bolstered by religious fanaticism, and whose tactical skills (in attacking the weakest points of British squares, namely the corners) had led to ferocious hand-to-hand fighting. By defeating a remarkable enemy in this manner, Scottish soldiers like their English counterparts[70] had added further laurels to their heroic-warrior image. Yet Scots at home realised that many soldiers had been thoroughly dispirited by the loss of comrades and the failure to relieve Gordon. One Fifer composed a doleful account of his experience in the eastern Sudan:

> For Britain's honour we have fought,
>   And suffer'd heat, fatigue, and toil;

Defeated Osman's swarthy host,
  And made them quick disgorge their spoil.

While for companions loved we mourn,
  Struck down by roving Arab's spear;
To Britain we will glad return,
  From Afric's deserts, dry and dear.

With joy we'll hail our native land,
  The fields of Fife and Fortha's shore;
No more to tread the Red Sea strand,
  But meet the maiden we adore.

Oh! soon may War its horrors cease,
  No more may fields be drench'd in blood;
But happy nations live in peace,
  And dwell in social brotherhood![71]

Nor were the lasting images of the campaign distinctively Scottish. Although Prior sketched the Black Watch fighting at the battles of El Teb and Tamai, Godfrey Douglas Giles painted more memorable scenes from the battle of Tamai in 1885, neither of which involved the Scots. In one painting he depicted the dervishes (as they were now known) trying to operate a machine gun, and, in the second, the York and Lancaster regiment in action. Lady Butler painted some Highlanders but these were among the many images in the seven plates and eighteen sketches that she supplied for her husband's account of the war, *The Campaign of the Cataracts* (1887), and in her picture of the burial of Earle, Eyre and Coveny, *A Desert Grave* (1887).[72] The dominant image of the campaign remained that of Gordon himself. He had been depicted repeatedly in the illustrated press during the campaign, and George William Joy later produced an imaginative painting, *The death of General Gordon, Khartoum, 26th January 1885* (1894). Gordon also appeared in several statues (including one in Aberdeen) and in more popular forms through *tableaux vivants*, lantern shows and a waxworks creation in Madame Tussaud's.[73]

Politically, the failure of the Gordon relief expedition almost certainly exacerbated feelings in Scotland, and in Scottish regiments, as it did elsewhere in the United Kingdom. Lieutenant-Colonel Andrew C. P. Haggard, a King's Own Scottish Borderer, then attached to the Egyptian Army in Suakin, privately denounced 'our miserable government' over the fall of Khartoum. He later noted that the 'English papers of the 6th [February 1885]' were 'full of vengeance against the Government for the loss of Khartoum & Gordon',[74] feelings that the

Conservatives failed to exploit in the vote of censure. As H. Ivory, a Liberal election agent, assured Lord Rosebery, Scottish Liberals 'would not . . . turn out Mr Gladstone for any mistakes in Egypt;'[75] but they split one year later over Gladstone's proposals for Irish Home Rule (and so the Conservatives, who won only ten seats in Scotland in the general election of 1885, gained twelve with another seventeen seats for the Liberal Unionists in the election of July 1886).[76]

Scottish Conservatives, if thwarted over the Sudan, now saw profitable links emerging between imperialism generally and domestic politics. Imperial unity and access to overseas markets had sustained the trade and profits of many Scottish businessmen, particularly in Glasgow,[77] and concerns over imperial unity mounted in the mid-1880s when the Orange Order described home rule as the first step towards the break-up of the empire.[78] Opposing home rule, and preserving the empire, may have bolstered Orange support for the Conservative (and later Unionist) cause, especially in Glasgow and the west of Scotland, even if this support was still 'contingent' upon the handling of 'Protestant issues'.[79] The early campaigns in the Sudan had demonstrated that imperialist passions could resonate within Scotland, that the gallantry of Scottish soldiers still attracted widespread attention and could focus debate on imperial issues, and that this debate reverberated between and within the political parties north of the border.

Notes

1 Matthew, *Gladstone 1875–1898*, pp. 143–6; Earl of Cromer, *Modern Egypt*, 2 vols (London: Macmillan, 1908), 1, p. 443; Shannon, *Gladstone*, p. 327.

2 'Conservative Demonstration in Inverness', *Northern Chronicle*, 13 February 1884, p. 5; *Edinburgh Courant*, 21 January 1884, p. 4; *Inverness Courier*, 22 January 1884, p. 2; *North British Daily Mail*, 24 January 1884, p. 4; *Scotsman*, 21 January 1884, p. 4.

3 'General Gordon', *Highland News*, 11 February 1884, p. 4; *[Dundee] Weekly News*, 26 January 1884, p. 4; *Nairnshire Telegraph*, 23 January 1884, p. 2; *Falkirk Herald*, 23 January 1884, p. 2.

4 *Falkirk Herald*, 23 January 1884, p. 2; *Illustrated London News*, 8 March 1884, p. 218.

5 P. M. Holt and M. W. Daly, *A History of the Sudan: From the Coming of Islam to the Present Day* (Harlow: Pearson Education, 2000), p. 83; Wilkinson-Latham, *From Our Special Correspondent*, p. 185; *Northern Chronicle*, 20 August 1884, p. 4.

6 'Text of Osman Digna's Reply', 'A Letter from the Mahdi' and 'Letters from the Mahdi', *Scotsman*, 11 March 1884, p. 5, 16 January 1885, p. 5, 22 January 1885, p. 5; 'The Mahdi Interviewed', *Aberdeen Journal*, 22 March 1884, p. 3; 'The Mahdi at Home', *Dundee Courier & Argus*, 7 April 1884, p. 3; 'Letter of the Mahdi', *Dundee Advertiser*, 18 April 1884, p. 10.

7 *Edinburgh Courant*, 14 February and 15 March 1884, pp. 4 and 4; *Scotsman*, 13 March 1884, p. 4; E. M. Spiers, 'Dervishes and fanaticism: perception and impact', in M. Hughes and G. Johnson (eds), *Fanaticism and Conflict in the Modern Age* (London: Frank Cass, 2005), pp. 19–32.

8 D. W. R. Bahlman (ed.), *The Diary of Sir Edward Walter Hamilton 1880–1885*, 2 vols (Oxford: Clarendon Press, 1972), 2, pp. 554–6.

9 *Glasgow News*, 13 February 1884, p. 4; *North British Daily Mail*, 18 February 1884, p. 4; *Falkirk Herald*, 13 February 1884, p. 2.

10 Sandes, *Royal Engineers in Egypt and the Sudan*, pp. 59–60; H. Keown-Boyd, *A Good Dusting: A Centenary Review of the Sudan campaigns 1883–1899* (London: Leo Cooper, 1986), p. 26.

11 ' "The Daily Telegraph" War Correspondent', *Daily Telegraph*, 5 March 1884, p. 5; Wilkinson-Latham, *From Our Special Correspondent*, pp. 178–81.

12 B. Burleigh, *Desert Warfare: Being the Chronicle of the Eastern Soudan Campaign* (London: Chapman & Hall, 1884), pp. 46–7; 'The Great Battle', *Evening Standard*, 3 March 1884, p. 8; 'The War in the Soudan', *Illustrated London News*, 8 March 1884, p. 222.

13 'The Great Battle', p. 8; 'British Victory at El Teb' and 'The Battle at El Teb', *Daily Telegraph*, 3 and 5 March 1884, pp. 5 and 5; 'Military Notes on the Battle of Teb', *Scotsman*, 3 March 1884, p. 6; 'The Battle of Teb', *Edinburgh Courant*, 4 March 1884, p. 2.

14 TNA, PRO, WO 33/42, 'Correspondence relative to the Expedition to Suakin', Sir G. Graham to Secretary of State for War, 2 March 1884, p. 45; Keown-Boyd, *A Good Dusting*, p. 27.

15 'The Defeat of Osman Digna', *Edinburgh Courant*, 15 March 1884, p. 5.

16 'The Soudan', *[York] Evening Press*, 14 March 1884, p. 3; 'Recent British Battles', *Strathearn Herald*, 22 March 1884, p. 2; Keown-Boyd, *A Good Dusting*, p. 32; D. Featherstone, *Khartoum 1885: General Gordon's Last Stand* (London: Osprey, 1993), p. 52.

17 Prior, *Campaigns of a War Correspondent*, p. 196; Burleigh, *Desert Warfare*, pp. 174–5; 'Gallantry of the Black Watch', *Highland News*, 17 March 1884, p. 2; 'Incidents of the Battle', *Stirling Observer*, 20 March 1884, p. 6; 'Heroic Deeds by Highlanders', *Strathearn Herald*, 22 March 1884, p. 2.

18 Wilkinson-Latham, *From Our Special Correspondent*, pp. 184–5; 'Great Battle in the Soudan', *Standard*, 14 March 1884, p. 8; see also 'Lessons of the Fight', *Edinburgh Courant*, 15 March 1884, p. 5; 'The

Cause of the Repulse', *Western Mail*, 14 March 1884, p. 3; *Dundee Courier & Argus*, 14 March 1884, p. 4.

19 *Scotsman*, 15 March 1884, p. 8.

20 'Sir Charles McGregor and Sir Archibald Alison on the Highland Regiments', *Scotsman*, 24 March 1884, p. 4; see also 'The War in the Soudan', *Illustrated London News*, 84 (12 April 1884), p. 346.

21 'Letters from Egypt', *Ross-shire Journal*, 4 April 1884, p. 3.

22 GHM, PB 173, McRae Mss, Private McRae to his aunt, 20 April 1884; see also PB 64/5, Denne Mss, Denne to his father, 6 March 1884.

23 'Letter from Another Welsh Soldier', *Western Mail*, 10 April 1884, p. 3; BWRA, 0204, Coveny, 'Letters From Egypt and the Soudan', 9 June 1884; see also GHM, PB 64/5, Denne Mss, Denne to his father, 6 March 1884.

24 'The Battle of Tamai in the Sudan', *Strathearn Herald*, 12 April 1884, p. 2; 'The Battle of Tamasi [sic]', *Dover Telegraph*, 23 April 1884, p. 7; 'Letter from a Soldier of the Black Watch', *Falkirk Herald*, 5 April 1884, p. 2.

25 Colonel Sir P. Marling, *Riflemen and Hussar* (London: John Murray, 1931), p. 112; GHM, PB 173, McRae Mss, McRae to his mother, 17 March 1884.

26 'Gallantry and Narrow Escapes from the Destruction of the Black Watch', *Edinburgh Courant*, 5 April 1884, p. 5; BWRA, 0203/1, Barwood diary, Barwood to E, 22 September 1884, pp. 80–1.

27 *Scotsman*, 2 April 1884, p. 7; *Edinburgh Evening News*, 7 April 1884, p. 4; *York Herald*, 8 April 1884, p. 5; *[York] Evening Press*, 8 April 1884, p. 3; *Strathearn Herald*, 12 April 1884, p. 2; *[Dundee] Weekly News*, 12 April 1884, p. 6; *Sussex Daily News*, 14 April 1884, p. 2.

28 BWRA, 0641, 'Account of the Battle of Tamai', Captain A. Scott Stevenson to his wife, 16 March 1884.

29 Ibid; see also BWRA, 0203/1, Barwood diary, 30 August 1884, pp. 69–74; TNA, PRO, WO 33/42, 'Correspondence relative to the Expedition to Suakim', Graham to the Secretary of State for War, 2 March 1884, p. 45.

30 GHM, PB 64/5, Denne Mss, Denne to his father, 6 March 1884.

31 GHM, PB 64/6, Denne Mss, Denne to his father, 15 March 1884.

32 'Fuzzy-Wuzzy', *Rudyard Kipling's Verse: Definitive Edition* (London: Hodder & Stoughton, 1946), pp. 400–1; E. & A. Linklater, *The Black Watch: The History of the Royal Highland Regiment* (London: Barrie & Jenkins, 1977), p. 127; GH Museum, PB 1832, Private E. Hawkins to his mother, 21 April 1884.

33 TNA, PRO, WO 33/42, 'Correspondence Relative to the Expedition to Suakim', Graham to the Secretary of State for War, 15 March 1884, p. 79; 'Lord Wolseley and the Black Watch', *Invergordon Times*, 16 July 1884, p. 4.

34 Compare the *Dunfermline Journal*, 8 and 29 March 1884, pp. 2 and 2, and *Aberdeen Journal*, 14 March 1884, p. 4, with the *Scotsman*, 28 March 1884, p. 4.

35 *Glasgow News*, 21 March 1884, p. 4; see also *Edinburgh Courant*, 31 March 1884, p. 4, and *Northern Chronicle*, 13 February 1884, p. 4.

36 Bahlman (ed.), *Hamilton*, 2, pp. 603, 610; see also A. Preston (ed.), *In Relief of Gordon: Lord Wolseley's Campaign Journal of The Khartoum Relief Expedition 1884–1885* (London: Hutchinson, 1967), pp. xxviii–xxxii, and J. Symons, *England's Pride: The Story of the Gordon Relief Expedition* (London: Hamish Hamilton, 1965), ch. 5.

37 *Parl. Deb.*, third series, 288 (12 May 1884), cols 54–8; *North British Daily Mail*, 13 May 1884, p. 4.

38 Sandes, *Royal Engineers in Egypt and the Sudan*, pp. 88–92: Symons, *England's Pride*, p. 106.

39 GH Museum, PB 64/7, Denne Mss, Denne to his father, 16 January 1885; see also Wilkinson-Latham, *From Our Special Correspondent*, pp. 186–7; 'The Soudan War', *Glasgow News*, 29 January 1885, p. 4.

40 *The Times*, 2 January 1885, p. 3; *North British Daily Mail*, 20 August 1884, p. 4; 'Disaster in the Soudan', *Aberdeen Journal*, 6 February 1885, p. 5; Symons, *England's Pride*, p. 168.

41 *Edinburgh Courant*, 29 January 1885, p. 4; Prior, *Campaigns of a War Correspondent*, pp. 215–16; 'The Battle of Abu Klea', *Daily Chronicle*, 25 February 1885, p. 5.

42 'Letter from a Member of the Black Watch', *North British Daily Mail*, 10 February 1885, p. 5; 'The Black Watch at Abu Dom', *Scotsman*, 11 April 1885, p. 7. Among the unpublished works are BWRA, 0808, Captain QM C. H. Sinclair, diary, and 0202, Lieutenant-Colonel J. MacRae-Gilstrap, diary.

43 BWRA 0203/1, Barwood, diary, pp. 87, 89–94, 113, 120–2, 124.

44 Symons, *England's Pride*, p. 144.

45 GH Museum, PB 64/7 and 64/10, Denne Mss, Denne to his father, 16 January and 16 March 1885.

46 Keown-Boyd, *A Good Dusting*, p. 79; Hamilton, *Listening for the Drums*, p. 176.

47 *North British Daily Mail*, 6 February 1885, p. 4; *Perthshire Advertiser*, 6 February 1885, p. 2; *Dundee Advertiser*, 6 February 1885, p. 4.

48 R. Hill, 'The Gordon Literature', *The Durham University Journal*, XLVII, no. 3 (1955), pp. 97–103; D. H. Johnson, 'The Death of Gordon: A Victorian Myth', *The Journal of Imperial and Commonwealth History*, 10, no. 7 (1982), pp. 285–310.

49 *Elgin Courant*, 6 February 1885, p. 2; *Kinross-shire Advertiser*, 14 February 1885, p. 2; *Glasgow News*, 6 February 1885, p. 4; *Falkirk Herald*, 11 February 1885, p. 2.

50 *North British Daily Mail*, 20 February 1885, p. 4; *Perthshire Advertiser*, 25 February 1885, p. 2; see also 'The Fall of Khartoum', *Scotsman*, 18 February 1885, p. 7, and *Edinburgh Courant*, 12 February 1885, p. 4.

51 *Glasgow News*, 11 February 1885, p. 4; *Falkirk Herald*, 14 February 1885, p. 2; *North British Daily Mail*, 12 February 1885, p. 4; *Scotsman*, 11 February 1885, p. 6; *Dundee Advertiser*, 7 and 11 February 1885, pp. 5 and 5.

52 'General Gordon', *Highland News*, 16 February 1885, p. 2; *Scotsman*, 11 February 1885, p. 6; *Kilmarnock Standard*, 14 February 1885, p. 2.

53 *Aberdeen Journal*, 13 February 1885, p. 4; P. M. Holt, *The Mahdist State in the Sudan 1881–1898* (Oxford: Clarendon Press, 1958), p. 205; Johnson, 'The Death of Gordon', p. 304; *Nairnshire Telegraph*, 18 February 1885, p. 2; *Dundee Courier & Argus*, 12 February 1885, p. 2; *Edinburgh Courant*, 21 February 1885, p. 4.

54 R. L. Stevenson to S. Colvin, 8 March 1885, in B. A. Booth and E. Mehew (eds), *The Letters of Robert Louis Stevenson*, 8 vols (New Haven and London: Yale University Press, 1995), 5, pp. 79–81.

55 *Glasgow News*, 10 and 11 February 1885, pp. 4 and 4.

56 *Perthshire Advertiser*, 13 February 1885, p. 2; *Dunfermline Journal*, 7 and 14 February 1885, pp. 2 and 2; *Kilmarnock Standard*, 28 February 1885, p. 2; *Kinross-shire Advertiser*, 14 February 1885, p. 2. For the opposition of Aberdeen's *Free Press*, see W. Hamish Fraser, 'The Press', in W. Hamish Fraser and C. H. Lee (eds), *Aberdeen 1800–2000: A New History* (East Linton: Tuckwell Press, 2000), p. 456.

57 *Dundee Courier & Argus*, 13 February 1885, p. 4.

58 Ibid.; *Falkirk Herald*, 14 February 1885, p. 2; *Aberdeen Journal*, 13 February 1885, p. 4.

59 *Glasgow News*, 13 February 1885, p. 4; see also *North British Daily Mail*, 13 February 1885, p. 4.

60 *Scotsman*, 13 February 1885, p. 4; *Elgin Courant*, 13 February 1885, p. 2.

61 *Elgin Courant*, 13 February 1885, p. 2; *[Dundee] Weekly News*, 14 February 1885, p. 4; *Glasgow News*, 13 February 1885, p. 4.

62 'The War in the Soudan – The Battle of Kerbekan', *Illustrated London News*, 21 March 1885, pp. 298–9.

63 The South Staffordshire lost five men killed and twenty-three officers and men wounded, Featherstone, *Khartoum 1885*, p. 80; *Strathearn Herald*, 14 February 1885, p. 2; *Dundee Courier & Argus*, 13 February 1885, p. 4; *Falkirk Herald*, 14 February 1885, p. 2.

64 'The Battle of Kirbekan', *Daily Telegraph*, 10 March 1885, p. 3; see also 'The Soudan Campaign', *Staffordshire Advertiser*, 7 March 1885, p. 6.

65 'The Black Watch at Abu Dom', p. 7.

66 Matthew, *Gladstone*, p. 149; Symons, *England's Pride*, pp. 268–70.

67 'A Soldier's Letter from Korosko', *Scotsman*, 18 April 1885, p. 7; 'Korosko', *The 79th News*, no. 198 (1932), pp. 171–3.

68 'Letter from a Soldier in the Soudan', *Kinross-shire Advertiser*, 2 January 1886, p. 2; 'Egypt and the Soudan', *Scotsman* 19 January 1886, p. 5 and 3 February 1886, p. 8.

69 'Egypt and the Soudan', *Scotsman*, 3 February 1886, p. 8; see also S. G. P. Ward, *Faithful: The Story of the Durham Light Infantry* (Edinburgh: Thomas Nelson, 1964), p. 274.

70 At the battle of Tofrik (22 March 1885) in the eastern Sudan, a half battalion of the Berkshire regiment was caught in the open and had to form a square rapidly to fight off a Mahdist assault. The regiment earned the title 'Royal' for its service in the field, F. Loraine Petre, *The Royal Berkshire Regiment*, 2 vols (Reading: The Barracks, 1925), 1, p. 337.

71 'A British Soldier in the Soudan', *Fife Herald*, 30 April 1884, p. 5.

72 Colonel Sir W. F. Butler, *The Campaign of the Cataracts: Being a Personal Narrative of the Great Nile Expedition of 1884–5* (London: Sampson Low, 1887), p. 342; Usherwood and Spencer-Smith, *Lady Butler*, pp. 158, 174–5; Prior, *Campaigns of a War Correspondent*, p. 196; 'The War in the Soudan', *Illustrated London News*, 22 March 1884, p. 273.

73 See portraits in the *Illustrated London News*, 22 March 1884 and 14 February 1885; Usherwood and Spencer-Smith, *Lady Butler*, p. 92; M. Pugh, *The Tories and the People 1880–1935* (Oxford: Basil Blackwell, 1985), p. 91.

74 King's Own Scottish Borderers (KOSB) Museum, T4/35, 'The Suakim Diary of Lt. Colonel Andrew Charles Parker Haggard', 5 and 20 February 1885.

75 National Library of Scotland (NLS), Rosebery Mss, Ms. 10037, ff. 96–8, 109–10, H. Ivory to Lord Rosebery, 20 March and 17 June 1884.

76 J. F. McCaffrey, 'The origins of Liberal Unionism in the west of Scotland', *Scottish Historical Review*, 50 (1971), pp. 47–71; D. C. Savage, 'Scottish Politics, 1885–6', *Scottish Historical Review*, 40 (1961), pp. 118–35.

77 McCaffrey, 'The origins of Liberal Unionism', pp. 53 and 67; Fry, *Patronage and Principle*, p. 110.

78 'Irish Orangemen's Manifesto', *Glasgow News*, 22 December 1885, p. 5.

79 E. McFarland, ' "A Mere Irish Faction": The Orange Institution in Nineteenth Century Scotland', in I. S. Wood (ed.) *Scotland and Ulster* (Edinburgh: Mercat Press, 1994), pp. 71–87 and ' "Outposts of the Loyalists of Ireland": The Orangemen's Unionist Vision', in C. M. M. Macdonald (ed.), *Unionist Scotland 1800–1997* (Edinburgh: John Donald, 1998), pp. 27–51; Hutchison, *Political History of Scotland*, pp. 122–3.

6

COMMEMORATION, PROMOTION AND THE STORMING OF DARGAI HEIGHTS

◞

Eleven years elapsed between the battle of Ginnis and the storming of Dargai Heights, years that represented a watershed in the late-Victorian history of the Scottish soldier. Although many battalions garrisoned outposts of the empire in the Mediterranean, Africa and India, they served in relatively minor campaigns (like the 1st Royal Scots in the bloodless Bechuanaland expedition and later in Zululand, and the 2nd Seaforth in the Black Mountain expeditions of 1888 and 1891) or engaged in unspectacular counter-guerrilla operations (like the 2nd Royal Scots Fusiliers in the Third Burma War of 1885–7). They earned unwonted publicity, too, in the debates about the Cardwellian army, particularly when attention centred upon Scottish recruiting difficulties. Lacking opportunities to earn further martial renown, and facing jibes about a purported dependence on 'Whitechapel highlanders',[1] Scottish regiments might have struggled to maintain their profile as prominent instruments of the imperial mission and as icons of Scottish nationhood. In fact, they managed to do so partly on account of their own efforts, partly on account of others with the commemoration of recent imperial achievements and the promotion of their image throughout the United Kingdom, and then in stunning military actions on the North-West Frontier, first in the Chitral and later in the storming of Dargai Heights.

The profile embellished in these years ensured not only extensive coverage of their service in the subsequent Sudanese and South African wars but also fuelled the surge of imperialist passions that swept through Scotland during the South African War. In studies of this phenomenon, which caused acute divisions within Scottish Liberalism, the impact of imperialism with all its martial connotations of the 1880s and 1890s appears almost *de novo*. Despite references to Glasgow's longstanding reputation as the 'second city of the empire', reflected in its imperial exhibitions and its shipbuilding and heavy engineering industries that prospered through colonial trade, as well as Scotland's imperial contribution through banking, engineering and missionary work, the military dimension receives scant coverage.[2] By reviewing the legacy of the Egyptian and Sudanese campaigns, and the image of the Scottish soldier in the years preceding the South African War, more insights may be gleaned about the recognition of Scotland's military achievements, not merely in Britain but across the empire, and about the role of Scottish regiments as representatives of Scotland within a greater imperial mission.

Even without the active involvement of Scottish regiments, the Scottish press displayed an enduring interest in Egyptian affairs, with reports and editorial commentary on the defeat of a Mahdist invasion of Egypt by an Anglo-Egyptian army at the battle of Toski (3 August 1889).[3] Various localities also honoured the martial achievements of Scottish regiments in the Egyptian and Sudanese campaigns. Within two years Aberdonians raised the requisite funding to erect a monumental cross in Duthrie Park in memory of the fallen Gordon Highlanders, a civic event that earned coverage in the metropolitan press.[4] In March 1886, Major John Menzies (10th Lanark, Glasgow Highlanders) launched a public campaign to erect a monument to the Black Watch near the site of its first encampment at Aberfeldy. In eighteen months his committee raised sufficient resources, including donations from Jamaica, Cape Town, New York, and the largest in proportional terms from New Zealand, to erect a memorial cairn, thirty-five feet high, surmounted by a life-size figure of a Highlander dressed in the original uniform of the Black Watch. This cairn, designed by the Edinburgh sculptor J. B. Rhind, commemorated the fighting history of the regiment from the battle of Fontenoy (1745) to Kirbekan, and the unveiling ceremony on 12 November 1887 attracted thousands of visitors, travelling by special trains from Glasgow, Edinburgh, Dundee and Perth. In unveiling the monument, the Marquis of Breadalbane described it as a means of inspiring young men to join such a distinguished regiment, as an attraction that would lure thousands of visitors to 'our picturesque and romantic district' and as a fitting memorial in the year of the queen's Golden Jubilee. To loud cheers, he read a letter from Wolseley stating that 'Perthshire has good reason to be proud of this regiment, for it is, without any doubt, the finest that has ever worn royal uniform.'[5]

Equally impressive was the unveiling on 14 July 1893 of the Cameron Monument in Inverness. Based on subscriptions from the officers and men of the regiment, this statue of a Cameron Highlander commemorated comrades who had fallen in action or died from disease or wounds in the Egyptian campaigns. Unveiled by Lochiel, chief of clan Cameron, on market day, it attracted a 'vast crowd of citizens', including 'farmers and others from all parts of the High- lands'. They came to witness the first piece of public art erected in the burgh, and located centrally in Station Square. Among the many trib- utes to the regiment Dr Norman Macleod, chaplain of the 1st Volunt- eer Battalion, Cameron Highlanders, claimed that Egypt, despite the 'betrayal and abandonment of Gordon', was now enjoying 'the ever- widening freedom and increasing prosperity which British rule and protection have secured for her'. He earned great applause in declar- ing that the British soldier had distinguished himself in 'the promo- tion of true freedom and justice', in opening up the African continent to the 'benign influence of civilisation and Christianity' and in making sacrifices 'on behalf of the magnificent commonwealth of which we are all so justly proud'.[6] The imperial mission had its adherents in Inverness.

This high esteem of the army as an instrument of imperialism contrasted sharply with the low regard for the army as a career, a reflection primarily of the limited appeal of army pay, terms, and con- ditions of service. Lochiel, who deplored the inability of the Cam- erons to find recruits in the traditional recruiting area of Lochaber, maintained, as others did, that if a regiment could be based in the Highlands then recruiting would improve.[7] Yet the scope for domes- tic postings was limited by the lack of adequate barrack accommo- dation in parts of the Highlands and by the deployment of a disproportionate number of battalions overseas, which wrecked the intended balance of battalions at home and abroad. Recruiting parties still marched through their regimental districts and small assault-at-arms teams conducted displays at public gatherings, but they sometimes encountered mixed receptions. On 19 August 1893 the *Highland News* reported on the Strathpeffer gathering wherein twenty-six 'strapping Highlanders' performed various military exer- cises, enacted scenes from the Zulu war, boxed each other and sang patriotic songs and Gaelic melodies. The newspaper then focused upon the recruiting dearth in Inverness-shire and ascribed the lack of recruits to 'the increase of legitimate labour, the dawn of better social arrangements at home, and a growing self-respect' which had dimin- ished the appeal of 'the least desirable, and worst paid of employ- ments . . . Is it not a fact that, all over the north and west, for a man to enter the army has always been regarded as equivalent to throw- ing himself away?'[8]

Military participation, though, extended beyond the regular army, and, as Hugh Cunningham has demonstrated, the Volunteers attracted a much higher proportion of the available population in Scotland than in England and Wales (and within Scotland, the Highland counties produced the highest rates of enrolment). By 1881 over 47,000 Scots (about 5.5 per cent of the available population) served in the Volunteers with the vast majority, like their English counterparts, coming predominantly from urban areas.[9] Given the ebb and flow of military crises (volunteering flourished during the invasion scare of 1884 and the Gordon controversy), the motivations included patriotism, a ready acceptance of martial values (wearing military uniform, learning elementary military duties and obeying orders) and, in some cases, a desire for comradeship, respectability and the opportunity to undertake rifle-shooting and other leisure pursuits.[10]

Some of these Volunteer values, coupled with the Victorian cult of the Christian Soldier,[11] found reflection in the Boys' Brigade, which was founded by William Alexander Smith in Glasgow in 1883. Smith, who was a Sunday school teacher of the Free Church and a member of the Glasgow Volunteer Regiment, the 1st Lanarkshire Rifles, had already been involved in young men's clubs and missions to the working-class districts of Glasgow. By establishing the Boys' Brigade, he sought to propagate the manly Christian virtues of obedience, reverence, discipline and self-respect through Sunday school and Bible class attendance, the wearing of uniform – pillbox cap, belt and haversack – and the inculcation of discipline and drill with dummy rifles. By 1890 there were 260 Boys' Brigade companies in Scotland (122 in England) and, by 1899, 276 companies in Scotland (470 in England and sixty-six in Ireland), involving 35,148 boys overall. The Scottish model would be developed, in even more militaristic and nationalist vein, by the Anglican Church Lads' Brigade (1891), and later the Jewish Lads' Brigade (1895) and the Catholic Boys' Brigade (1896).[12]

Discipline and drill were hardly novelties for Scottish children. Quite apart from the discipline of the Victorian classroom, drill and physical education were taught, sometimes by ex-soldiers employed as school janitors. If radicals on school boards periodically deplored any stimulation of the militarist spirit, Henry Craik, the influential secretary of the Scottish Education Department, defended drill as inculcating

> habits of comradeship, of responsibility, and of individual resource . . . Indirectly they bring the individual into contact with the principles which

lie at the foundation of national defence, and they bring home to him his duties and responsibilities as a citizen of the Empire. . . .[13]

The empire also fulfilled an important function within the teaching curriculum; as R. D. Anderson argues, it served 'as a kind of synthesis of English and Scottish histories', reflecting a predominantly Unionist perspective that the empire had provided a common purpose, submerging ancient animosities.[14]

Complementing the drilling of young boys was a diffusion of martial values through various media. A Scottish dimension or theme was prominent in various literary forms. Archibald Forbes, the former war correspondent, wrote a biography of Gordon (1884) that was in its twelfth edition within a year of publication, another biography of Colin Campbell and a popular history of the Black Watch.[15] James Cromb rewrote the history of Majuba, refuting allegations of 'funk' by the British soldiers and describing 'a story of Highland Heroism'. Using correspondence from officers of the Gordon Highlanders to Colonel White after the battle, he quoted from Captain (later Major) Macgregor but ignored his claims that the soldiers had 'enough ammunition' throughout the battle, and that in the retreat over broken ground, 'Every man had to look after himself . . .'[16] Several authors wrote regimental histories, or memoirs of their service in the Crimea and Indian Mutiny,[17] but probably more influential was the rapid expansion of juvenile literature, with its prominent themes of adventure and imperialism. This was a truly British phenomenon as reflected in the sales of the *Boy's Own Paper* (1879), which enjoyed a circulation of 200,000 initially, and the publication of over 900 new books annually by the early 1880s. Scottish heroes were prominent in the voluminous literature, not least in the writing of Dr Gordon Stables. Like G. A. Henty, the doyen of this literature, Stables was a proponent of 'aggressive militarism'; he wrote nearly one hundred adventure tales, many of them beginning in the Highlands with a Scottish lad as hero, who would undertake a harrowing journey to a distant land, and help create or maintain the empire, before returning to Scotland 'with a moral precept . . . on the virtues of manliness and muscular Christianity'.[18]

Manliness was an evolving Victorian concept which had assumed distinctly robust qualities by the late nineteenth century. These qualities included physical prowess, courage, fortitude, nerve, loyalty, patriotism, unselfishness and self-control – all qualities deemed necessary for those destined for imperial service and largely consistent with the image of the Highland soldier (though Campbell's charge of impulsiveness seemed replicated at the battle of Tamai). For potential officers, these qualities were thought to be inculcated in Victorian public schools like Loretto School near Musselburgh, under its head-master Hely Hutchinson Almond, where the playing of team games, and learning to 'play the game', were thought to develop hardiness, team spirit and 'character'. Former pupils were expected to emerge with gentlemanly ideals, a sense of noblesse oblige and a chivalrous code of conduct. This public school ethos, linked to notions of impe-rial service, was popularised and promoted through adventure books and boys' magazines.[19]

Admittedly, this literature may have served as an 'escapist narcotic' for many lower middle or working-class readers whom, in later life, neither rushed to the colours in peacetime nor emerged as ardent imperialists.[20] It confirmed nonetheless popular stereotypes, includ-ing the 'Scots as warlike', and contributed, as Dave Russell argues in respect of the writers of popular patriotic songs, towards a 'positive acquiescence' in imperial sentiments and so 'constructed, reflected and reinforced' popular attitudes.[21] The more specific image of the heroic, chivalrous Scottish soldier was disseminated on the stage, in the music hall, in songs, poetry, popular art, engravings and adver-tisements. If the lavish spectacles that transmitted images of the Crimean War in mid-century were less prominent by the 1890s,[22] melodrama with its strong passions, vigorous action and moral themes remained immensely popular. Highland heroes appeared in several productions, with the poster for *One of the Best*, performed at the Adelphi theatre, London in 1895, showing a Highland soldier proclaiming 'You can take my life – But you can never take from me my Victoria Cross'.[23] In *The Girl I left Behind Me*, a balletic version of a Drury Lane melodrama, the hero, who is ruined by gambling on horses, enlists in a Highland regiment to sail for Burma and win the Victoria Cross and later the hand in marriage of his faithful girl. The 'military evolutions of the mimic Highlanders', wrote the critic of *The Times*, earned 'unstinted' applause from the audience on opening night (27 September 1893) and the production ran for fifty-three weeks.[24]

Highland soldiers featured in various jubilee productions, includ-ing Sir Arthur Sullivan's *Victoria and Merrie England* (25 May 1897) and the Empire theatre's *Under One Flag* (21 June 1897). Scottish military bands performed across the country at exhibitions, tattoos and the Military Tournament. In the heyday of the music hall and patriotic songs, the bravery and heroism of Scottish regiments found reflection on the stage, often in the form of dramatic tableaux. The Gordon Highlanders became the theme of several works, especially in the wake of the Dargai charge, as well as musical versions of ballads by Gerard F. Cobb like *The Gay Gordons* (1897) and his march *The Charge at Dargai* (1898). [25] After Dargai an entertainment in aid of the Gordons' benevolent fund was held in Aberdeen's music hall (17 December 1897), involving songs by leading Scottish performers, dance, instrumental music from the Volunteer pipers, a cinematograph involving thirty-six animated photographs, as well as a bayonet exercise and drill by a detachment of the regiment. It attracted a large gathering and 'vociferous applause' for many parts of the programme. [26]

Less dramatic but no less important in confirming both the identity of the Scottish soldier and his distinctiveness within the British army, were the multitude of images disseminated throughout the United Kingdom. Whether in the dramatic imagery of R. Caton Woodville, often illustrating scenes from the Peninsular or Indian wars, or photographs in magazines like *Navy and Army Illustrated*, or in the illustrations of the remarkably prolific Harry Payne, Scottish soldiers were highly conspicuous. [27] Payne, who was renowned for the accuracy of his work, received commissions from Scottish regiments to prepare drawings of their recent campaigns, notably from the 1st Battalion, Royal Scots as mounted infantry in Bechuanaland (1885), Natal (1886–7) and Zululand (1888–91). He composed illustrations for the 'Illustrated Histories of the Scottish Regiments' (1893–5), children's books including *With Claymore and Bayonet* (1895) and *Scotland for Ever* (1897), and official histories of Scottish regiments, including Lieutenant-Colonel Greenhill Gardyne's history of the Gordon Highlanders. He also illustrated court cards, postcards, cigarette cards and scraps for children's albums, all of which circulated in vast numbers during the halcyon days of printed relief and the picture postcard. 'The Harry Payne Toy Books', produced by lithography from 1897 onwards, were among his most colourful works, including depictions of the Scots Fusilier Guards parading at Buckingham Palace before their departure for the Crimea and the 93rd in the relief of Lucknow. [28] The picturesque Scots were also a feature of contemporary advertising, and if the use of military imagery grew significantly during the South African War (with Highlanders advertising products as disparate as Bovril, cocoa and whisky), pre-war advertising, whether promoting biscuits or blended whisky, used Highlanders and the Scots Greys. Unlike the subsequent, wartime depiction of khaki-clad Highlanders set in mundane South African locations, much of the pre-war advertising was more stylised and involved images of Highlanders in feather bonnets and full Highland costume.[29]

However pervasive these images, the fighting reputation of the Scottish soldier rested primarily on its vindication in battle. Although the Black Mountain expeditions produced evocative photographs of Seaforths on mountainsides,[30] they did not involve the heavy fighting that characterised the Chitral relief expedition of 1895. The British had become involved in civil strife over the succession to this small state in the far north of British India. Following the murder of its ruler, the Mehtar, in January 1895, an uncle of the murdered ruler invaded the state, assisted by the Pathan chief, Umra Khan of Jandol. By early March Surgeon-Major Scott Robertson, the British agent, found himself besieged in Chitral fort, protecting the ten-year-old ruler, Shuja, and about a hundred Chitrali civilians. The image of a small, isolated garrison, with a few British officers and loyal native soldiers holding out against overwhelming odds, evoked comparisons with Khartoum,[31] and pressure mounted for the dispatch of a relief force. Major-General Sir Robert Low duly mobilised a force of 15,000 men at Peshawar (including the 2nd Battalion, King's Own Scottish Borderers and the 1st Battalion, Gordon Highlanders) prior to con- centrating at Nowshera (1 April) for a march over 160 miles across two rivers and several formidable mountain passes deep in snow.[32]

Another smaller relief force of the 32nd Punjab Pioneers (about 400 men and two guns) under Colonel Kelly actually reached the fort first (20 April) but the bulk of the reporting came from Low's divi- sion, where Lionel James reported for the Reuters' Agency, W. T. Maude for the *Graphic* and the Younghusband brothers for *The Times*.[33] Low's division undertook a series of hard-fought engage- ments, beginning with the storming of the Malakand Pass (3 April) held by an estimated 12,000 tribesmen. One officer, in a report filed by Reuters, described the assault launched by the Borderers in the central spur, the Gordons on the right and the 60th King's Royal Rifle Corps on the left as

> a horrible scramble up the steep hillside, but the Scotsmen, with marvel- lous agility, were over the rugged boulders and into the sangars in double- quick time. They accomplished more with the bayonet than the guns had done all day, and carried position after position with the greatest gal- lantry.[34]

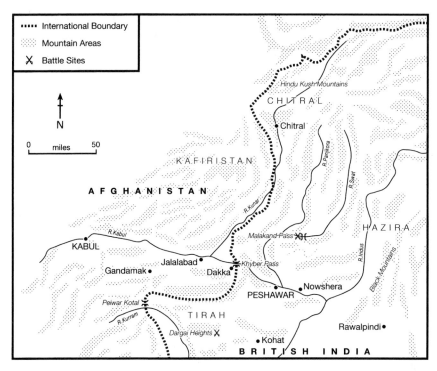

Map 8   *North-West Frontier, 1895–7*

Although the climb was extremely steep in places, varying in heights from 1,000 to 1,500 feet, artillery and Maxim machine guns covered much of the attack (until the final assault) and the new Lee Metford magazine rifles, with smokeless powder, 'did great execution'. The poorly armed enemy (less than half had rifles) suffered over 500 casualties compared with only sixty for Low's force.[35] A Borderers NCO recoiled at the sight on the summit: it was 'too horrible to describe ... The enemy were lying about in all directions. Every stone and rock was covered with blood.' The enemy, he added, were 'a brave race of men'.[36] The metropolitan press published few letters (as they arrived at least a fortnight after hostilities ceased), but in one account a sergeant of the Gordon Highlanders was less complimentary about the jeering Swatis and the 'fanatics of the Pathan race', who had guarded the hilltops. He described how the Gordons had climbed rapidly without cover up steep paths and reached the summit, in spite of bullets 'flying all around us', whereupon they 'shot down every nigger who showed himself . . .'[37]

Further actions were fought at the Swat and Panjkora rivers, but the storming of the Malakand Pass captured the public attention, not least when the Younghusband brothers produced their best-selling account of the *Relief of Chitral* in November 1895. Frank Younghusband had already made his name as an imperial traveller (and former political officer in the Chitral): he had also spoken out vigorously in favour of a relief action before the Royal Colonial Institute and the Royal Geographical Society in the previous March. This 'eyewitness' account, in which George Younghusband described the military exploits, proved immensely popular; it sold out two editions within a fortnight, praising the exploits of the Scottish soldier. At the Malakand Pass, he wrote, 'It was a fine and stirring sight to see the splendid dash with which the two Scotch regiments took the hill.' When the enemy counter-attacked at the Panjkora river (an action depicted in a double-page picture in the *Illustrated London News*), the Borderers and Gordons fired on the flanks: 'not a man got across, so steady and well directed was the flank fire of the British regiments'.[38] However briefly, the fighting prowess of the Scottish soldier had recaptured popular acclaim, focusing attention on the North-West Frontier and paving the way for the great imperial epic: the storming of Dargai Heights.

When frontier fighting erupted during the summer and autumn of 1897, involving attacks on convoys and forts, it prompted a series of punitive missions, the largest of which was the Tirah Field Force of Lieutenant-General Sir William Lockhart. The 2nd Battalion, King's Own Scottish Borderers and the 1st Battalion, Gordon Highlanders served in the striking force of two divisions that left Kohat on 11 October, planning to march through the country of the Afridis and Orakzais. Within a week they encountered their first major natural obstacle, the almost perpendicular heights below the village of Dargai, approachable only by a narrow steep footpath after crossing a glacis some fifty yards wide. On 18 October the 3rd Gurkhas, followed by the Borderers, briefly seized the heights with minimal losses before the Afridis reappeared in their thousands, forcing a precipitate retreat. Lance-Corporal Waddington (KOSB) praised the Gurkhas after this feat as 'the bravest soldiers England possesses . . .'[39] Forced to relaunch the attack on 20 October against an estimated 12,000 Afridis, Lockhart sent fresh troops into action, covered by three batteries of mountain guns, but the attacks of the 1st/2nd Gurkhas, 2nd Derbyshire and 1st Dorsetshire all failed before the Gordons were called into action. After a bombardment lasting three minutes, Lieutenant-Colonel H. H. Mathias exhorted his men: 'The general says this hill must be taken at all costs – the Gordon Highlanders will take it!' The men cheered and followed their colonel as he sent his pipers forth. The Gordons crossed the fire-swept glacis and stormed the heights, losing three officers and men killed and forty-one wounded (four of whom later died of their wounds) out of a total of 195 casualties.[40]

Although soldiers served in the Tirah valley until December 1897, this charge captured the imagination as few imperial events had ever done before or since. The early telegrams highlighted a 'splendid feat of arms', acts of 'individual heroism' and the 'great gallantry of the Gordons'.[41] The Scottish press revelled in 'a magnificent piece of derring-do' (*Falkirk Herald*), which proved that 'heroism on the field of battle is still possible' (*Nairnshire Telegraph*) and would be revered in 'Aberdeen and Aberdeenshire' (*Aberdeen Journal*). If the charge confirmed the traditional image of heroic Scottish warriors, led by their officers in a daring assault, it carried even greater resonance because the Gordons had responded to an exhortation 'thoroughly in the pithy style of Sir Colin Campbell', and to a piper who kept playing despite a serious ankle injury, before the battalion triumphed where others had failed.[42]

Even Scottish Liberals, who condemned the 'forward' policy and the costs of the war, hailed the Gordons. James Bryce, the MP for Aberdeen South, praised the 'splendid feats of heroism' of his local regiment in 'the present deplorable war'.[43] Similarly Glasgow's *North British Daily Mail*, though a fierce critic of the costly war, acknowledged the 'thrilling' achievements of the Gordons, the echoes of Colin Campbell in the address of Colonel Mathias, the recognition of the Gordons' bravery by 'the impromptu ovation from the assembled troops who had watched their attack', and further plaudits among 'fellow countrymen at home'.[44] What impressed many Scots was the extent of the recognition. As the 'London Notes' of the *Highland News* confirmed: 'The Gordon Highlanders are the heroes of the hour. Their brilliant conduct is the talk of Scotsmen wherever they meet, and even the average Englishman cannot refrain from expressing his admiration for such daring and gallantry as was displayed at Dargai.'[45]

The metropolitan press, having recently revelled in the Diamond Jubilee celebrations with the spectacular display of military forces and imperial unity in the capital, now praised the Gordons, illustrated their achievements, and printed histories of the regiment.[46] The

Scottish newspapers reprinted tributes from *The Times, Morning Post, Pall Mall Gazette, Evening News, St James's Gazette, Daily Graphic, Sun, Daily News* and *Daily Chronicle*, and reflected the burgeoning interest in the identity of the wounded piper. [47] They also reported plaudits paid to the Gordons in the service clubs, a representation of the attack at Madame Tussaud's and the poems composed in honour of the regiment, including *At Dargai* by Sir Edwin Arnold,[48] the poet laureate. The tenth and eleventh verses described:

> Fierce, splendid, faithful, stream our Scots
> > To lightsome, homely Highland lilt;
> Too swift for Fate, too bold to fail,
> > Rush buskin, plume, and kilt.
> The fifty yards of fire are passed:
> The savage ridge is gained at last!
>
> Down from the emptied sangars fly
> > Those rebel hordes: the flaming hill
> Is cleared! the grim position seized
> > As was the General's will.
> The Colonel's simple word did make it,
> 'The Gordon Highlanders will take it!'

Scots, whether at home or overseas, followed suit and composed numerous poems in honour of the Gordons and their piper.[49]

Equally gratifying were the tributes paid to the regiment which were passed on to the men encamped in the Tirah valley. As several Gordons recalled, there were commendations from the queen-empress, Lockhart, Wolseley (now commander-in-chief), fellow Scottish regiments, the 2nd and Volunteer Battalions of the Gordons, the Rifle Brigade, 9th Lancers, 'old and present officers' of the regiment, Lord Saltoun, friends from Ceylon, and Caledonian societies in Johannesburg, Durban, Cape Town and even the United States. At a ball of the Highland society in Johannesburg there were reportedly cheers for the regiment and its 'brave piper'.[50] The Gordon Highlanders, claimed the *Northern Chronicle*, had become, for the moment, 'the selected champions of the British Empire'.[51]

Given this adulation and the continuation of the campaign for another two months, the letters of Gordon Highlanders proved in great demand, and wounded or time-expired soldiers were interviewed on their return home. Band Corporal Douglas Hunter, like others, remembered the daunting spectacle of the heights, which resembled 'a second Gibraltar'.[52] They recalled the colonel's speech (even if accounts of it varied enormously)[53] and, on reaching the summit, the cheers for Mathias, whom Corporal Pique described as 'a true soldier and a great commander'.[54] Lance-Corporal Low, like others, thought they had advanced to the strains of 'The Cock o' the North', but some neither saw nor heard the wounded piper who continued playing: Corporal Esslemont conceded that if the piper claimed he was playing 'The Haughs of Cromdale', then 'he should know best . . .'[55] The charge, claimed a Glaswegian sergeant, would 'never . . . be forgotten' by the survivors;[56] it was a 'splendid rush of tartan', recalled Lieutenant George D. MacKenzie,[57] and one undertaken by sections of soldiers, following their officers, across the fire-swept glacis. As Private John Bennett, a Gordon Highlander from Leeds, recollected, those who managed to cross the pass, strewn with the dead, dying and wounded, gathered under cover of the ridge and 'cheered those who were rushing across. The din altogether was frightful. When we had reformed under the ridge we started off up the hill in small rushes again in the face of a terrible fire. Many of us were bowled over . . .'[58] Once they reached the summit (a succession of ridges on which the men could reform and advance in numbers) Colour-Sergeant William Patterson, who was in the first party just behind Colonel Mathias, described how the enemy fled at once and 'we followed them with a few volleys which helped to accelerate their movements'.[59] Some admitted that various Sikhs, Gurkhas, Derbys and Dorsets joined the charge,[60] but most were delighted that the Gordons, as a regiment, had succeeded where others failed, and that fellow soldiers gave them an ovation when they retired from the hill.[61] Captain John L. R. Gordon (15th Sikhs) acknowledged that 'Even our men burst into loud cheers and it is seldom they show any emotion.'[62]

As the newspaper coverage was so extensive and flattering, it aroused resentment, not least as the newspapers, or comments from them, circulated among the soldiers in the Tirah. An Edinburgh man, serving in the King's Own Scottish Borderers, assured his brother that 'what you see in the papers about the Gordons is all lies'; another Borderer fumed that 'if we had kilts and Highlanders, no doubt you would see us in all the illustrated papers like the Gordons'; and many Borderers seemed to feel, as Private Alexander Ridgard added, that they had not received due credit for their seizure of Dargai on the 18th.[63] Of those who fought on the 20th, many did not begrudge the Gordons but maintained that the other regiments had done their duty too.[64] Some went further, complaining bitterly in letters to the Indian,

Dorset and Derbyshire press that the Gordons had been praised excessively: in the opinion of Captain Shaw (2nd Derbyshire), 'the Gordons have got every atom of credit for taking the position'.[65] These soldiers claimed that the 'leading groups' deserved more credit for bearing 'the heat and burden' of the fight, and that the 2nd Gurkhas deserved 'equal, if not greater glory' as they suffered the greatest number of killed and wounded.[66] Some insisted that the Gordons had only triumphed on account of the artillery support, and that various Gurkhas, Dorsets and Derbyshires had accompanied the final assault.[67] Among all this special pleading, an officer of the Derbyshires provided the most plausible commentary. Having commanded the company that provided fire support for the Gordons' charge, he had heard the exhortation of Mathias, the ringing cheers of the Highlanders, and then saw how the 'music of the pipes and inspiriting words had an extraordinary effect' as the Gordons followed their colonel, two majors and a lieutenant across the fire-zone. This Derbyshire officer soon followed, taking his company across in the wake of the Gordons.[68]

The Gordon Highlanders knew about the furore over the reporting. Some like Corporal Esslemont claimed that they were hardly to blame if the imaginations of various correspondents ran 'riot' in their reporting for 'the Evening papers at home'.[69] Nor was there much that they could do about jibes that this was hardly a triumph for Scotland as so many of their number were English or Irish (in fact most Gordons were Scots, although barely a quarter of the men came from the district of Aberdeenshire, Kincardineshire and Banffshire).[70] Colour-Sergeant Patterson, though willing to admit that the 'papers out here are enough to make us exhaust all our stock of blushes', asserted that

> It is no small boast to be able to say that we succeeded where the Dorsets, Derbys, Sikhs, and Gurkhas failed, and proved that the Highland regiments were as ready as ever to show the way to any others, despite the sneers of Mr Labouchere and others of his kidney. We don't say for a minute that we are alone among the Scots regiments who could have done it. Far from it! We feel sure that any of our regiments, Black Watch, 93d, King's Own Scottish Borderers, Seaforths, or any other regiment would have done it just as we did, sustained by the feeling of esprit de corps which is, in my opinion, stronger in Scottish regiments than in most English regiments.[71]

His distaste for the criticisms of Henry Labouchere, MP, found reflection in another letter of a Gordon Highlander from Camp Maidan in the Tirah, complaining that their division had suffered over 400 casualties by 19 November, 'which is pretty warm considering we are (to quote Mr Herbert Gladstone) only fighting unarmed savages'.[72]

The Gordons, like other units, endured the subsequent campaigning, with minimal rations, as conditions became increasingly cold. They wrote of their duties in surveying the territory, foraging, and skirmishing with the enemy, suffering from the recurrent sniping at foraging parties and nightly fusillades and undertaking reprisal missions, blowing up houses, burning villages and 'ringing' trees (that is, cutting off layers of bark to prevent their 'fruiting' in future years).[73] Although the Ozarkais submitted, paying the levied fines – in rifles and cash – by the end of November, the Afridis proved more recalcitrant. They 'follow us', wrote a Gordon from Kirkcaldy, 'are wonderfully good shots, . . . judge distance only too well . . .' and seemed impervious to pressure: as a Glaswegian sergeant recalled, 'All the Maidan Valley is burned or on fire now, and there is nothing else we can do with these people, for they don't intend giving in or paying a fine and giving up their arms.'[74] When Lockhart withdrew his force in early December to avoid the onset of winter, the Afridis harried the rearguard, including the Gordons who fought a rearguard action for two days over eleven miles. In Private John Allen's view, this was 'ten times worse' than Dargai.[75]

Yet Dargai remained the focus of attention, partly because it took a couple of months to identify the piper correctly. The original telegrams came from correspondents who were a mile in the rear with Lockhart, and only knew of the regiment's success through a signal from Mathias, claiming that 'the Gordons have taken the position'.[76] Having heard of the piping incident, they later misidentified the piper from the casualty returns as Lance-Corporal Patrick Milne, with Gordons, like Private James Forsyth, compounding the error because they never really knew who was piping among 'the bodies of our dead and wounded comrades'.[77] Eventually the pipers clarified matters; Milne, in a letter to his brother in Vancouver, explained that he had led the pipers out but was shot through the lung, whereas Piper George Findlater, though shot through an ankle with a dum dum bullet, was able to keep playing. As Findlater added, 'it was a wonder I got away with my life, for I was sitting right in the open, and the bullets were glancing around me in all directions'.[78]

Findlater now became an imperial hero, sustaining public interest in Dargai for over a year or more. His photograph appeared in the illustrated press with placards displayed in London and the county towns. On learning of his gallantry, Scotsmen in Cape Colony raised a public subscription for him, and a wealthy lady in Indian society reportedly offered her hand in marriage.[79] The Marquis of Huntly launched another subscription fund, raising some 3,843 rupees by April 1898 for the sick, wounded and the widows and dependants of the Gordon Highlanders.[80] When Findlater and the other wounded soldiers were brought back to England for further treatment in the Royal Victoria Hospital at Netley, reporters rushed to interview him, to hear him play on the chanter and to see his kilt still bearing splotches of blood. They also reported on the queen's visit, when she conferred the Victoria Cross on Findlater and he again played the 'Haughs o' Cromdale'.[81] Once fit to leave Netley, Findlater found himself in immense demand, playing the pipes in the Military Tournament, where royal personages and generals shook his hand, and at the Alhambra music hall, Charing Cross Road, where he performed several times nightly. Although the adjutant-general deplored his music-hall activities, Findlater acquired agents to manage his tours of the music halls in Ireland, England and Scotland until his public acclaim began to diminish over a breach-of-promise suit. He was harassed over the affair by a huge crowd in Union Street, Aberdeen, and booed by a section of the audience at the Empire Palace Theatre, Glasgow, before the case was settled out of court. Eventually a post was found for him in the queen's household, enabling him to retire to his Scottish croft.[82]

Findlater's heroism and public acclaim, nonetheless, sustained interest in the Dargai charge, which became the theme of several paintings. Although Findlater only appeared in the background of Allan Stewart's *The charge of the Gordon Highlanders* (1898), he was a central figure in Stanley Berkeley's *Charge of the Gordon Highlanders* (1897), Vereker Hamilton's *Piper Findlater at Dargai* (1898), Woodville's *'The Cock o' the North'; storming of Dargai Heights by the 1st Battalion Gordon Highlanders* (1898) and Edward Matthew Hale's *Piper Findlater winning the Victoria Cross at Dargai* (1898). Woodville also composed a partially coloured, double-page illustration of 'The Gordon Highlanders at Dargai' for the *Illustrated London News* of 2 April 1898, with Piper Findlater in the centre of the picture.[83] The lone, injured piper had provided a personal and focal point for these paintings that had rarely been exploited in a similar way before.

Complementing the battle paintings were numerous representations of the Gordons in prints and popular art – even a set of Christmas cards[84] – popular histories and songs composed in their honour.

Figure 6 Piper Findlater at Dargai *(Vereker Hamilton, reproduced by permission of the Gordon Highlanders' Museum)*

This extraordinary response confirmed the failure of what J. M. Bulloch described as 'the necessary reaction' (in the letters from rival regiments) to the first wave of romantic reports about the Dargai charge. 'The great mass of the public', he argued, was 'disinclined to correct its first impressions',[85] a response that may have reflected the legacy of imperial enthusiasm aroused by the Diamond Jubilee celebrations, which had occurred throughout most of the United Kingdom and empire (despite some protests in Dublin). The 2nd Battalions of the Seaforth and Gordon Highlanders had lined streets in London during the royal procession of 22 June 1897, a conspicuous Scottish presence within the imperial pageant.[86] The 1st Battalion, Gordon Highlanders had now assisted in the defence of imperial unity, achieving thereby an iconic status not only in Scotland but also in much of the United Kingdom (save in those areas chafing at the neglect of their county regiments) and in the Scottish imperial diaspora. The Scottish press appreciated the impact: even the *North British Daily Mail*, now the principal organ of Liberalism in Glasgow and a fierce critic of the Tirah campaign, asserted:

It has been suggested that our plaudits [for the Gordon Highlanders] have been a little overstrained, but we need not be afraid of that. Nothing heartens a soldier better than deserved praise and the knowledge that whatever merit he displays will be appreciated.[87]

Notes

1 On this issue, see A. V. Tucker, 'Army and Society in England, 1870–1900: A Reassessment of the Cardwell Reforms', *Journal of British Studies*, 2 (1963), pp. 110–41, and Skelley, *The Victorian Army at Home*, pp. 288–9. On the Burmese operations, see J. Buchan, *The History of The Royal Scots Fusiliers (1678–1918)* (London: Thomas Nelson & Sons, 1925), pp. 250–1.

2 J. F. McCaffrey, *Scotland in the Nineteenth Century* (Basingstoke: Macmillan, 1998), pp. 105–6; S. J. Brown, ' "Echoes of Midlothian": Scottish Liberalism and the South African War, 1899–1902', *Scottish Historical Review*, 71 (1992), pp. 156–83.

3 *Scotsman*, 6 August 1889, p. 4; 'Great Battle in the Soudan', *Dumfries and Galloway Courier and Herald*, 7 August 1889, p. 7.

4 *Illustrated London News*, 12 July 1884, p. 46.

5 'The Black Watch Memorial', *Perthshire Advertiser*, 14 November 1887, p. 3.

6 'The Memorial to the Cameron Highlanders', *Inverness Courier*, 18 July 1893, p. 5; 'The Unveiling of the Cameron Monument at Inverness', *Northern Chronicle*, 19 July 1893, p. 6; N. Newton, *The Life and Times of Inverness* (Edinburgh: John Donald, 1996), pp. 133–4.

7 'The Unveiling of the Cameron Monument at Inverness', p. 6; 'Clan Cameron Gathering in Glasgow', *Northern Chronicle*, 9 February 1898, p. 3; 'Opinion of Mr Bryce, M.P.', *Aberdeen Journal*, 15 December 1897, p. 5.

8 'The Strathpeffer Gathering' and 'Recruiting in the Highlands', *Highland News*, 19 August 1893, p. 2.

9 H. Cunningham, *The Volunteer Force: A Social and Political History, 1859–1908* (London: Croom Helm, 1975), pp. 46–9.

10 Ibid., ch. 6.

11 O. Anderson, 'The growth of Christian militarism in mid-Victorian Britain', *English Historical Review*, 86 (1971), pp. 46–72.

12 J. O. Springhall, *Youth, Empire and Society: British Youth Movements, 1883–1940* (London: Croom Helm, 1977), pp. 17, 22–8, 37.

13 H. Craik, 'Physical Education in Schools', 3 February 1900, in PP, *Report of The Committee of Council on Education in Scotland*, 1899–1900, Cd. 170 (1900), XXIV, p. 263.

14 R. D. Anderson, *Education and The Scottish People 1750–1918* (Oxford: Clarendon Press, 1995), pp. 212–20.

15 A. Forbes, *Chinese Gordon: A succinct record of his life* (London:

Routledge & Sons, 1884); *Colin Campbell*; and *The Black Watch* (London: Cassell, 1896).

16 J. Cromb (ed.), *The Majuba Disaster: A Story of Highland Heroism, Told By Officers of the 92nd Regiment* (Dundee: John Leng, 1891); BL, White Mss Eur F108/91, Captain Macgregor to White, 6 May 1882.

17 Wimberley, *Some Account of the Part taken by the 79th Regiment*; Forbes-Mitchell, *Reminiscences of the Great Mutiny 1857–9*; Gordon-Alexander, *Recollections of a Highland Subaltern*; A. Robb, *Reminiscences of a Veteran: Being the Experiences of a Private Soldier in the Crimea, and during the Indian Mutiny* (Dundee: W. & D. C. Thomson, 1888).

18 P. A. Dunae, 'Boys' Literature and the Idea of Empire, 1870–1914', *Victorian Studies*, 24 (1980), pp. 105–22, and 'New Grub Street for boys' as well as J. Richards, 'Introduction', in J. Richards (ed.), *Imperialism and juvenile literature* (Manchester: Manchester University Press, 1989), pp. 5, 18 and 21. For the debate about the *BOP*'s circulation, see J. McAleer, *Popular Reading and Publishing in Britain 1914–1950* (Oxford: Clarendon Press, 1992), pp. 20, 215–19.

19 J. A. Mangan, *The Games Ethic and Imperialism: Aspects of the Diffusion of an Ideal* (Harmondsworth, Middlesex; Viking, 1986), pp. 23–8, 69–70; J. O. Springhall, 'Building character in the British boy: the attempt to extend Christian manliness to working-class adolescents, 1880–1914', in J. A. Mangan and J. Walvin (eds), *Manliness and morality: Middle-class masculinity in Britain and America 1800–1940* (Manchester: Manchester University Press, 1987), pp. 52, 66–7.

20 J. Rose, *The Intellectual Life of the British Working Classes* (New Haven: Yale University Press, 2001), pp. 8, 331–5, 341; McAleer, *Popular Reading*, pp. 29–30.

21 D. Russell, *Popular music in England, 1840–1914* (Manchester: Manchester University Press, 1997), pp. 160, 164; K. Boyd, *Manliness and the Boy's Story Paper in Britain: A Cultural History, 1855–1940* (Houndmills, Basingstoke: Palgrave Macmillan, 2003), pp. 123–4.

22 J. S. Brattan, 'Theatre of war: the Crimea on the London stage 1854–5', in D. Bradby, L. James, B. Sharratt (eds), *Performance and politics in popular drama* (Cambridge: Cambridge University Press, 1980), pp. 119–37.

23 G. Rowell, *Theatre in the Age of Irving* (Oxford: Basil Blackwell, 1981), p. 145.

24 *The Times*, 28 September 1893, p. 3; J. Richards, *Imperialism and music: Britain 1876–1953* (Manchester: Manchester University Press, 2001), pp. 258–9.

25 Richards, *Imperialism and music*, pp. 31–2, 179, 222, 259, 335, 354; Russell, *Popular music*, pp. 148, 163; and 'We carved our way to glory', in MacKenzie (ed.), *Popular Imperialism*, p. 60.

26 'Gordon Highlanders' Benevolent Fund', *Aberdeen Journal*, 18 December 1897, p. 5.

27 'Carrying Sir John Moore from the Battlefield' and 'The 42nd Highlanders Driving the French out of Elvina', *Illustrated London News*, 7 September 1895, pp. 301, 305; P. Warner, *Army Life in the '90s* (London: Hamlyn, 1975), pp. 27, 52–3, 84, 127; M. Cane, *For Queen and Country: The Career of Harry Payne Military Artist 1858–1927* (Kingston, Surrey: private, 1977).

28 Cane, *For Queen and Country*, pp. 28–32, 40, 44, 51, 54, 62; T. and V. Holt, *Picture Postcards of the Golden Age: A Collector's Guide* (London: MacGibbon & Kee, 1971), pp. 36–7, 81–2; A. Allen and J. Hoverstadt, *The History of Printed SCRAPS* (London: New Cavendish Books, 1983), pp. 25, 39, 162, 235.

29 L. Anne Loeb, *Consuming Angels: Advertising and Victorian Women* (Oxford: Oxford University Press, 1994), pp. 12, 83–5; D. and G. Hindley, *Advertising in Victorian England 1837–1901* (London: Wayland, 1972), pp. 118–19; *Daily News*, 23 January 1900, p. 10; M. J. Franklin, *British Biscuit Tins 1868–1939: An Aspect of Decorative Packaging* (London: New Cavendish Books, 1979), p. 51; and advertisements for whiskies in the *Illustrated London News*, 16 November 1895, p. 671, 14 December 1895, p. 750, 26 June 1897, pp. 899, 900; and J. Murray, *The Art of Whisky: A De Luxe Blend of Historic Posters from the Public Record Office* (Kew, Surrey: PRO Publications, 1998), pp. 34–5, 56.

30 See photographs from the National Army Museum reproduced in Beckett, *Victoria's Wars*, p. 63, and Barthorp, *Afghan Wars*, p. 95.

31 P. French, *Younghusband: The Last Great Imperial Adventurer* (London: HarperCollins, 1994), pp. 114–15.

32 Ibid., pp. 115–16; see also Barthorp, *Afghan Wars*, pp. 107–17.

33 Wilkinson-Latham, *From Our Special Correspondent*, p. 210.

34 'Chitral Campaign: An Officer's Narrative of the Fighting', *Daily Telegraph*, 6 April 1895, p. 5; Captain H. L. Nevill, *Campaigns on the North-West Frontier* (London: John Murray, 1912), p. 191.

35 'Storming the Malakand', *Daily Graphic*, 30 April 1895, p. 8; T. R. Moreman, *The Army in India and the Development of Frontier Warfare, 1849–1947* (Houndmills, Basingstoke: Macmillan, 1998), p. 51; R. Woollcombe, *All The Blue Bonnets: The History of The King's Own Scottish Borderers* (London: Arms and Armour Press, 1980), pp. 66–7.

36 GH Museum, PB 378/132, press cuttings on the storming of the Malakand Pass, including a letter, n.d., from an NCO of the KOSB published in the Indian press.

37 'A Sergeant's Story', *Evening News*, 9 May 1895, p. 2.

38 French, *Younghusband*, p. 130; Captain G. J. Younghusband and Captain F. E. Younghusband, *The Relief of Chitral* (London: Macmillan,

1897), pp. 66, 81; see also 'The Chitral Campaign', *Illustrated London News*, 25 May 1895, pp. 648–9.

39 'A West Hartlepool Man at the Frontier', *Newcastle Daily Chronicle*, 16 November 1897, p. 8.

40 Greenhill Gardyne, *Life of a Regiment*, 2, pp. 292–3; Barthorp, *Afghan Wars*, pp. 132–3; for retrospective and transcribed diaries on the campaign, see GH Museum, PB 167, Lieutenant G. D. Mackenzie, 'A Retrospect' (An Account of the Tirah expedition & battle of Dargai August 1897–February 1898); PB 180, Bandsman W. Marr, diary; and PB 625, Corporal J. Esslemont, diary.

41 'Storming of Dargai' and 'Frontier Fighting', *Daily Telegraph*, 22 and 23 October 1897, pp. 7 and 7; 'Great Gallantry of the Gordons', *Aberdeen Journal*, 21 October 1897, p. 5.

42 *Falkirk Herald*, 30 October 1897, p. 4; *Nairnshire Telegraph*, 27 October 1897, p. 2; *Aberdeen Journal*, 23 October 1897, p. 4.

43 'Mr Bryce and his Constituents', *Aberdeen Journal*, 16 November 1897, p. 6.

44 *North British Daily Mail*, 23 October 1897, p. 4; see also 'Gallantry of the Gordon Highlanders', *[Dundee] Weekly News*, 30 October 1897, p. 9.

45 *Highland News*, 30 October 1897, p. 2.

46 *Daily News*, 26 October 1897, p. 4; 'Gallant Gordons' and 'Thin Red 'Eroes', *Evening News*, 25 and 26 October 1897, pp. 2 and 2; 'Gordons' Conduct in Campaigns', *Aberdeen Journal*, 26 October 1897, p. 6; Prior, *Campaigns of a War Correspondent*, p. 268.

47 *Scotsman*, 16 November 1897, p. 5; *North British Daily Mail*, 17 November 1897, p. 4; 'The Press on the Brave Gordons', *Aberdeen Journal*, 28 October 1897, p. 5; 'The Indian Frontier War', *Edinburgh Evening News*, 16 November 1897, p. 4; 'How the Gordons Stormed Dargai', *[Dundee] Weekly News*, 20 November 1897, p. 9; 'The Indian Frontier War', *Northern Chronicle*, 17 November 1897, p. 6.

48 'At Dargai', *Daily Telegraph*, 26 October 1897, p. 9, reprinted in *Aberdeen Journal*, 27 October 1897, p. 5; see also 'The Gordons' Charge', 'The Storming of Dargai', 'A Deed for the Brave to Feel', *Aberdeen Journal*, 26 October 1897, pp. 5–6; 'Scots Wha Hae' and 'Gay Goes the Gordon to a Fight', *Aberdeen Journal*, 28 October 1897, p. 5; 'To-Day's London Letter', *Edinburgh Evening News*, 23 December 1897, p. 2; 'At Dargai: and a Nation's Gratitude', *Northern Chronicle*, 17 November 1897, p. 6.

49 'The Gordons' Charge at Dargai', 'The Afridi and the Gordons' and 'The Pipers of Dargai', *Aberdeen Journal*, 8 November 1897, p. 5; 'The Gordons at Dargai', *Aberdeen Journal*, 9 November 1897, p. 5; 'A Patriotic Scot', *Aberdeen Journal*, 13 January 1898, p. 5.

50 'Honour for the Gordons in South Africa', 'The Gordon Highlanders on

the Frontier' and 'The Gordon Highlanders', *Aberdeen Journal*, 23 November 1897, p. 6, 30 November 1897, p. 5, and 7 December 1897, p. 5; 'With the Gordon Highlanders on the Frontier', *Scotsman*, 4 December 1897, p. 9; GH Museum, PB 1215, field telegrams on Dargai, 1897, and PB 180, Marr, diary, 5 November 1897; Greenhill Gardyne, *Life of a Regiment*, 2, p. 294.

51 *Northern Chronicle*, 27 October 1897, p. 4.

52 'The Charge at Dargai', *North British Daily Mail*, 17 November 1897, p. 5; 'How the Gordons stormed Dargai', *Edinburgh Evening News*, 16 November 1897, p. 4.

53 'How the Gordons stormed Dargai', p. 4; 'Another letter from the Front', *Aberdeen Journal*, 4 December 1897, p. 5; 'The Gordon Highlander at Dargai', *Nairnshire Telegraph*, 8 December 1897, p. 3; 'The Story of Dargai', *Invergordon Times*, 23 March 1898, p. 4; NAM, Acc. 1973–07–39, Officer of the Gordon Highlanders, n.d.

54 'Interview with Gordon Highlanders', *Aberdeen Journal*, 16 February 1898, p. 5; 'The Gordon Highlander at Dargai', p. 3.

55 'The Gordon Highlanders' and 'Exciting Incidents and Gruesome Experiences', *Aberdeen Journal*, 13 January 1898, p. 5, and 19 February 1898, p. 6; 'Interview with Gordon Highlanders', p. 5; GH Museum, PB 625, Esslemont, diary, 20 October 1897; 'The Story of Dargai'. p. 4.

56 'A Gordon Highlander's Description of Dargai', *Scotsman*, 23 November 1897, p. 5.

57 GH Museum, PB 167, MacKenzie, 'A Retrospect', p. xi.

58 'The Story of Dargai', p. 4.

59 'The Gordon Highlander at Dargai', p. 3.

60 GH Museum, PB 167, MacKenzie, 'A retrospect', p. xi; NAM, Acc. 1973–07–39, Officer of the Gordon Highlanders.

61 'Luckiest Man in the Gordons', *Evening News*, 27 November 1897, p. 2; 'Another Letter from the Front', p. 5; GH Museum, PB 625, Esslemont, diary, 20 October 1897; 'The Gordon Highlander at Dargai', p. 3.

62 GH Museum, PB 2476, Captain J. L. R. Gordon, 'Diary of the Tirah Campaign', p. 34; see also 'Gordons at the Front', *Aberdeen Journal*, 25 November 1897, p. 5.

63 'An Edinburgh Man's Experience', *Aberdeen Journal*, 20 January 1898, p. 6; 'The Scottish Borderers and the Gordon Highlanders', *Aberdeen Journal*, 13 January 1898, p. 5; 'A Derbyshire man at Dargai', *Derbyshire Times*, 29 January 1898, p. 3.

64 'The Dorsets at Dargai Ridge' and 'The Dorsets and the Capture of Dargai', *Dorset County Chronicle*, 2 December 1897, p. 12, and 30 December 1897, p. 11; 'The Capture of Dargai', *Aberdeen Journal*, 2 December 1897, p. 5.

65 'True Story of the Storming of Dargai', *Derby Daily Telegraph*, 31 December 1897, p. 2; 'The Dorsets and the Capture of Dargai', p. 11,

and 'A Dorsetshire Man Claims Credit for his Regiment', *Dorset County Chronicle*, 6 January 1898, p. 12.

66 'The Story of Dargai', *Dorset County Chronicle*, 17 February 1898, p. 12; 'Letters to the Editor', *Daily News*, 18 November 1897, p. 6; 'A Chesterfield Man at Dargai', *Derbyshire Times*, 19 February 1898, p. 3; 'The Dargai Fight', *Scotsman*, 17 December 1897, p. 7.

67 'The Capture of Dargai', p. 5; 'The Dorsets at Dargai Ridge', p. 12, and 'In Defence of the Dorsets', *Dorset County Chronicle*, 16 December 1897, p. 11; 'Yorkshire Soldier's Letter to his Mother', *Derby Daily Telegraph*, 26 November 1897, p. 2.

68 'Real Story of Dargai', *Daily Mail*, 14 January 1898, p. 5.

69 GH Museum, PB 625, Esslemont, diary, 20 October 1897.

70 'In Defence of the Dorsets', p. 11; 'Letters to the Editor', *Edinburgh Evening News*, 23 December 1897, p. 2; 'Aberdeenshire and the Gordon Highlanders' and 'The Composition of Highland Regiments', *Aberdeen Journal*, 4 November 1897, p. 5, and 31 January 1898, p. 5.

71 'With the Gordon Highlanders on the Frontier', *Scotsman*, 4 December 1897, p. 9.

72 'With the Gordon Highlanders', *Scotsman*, 17 December 1897, p. 7.

73 'With the Gordon Highlanders' and 'A Gordon Highlander's Experiences', *Aberdeen Journal*, 28 December 1897, p. 5, and 5 January 1898, p. 6; 'A Borderer's Experiences in the War', *Edinburgh Evening News*, 28 December 1897, p. 2.

74 'With the Gordon Highlanders', *Scotsman*, 17 December 1897, p. 7; 'With the Gordon Highlanders', *Aberdeen Journal*, 15 December 1897, p. 5.

75 'Another Peterhead Man at the Front', *Aberdeen Journal*, 10 February 1898, p. 6.

76 'Two Views on Dargai', *Aberdeen Journal*, 10 February 1898, p. 6.

77 'The Hero of Dargai', *Evening News*, 18 November 1897, p. 3; 'Interesting Letter from an Insch Soldier', *Aberdeen Journal*, 1 December 1897, p. 4.

78 'Letters from the Pipers of Dargai', *North British Daily Mail*, 10 December 1897, p. 5; 'Letter from Piper Milne' and 'The Heroes of Dargai', *Aberdeen Journal*, 22 December 1897, p. 5, and 3 January 1898, p. 5; 'The Pipers of Dargai', *Huntly Express*, 11 December 1897, p. 6; 'The Dargai Charge', *Inverness Courier*, 21 January 1898, p. 3.

79 'The Wounded from India', *The Navy and Army Illustrated*, 30 April 1898, pp. 135–6; 'The Dargai Charge', *Inverness Courier*, 21 January 1898, p. 3.

80 'The Gallantry of the Gordon Highlanders', *Nairnshire Telegraph*, 17 November 1897, p. 4; 'The Gordon and Gurkha Fund', *Invergordon Times*, 11 May 1898, p. 4.

81 'Piper Findlater', *Scotsman*, 11 April 1898, p. 9; 'The Queen at Netley

Hospital', *Aberdeen Journal*, 16 May 1898, p. 5.'The Queen and Her brave Soldiers', *Northern Chronicle*, 18 May 1898, p. 6.

82 'Piper Findlater', *Ross-shire Journal*, 27 May 1898, p. 7; Greenhill Gardyne, *Life of a Regiment*, 2, p. 294; 'Piper Findlater, V.C. in Aberdeen' and 'Piper Findlater in Aberdeen', *[Dundee] Weekly News*, 3 and 10 September 1898, pp. 7 and 6; 'Piper Findlater's Breach of Promise Case', *Lincolnshire Chronicle*, 18 November 1898, p. 4.

83 Harrington, *British Artists and War*, pp. 256–61.

84 'The "Gay and Gallant" Gordons', *Aberdeen Journal*, 1 December 1897, p. 4.

85 J. M. Bulloch, 'The Gay Gordons: A Study in Inherited Prestige', *Blackwood's Edinburgh Magazine*, 163 (1898), pp. 254–61.

86 *The Times*, 23 June 1897, pp. 10–11, 13–14.

87 *North British Daily Mail*, 15 November 1897, p. 4.

7

RECONQUERING THE SUDAN

֍

While the last remnants of fighting on the North-West Frontier persisted into 1898, another major colonial operation approached its climax, namely the reconquest of the Sudan under the Sirdar, Major-General Sir Horatio Herbert Kitchener. The campaign had begun in March 1896 with an incursion into the northern province of Dongola, a move intended to distract Mahdist attention from the Italian garrison at Kassala after the rout of Italian forces at Adowa (1 March 1896). Scottish units were neither involved in the capture of Dongola (23 September 1896) nor, in 1897, when Kitchener authorised the laborious construction of a railway (with accompanying telegraph) from Wadi Halfa across 230 miles of the Nubian Desert to Abu Hamed. Accordingly the Scottish press, like its English counterpart, largely followed wars in other theatres, especially the dramatic events at Dargai. There was scant awareness that these careful preparations would lead to the most spectacular battle in the 'scramble for Africa' and the emergence of a new imperial hero in Scotland.

Kitchener's railway, later extended to Fort Atbara, would be described as 'the deadliest weapon ever used against Mahdism',[1] as it shortened the journey to Abu Hamed from eighteen days by camel and steamer to twenty-four hours (depending on the serviceability of the engines) and enabled Kitchener to move his forces into the heart of the Sudan regardless of season or the height of the Nile. As Kitchener pressed southwards, deploying forces in Berber before the end of 1897, he feared confrontation with the armies of Khalifa 'Abdullahi. Hence, at the beginning of 1898, he sought and received British reinforcements, namely a first brigade composed of the 1st Battalions, Cameron Highlanders, Seaforth Highlanders, Royal Warwickshire and Lincolnshire. Even this deployment attracted little attention as domestic news, including the death of Gladstone, dominated newspaper coverage and war-reporting followed events elsewhere (with depictions of Dargai appearing in the *Illustrated London News* as late as 2 April 1898). Although the Sudan campaign had two highly dramatic moments, the battles of the Atbara (on Good Friday, 8 April 1898) and Omdurman (2 September 1898), followed by the diplomatic incident between Britain and France at Fashoda, press attention still switched to the Spanish-American War from late April to early August 1898.[2] So there was never the sustained intensity of coverage on this war as there had been on others, but the issues at stake could hardly have aroused greater emotions, namely the smashing of the Mahdist state, the avenging of Gordon's murder, and the massive expansion of Britain's imperial presence in Africa. The campaign also involved Scottish soldiers serving in the heart of the Sudan and facing a battle-hardened enemy in another major test of their fighting prowess.

Although the intense anguish generated by Gordon's death had largely dissipated by the early 1890s, British interest in the Mahdist regime had revived on account of the sustained propaganda campaign waged by Major F. Reginald Wingate, director of military intelligence in the Egyptian Army, and two escapees from Omdurman, Rudolf Slatin, the former Austrian governor of Darfur, and Father Joseph Ohrwalder. They wrote several widely read books which chronicled (and exaggerated) the debauchery, depravations, decay and divisions of the Khalifa's regime. Slatin and Ohrwalder proffered support for Wingate's claim that 'rapine, bloodshed and horrors filled the land', thereby sustaining the moral imperative for intervention; they also emphasised that the Mahdist state was becoming increasingly vulnerable, suffering from the effects of famine and internal revolts.[3]

Accordingly, as soon as Kitchener's intervention reached a decisive stage, involving the prospect of action involving the British brigade, interest in the campaign revived. Most soldiers, apart from a few veterans of earlier Sudanese campaigns, were new to Sudanese conditions, and they recorded how the battalions, in spite of good-natured rivalry, worked with each other in adverse and demanding circumstances. Many found the journey south and the acclimatisation, which was much more rapid than in previous campaigns, extremely stressful. After leaving Cairo, a Cameron Highlander described how 'We were 42 hours on the train, and 10 days on the barges, and it just about "fed us all up". We were packed like herrings in a box, and I was not sorry a bit when we finished the voyage.' After an equally cramped journey on the Sudan Military Railway, the soldiers found themselves in the heart of the Sudan: 'nothing but sand' and an 'awful' climate, 'roasted one minute and frozen the next', and tormented by flies.[4]

In these conditions the Highlanders displayed their customary fortitude (other than an elderly and hard-pressed quartermaster who 'blew out his brains', reportedly after 'a choking off that the Colonel gave him').[5] They drilled and trained regularly under a martinet from the Chitral, Major-General William F. Gatacre, who had the men spend several hours each day filing the tips off their ammunition to produce dum dum bullets. As a Cameron Highlander explained, displaying a penchant for Kiplingesque vocabulary, 'Each company does about three boxes a day, and we have just finished the last box to-day; so that is 300 boxes of Dum Dums for Fuzzy Wuzzy to stomach . . .' He also noted that 'the Gordons have been getting their name up, and I hope we are going to follow their example'.[6] Gatacre soon dispatched the battalions on a forced march over ninety-six miles in four nights in full kit with minimal food and water to Berber (in the mistaken belief that it was under imminent threat). As Private D. MacDonald recollected, 'What made the marching worse was that the most of it was done on our bare feet, as we had no shoes or sox on.'[7] When the Seaforths finally left to join the other British battalions, they tried to make up time after the second rail journey by travelling by camel around a cataract at night. Camels, as a Dingwall soldier recalled, 'were horrible things to ride, and we were falling off in dozens, and with all our straps round our necks we were nearly strangled; but worst of all we were all in the kilt . . .'[8] The Seaforths, nonetheless, appreciated the 'very hearty reception' on their arrival at Kunour from the British, Egyptian and Sudanese soldiers.[9]

Following the arrival of the Seaforths on 16 March, Kitchener resolved four days later to meet the *ansar* of 16,000 men under Emir Mahmoud which had been advancing slowly northwards. The subsequent battle on 8 April, when Kitchener's Anglo-Egyptian army attacked Mahmoud's encampment on the bank of the Atbara River, caused a sensation in the British press. Following a preparatory artillery bombardment, the three brigades (two Egyptian and one British) launched their assault. The Camerons advanced in line formation to the strains of 'The March of the Cameron Men'; they fired volleys and led the British formation, with the Seaforths, Warwicks and Lincolns following in columns. The Camerons tore holes in the zareba, allowing the supporting forces to storm the encampment and inflict between two and three thousand Mahdist fatalities for some eighty-one killed and 478 wounded.[10]

The 'Good Friday' victory earned plaudits across the United Kingdom. Following the telegrams published in the metropolitan

Figure 7 Cameron Highlanders Storming the Zariba at the Battle of the Atbara
(Stanley Berkeley)

press and reprinted in Scottish newspapers, editors lauded the bravery and achievements of the Scottish soldiers. As the Scots bore the brunt of the British casualties, with the Camerons suffering most of the fatalities and nearly half of the wounded, the Scottish press extolled their achievements. They praised acts of 'sublime' heroism (such as Major Urquhart, though mortally wounded, exhorting his men: 'go on lads; never mind me', Private Cross who bayoneted a dervish aiming point-blank at General Gatacre, and Piper Stewart who continued piping on a knoll until shot dead, pierced by seven bullets) and paid extensive tributes to the fallen (even printing pulpit sermons to them).[11] The *Scotsman* reported Kitchener's praise for the steady, determined advance of the Camerons as 'one of the finest feats performed for many years', and, like other Scottish newspapers, made comparisons with Dargai Heights.[12] The *Scotsman*, now a leading organ of Liberal Unionism in Scotland, intermingled Scottish and British identities in striking phraseology:

> The country has once again reason to be proud of its soldiers. Scotland has again special reason to be proud of the part played by her sons . . . we can rejoice at the proof yielded by the Soudan as by the Indian campaign that the spirit of the British soldier and of the British people has in no way fallen off . . .[13]

The Scottish soldier was clearly perceived as part of a great British, imperial enterprise and his 'dash, energy and 'pluck' were seen as crucial to ensuring success.[14] Even a staunchly Liberal newspaper like the *Kinross-shire Advertiser*, though ready to advise its readers not to dwell upon victory 'in a vain-glorious Jingo spirit', insisted that Scots could take 'an honest pride in ourselves . . . The Jubilee left a lasting and wholesome effect upon those who witnessed it, by teaching us to understand that we are units in a mighty empire.' It argued, too, that the cause was just, vindicating the memory of Gordon 'as true a soldier of the Cross as any Crusader', and as a means of releasing 'a people from slavery' in 'a righteous war'. Good Friday, it added, seemed a 'curiously appropriate day for a victory', and then, in a passage of pure euphoria, claimed: 'Throughout the land the church bells summoned the faithful to commemorate the greatest event that ever took place in the world's history.'[15]

The metropolitan press, however, led the way with tributes, photographs, poetry and accounts of the Highlanders. According to Captain Douglas Haig, then commanding a squadron of Egyptian cavalry, Bennet Burleigh of the *Daily Telegraph* 'went to the Seaforths after the fight & asked for the name of a piper stating that he had to write about a piper after the Dargai incidents'.[16] George Warrington Steevens of the *Daily Mail* produced some of the most florid commentary in Victorian war-reporting:

> The bugle sang out the advance. The pipes screamed war, and the line started forward . . . the bullets were swishing and lashing now like rain on the river. But the line of khaki and purple tartan never bent or swayed; it just went slowly forward like a ruler. The officers at its head strode self-containedly: they might have been on a hill after grouse . . . And the unkempt, unshaven Tommies, who in camp seemed little enough like Covenanters or Ironsides, were now transformed . . . whether they aimed or advanced, they did it orderly, gravely, without speaking. The bullets had whispered to raw youngsters in one breath the secret of all the glories of the British Army.[17]

Haig, if reasonably well disposed to his fellow Oxonian, Steevens, despaired of the press coverage in general: 'What rubbish the British public delights to read! The exaggeration of some of the reports almost makes a good day's work appear ridiculous. The headings of the D[aily] T[elegraph] are so overdrawn that instinctively one says: "Waterloo Eclipsed".'[18] Ordinary soldiers disagreed; they eagerly awaited mail and newspapers from home, and some read accounts of the battle to illiterate comrades: as a Cameron Highlander remarked, 'it cheered us very much to think the people at home were thinking of us'.[19] They also realised that the provincial press would wish to supplement their coverage of the war with letters from the front.

English and Scottish newspapers duly printed a profusion of letters about Atbara and its aftermath. Private D. Macdonald (Camerons), like several Scots, recalled Kitchener's pre-battle exhortation: 'Remember Gordon' and the men in front are 'his murderers'.[20] Highly motivated, they had advanced in the wake of a preparatory artillery bombardment, the first time in action for many young soldiers. Private J. Turnbull (Camerons) admitted that 'It felt a bit funny at first hearing the bullets whistling round a fellow's ears, and seeing a chum drop beside a fellow . . .', but, as a Seaforth officer added, at least the 'Camerons had the excitement of firing', his young soldiers 'following 50 to 60 yards in rear had nothing to do, except to watch their men dropping, and all the bleeding and doctoring and stretcher work . . .'[21] Nevertheless, Seaforth and English soldiers lauded the Camerons for advancing 'in splendid style', fighting 'like demons' and bearing the brunt of the casualties.[22] They also commended the gallantry of Kitchener, Gatacre and their own officers, who led from the front (although a Seaforth lance-sergeant ruefully admitted that there was little chance of winning a Victoria Cross as 'there were too many officers trying for it, as could easily be seen from the account of the wounded').[23]

Once the zareba was breached, Sergeant Roderick Morrison (Seaforths) confirmed that 'Everything got mixed . . . Camerons and Seaforths were all through one another', and the fighting, as fellow Sergeant Roderick Mackenzie added, was 'severe . . . a lot of it hand to hand'.[24] Camerons admitted that they disobeyed orders to pull down the zareba and let the others through: 'we took no notice of that', wrote Private Macdonald, and another noted: 'We were at fixed bayonets; we did not want any orders to charge but went for them for all we were worth like devils.'[25] Bandsman P. Learmonth (Seaforths) was not alone in describing the enemy as indifferent marksmen but 'brave men' who died 'without a groan'; Corporal Farquharson (Seaforths) agreed that 'Some of them made a very good stand, but not one of them was shown any mercy. Our fellows had revenge for Gordon right enough,' both in the zareba, and as they tried to retreat across the river whereupon the shooting 'reminded me of a rabbit drive at home'.[26] Scots justified such ruthlessness as necessary to avenge Gordon and fallen comrades, to retaliate against a 'treacherous' foe who, if wounded or shamming death, was liable to attack any passing soldier, and to suppress an enemy capable of barbarous acts (Colonel R. H. Murray noted several heads impaled on poles in the zareba).[27] Yet Captain Neville Cameron (Cameron Highlanders) reckoned that 'the Dervishes' (by virtue of fighting behind a zareba and reserving their fire until the final assault) 'have lost nearly all that deep fanaticism of former years', a view contradicted by Sergeant John Philip, an Aberdonian Guardsman, who had instructed the Egyptian Army for the past eighteen months: as he informed his father, 'Everyone is agreed that it was the hardest fight we have ever had in the Soudan.'[28]

Many Highlanders, though, were brutally frank about the aftermath of the battle, namely the appalling smell from the 'camels, donkeys and dead dervishes, lying thick'[29] and the terrible sight of the camp partially ablaze with roasting corpses and exploding ammunition. As Bandsman Learmonth observed: 'The scene inside the zareba was indescribable. The people in our quiet homes in Scotland could never think that such a thing could be, and I hope never to see such a sight again.'[30] Following the grim burial of the dead, they had to bivouac in the desert until 5 p.m. before they could march back to their own camp. As a Seaforth officer recalled, this was

> No joke; absolutely no shade. We marched back to our camp at five o'clock but did not reach it until midnight, having had no sleep for 36 hours. All ranks were practically exhausted. If it was bad for us, it was a thousand times worse for the wounded, who suffered much.[31]

All this testimony to the spirit, fortitude and resolve of the Highlanders, with letters appearing in the press throughout May and into June, sustained the impact of the initial reporting (even if the main focus of international news switched to the Spanish-American War). Scottish regiments sought to exploit the publicity, and hopefully attract more recruits, by sending recruiting parties with pipes and drums through their regimental districts. The Argylls, who had marched from Maryhill to Glasgow Green in the wake of Dargai, now attracted 'considerable attention' as they marched through Glasgow on 3 May 1898, 'the whole route being lined with large crowds of admiring onlookers'.[32] The newly formed 2nd Battalion, Queen's Own Cameron Highlanders also sent a company on a march from Aberdeen to Fort George, drawing large crowds at the various towns and villages along the route, and stimulating, as the *Aberdeen Journal* described, a 'remarkable manifestation of public feeling and patriotic enthusiasm'.[33]

Feelings were rather different in the Sudan. As soldiers settled into their 'summer quarters' – the Highlanders at Darmali and the English battalions at Es Sillem – some dwelled on their relative contributions in battle. If Colonel Murray was quick to praise the contribution of other units, especially the Lincolns, Lance-Sergeant Colin Grieve, who never served in the battle, claimed that 'the Lincolns & Warwicks had scarcely any wounded as the Jocks were in the trenches first'.[34] Even among the Jocks, as Lieutenant A. J. McNeill admitted, 'great was the friendly rivalry between us', with Major Granville Egerton and Captain J. Spencer Ewart 'never ceasing to "chip" one another about' the prowess of their respective battalions in the battle.[35] Some Warwickshire and Lincoln rankers complained about the way in which the press extolled and illustrated the achievements of the Highlanders: 'Of course, they always mention a Scotch Regiment first', as one Lincoln averred.[36] Another Scot, Major-General Archibald Hunter (Egyptian Army) deplored the failure to recognise the services of the Egyptian brigades.[37] The British reinforcements, required for the final push on Omdurman, were possibly even more aware of the press coverage. While en route to Egypt, Sergeant Shirley (1st Battalion, Grenadier Guards) wrote: 'I hope we shall be able to give a good account of ourselves (so as to cut the Highlanders out; one can read nothing else but about the canny Scot).'[38]

Finally, Scots joined the recriminations over Gatacre's mode of attack. If no one doubted Gatacre's bravery – he was 'made of steel and ignorant of the word fear', as Captain John Spencer Ewart (Camerons) claimed[39] – several officers, including Haig, Hunter and Egerton, deplored his attack formation at the Atbara. Hunter maintained that 'it was as bad as bad could be', producing an advance 'as slow as a funeral' and one in which 'everybody got jumbled together', with inadequate fire effect.[40] In short, Scottish officers realised that Gatacre had failed to adopt an attacking formation that maximised the impact of their soldiers' discipline, manoeuvrability and fire power.

However deeply felt, these sentiments hardly distracted soldiers from their daily round of training, fatigues and early-morning marches twice a week. Faced with a protracted halt in extreme climatic conditions, Lance-Sergeant W. Briggs (Seaforths) recognised that 'The General is doing all he can for the comfort of the troops during the warm weather, and at the same time he is keeping us as fit as possible for our march to Khartoum.' He also claimed that 'all the troops at Darmali are in good health',[41] but this was far from true as large numbers of men suffered from diarrhoea after drinking unfiltered water at the Atbara, and later from an outbreak of typhoid fever that swept through the camp. By early August there were some fifty graves in the cemetery, prompting Spencer Ewart to observe that: 'Our stay at Darmali had cost more lives than the battle of the Atbara; it is ever so in war; the climate is the soldier's most deadly foe.'[42]

Maintaining morale in these circumstances was imperative as the good-natured rivalry was channelled into sporting competition and sustained efforts were made to improve camp conditions, including the construction of mud huts to escape from the midday heat, and the provision of a more varied diet. Several Seaforths testified to such improvements as early as mid-April, with Sergeant Thomas Christian conceding that 'You'd hardly recognise us as Highlanders, some with boots, no spats, no hose; some no kilts, wearing trews borrowed from anywhere, belts brown, buttons sand colour; nearly all with beards, for we don't shave.'[43] The Camerons resumed their cordial relations with the 9th Sudanese, who had fought alongside them at the battle of Ginnis. When the 9th, 10th and 11th Sudanese Battalions passed through Darmali on 31 July, Spencer Ewart recorded that 'It was a grand and impressive sight to see these three magnificent black regiments – the finest fighting troops in the world – pass through by moonlight with their bands playing Scottish airs'.[44] The Scots also welcomed the British reinforcements brought in for the final push on Omdurman, particularly the 2nd British Brigade,[45] who would be followed by two batteries of field artillery, a Maxim machine gun detachment manned by Royal Irish Fusiliers, and the 21st Lancers. Finally, as Gatacre assumed divisional command, the 1st Brigade received a new commander in the highly popular Brigadier Andrew Wauchope, a Black Watch veteran of the Asante and Egyptian campaigns. Wauchope's fame extended beyond military circles as he had stood as the Conservative candidate for Midlothian against Gladstone in the general election of 1892, reducing the majority of the Liberal leader from 4,631 votes to 690.[46]

At least fifteen war correspondents accompanied this enlarged Anglo-Egyptian army, chronicling in words and pictures its final advance from Wad Hamed (24 August) to the decisive battle at Omdurman. Even so, the battle occurred earlier and proved more decisive than anyone had forecast (as Khalifa brought his army out of Omdurman to launch an abortive assault in daytime on Kitchener's army drawn up in a semi-circle formation, with its back to the Nile protected by gunboats). The Mahdist army of possibly 52,000 men was annihilated by 11.30 a.m., leaving some 10,800 corpses on the battlefield and at least 16,000 wounded, whereas the Anglo-Egyptian army (numbering about 25,000 men) lost only forty-eight officers and men killed and 382 wounded. The conclusive outcome at minimal cost in lives and financial resources impressed many Scots and some Liberal politicians as diverse in their views as Richard B. Haldane and John Morley.[47]

The Scottish press hailed Kitchener 'as one of the ablest strategists of the day', a general who 'saw the necessity of organised transport' and who exploited the strategic and tactical blunders of the Khalifa.[48] They commended the avenging of Gordon's death, the restoration of British prestige and the smashing of 'a cruel and barbarous tyranny'.[49] The destruction of the Mahdist state appealed to Liberals and Liberal Unionists alike, whether interpreted as freeing the 'Sudanese peasantry' from 'Dervish oppressors' (*Dundee Courier*) or removing a 'standing reproach and a standing menace to civilisation' (*Glasgow Evening News*) or helping to realise 'the vision of a continuous red strip on the map of Africa extending from the Cape to Cairo . . .' (*Scotsman*).[50] The 'conquest of Khartoum', added the *Scotsman*, had ensured 'that a great centre of the African slave trade has fallen into our hands and will harbour the nefarious traffic no more.'[51]

Such a decisive outcome reflected a remarkably one-sided battle in which the Highlanders had much less scope to distinguish themselves than at the Atbara. Like other soldiers, they had found the marches from Wad Hamed to Omdurman over difficult ground, and sometimes in torrential rain, 'very trying': 'lots of fellows', wrote Sergeant Christian, 'were quite knocked up days before the fight, but struggled on till the end'.[52] Once they reached the plain of Kerreri and encamped near the village of Egeiga, they formed part of Kitchener's firing line and were alerted on the night before the battle of the imminent attack. 'What with excitement and waiting for them', recalled Private Lison (Camerons), 'we got very little sleep'[53] and stood to arms at 3.45 a.m. As daylight broke, they first heard the war drums and yelling of the enemy before they saw, as Christian described,

> the great plain covered with white jebba-clad Dervishes, banners flying and drums beating – a splendid sight! We were ordered to kneel down, but could see through the zareba as they came on. It looked as if the whole of Africa was coming at us, for their front extended for miles.[54]

Following the first salvos of the artillery and machine guns, the Highlanders opened fire at about 1,400 yards: 'Of course', wrote

Lison, 'we knew that we were all right as long as we kept them at a distance.'[55] So in this 'magnificent triumph of scientific warfare', as described by the *Scotsman*,[56] there was little scope for the High-landers to live up to their heroic-warrior image.

None of the enemy, including their horsemen, reached the Anglo-Egyptian lines, but their bravery impressed correspondents and soldiers alike. After firing fifty-six volleys, Lance-Corporal A. Unsworth, a Mancunian Seaforth, was disappointed not to have 'another "blatter" at them',[57] but the second charge, launched at Kitchener's advancing army, would be met and defeated by the Sudanese battalions under Brigadier-General Hector Macdonald (with minimal help from the Lincolns), and the only hand-to-hand fighting involved the gallant, if costly, charge of the 21st Lancers. Even if the cavalry charge was a tactical blunder, as Haig asserted and the *Scotsman* suspected, it became the epic event of the battle and the scene depicted in numerous paintings and illustrations.[58] A Berwick trooper, Thomas Byrne, who would earn a VC for rescuing Lieutenant Molyneux during the charge, confirmed that his troop had suffered severely as it had crossed the part of the khor where 'the Dervishes were thickest'. In a second assault they drove the enemy off but found a 'horrible' sight thereafter: 'the Dervishes could not let our men die in quietness; they cut and hacked them as they lay on the ground'.[59] Private Donald Macpherson (Camerons) confirmed a widespread awareness of the enemy's penchant for mutilation, and their readiness to sham death on the battlefield. Accordingly, on crossing the battlefield, 'We finished them off, and the Soudanese finished them off, too', and, on the next day, when ordered to give water and biscuits to the 'wounded Dervishes . . . there was a perfect uproar, next to a riot. Instead of giving them water and biscuits, they should give each one a round of ammunition . . .'[60]

Such frank views might have contributed to the simmering controversy over the treatment of the dervish wounded and the Mahdi's disinterred skeleton (which was decapitated and the body thrown into the Nile to prevent a revival of his following), but the protests of Ernest Bennett of the *Westminster Gazette* prompted an impassioned defence of Kitchener and his conduct of the campaign.[61] The soldiers themselves believed that they had fought a just war and had seen sights that vindicated much of Wingate's pre-war propaganda. In Mahmoud's camp they saw mutilations, decapitations and slaves chained to logs; en route south they passed the deserted town of Metemmeh where Mahmoud's forces had massacred thousands of the

Jaalin tribe in 1897 and left the town strewn with skeletons; and in Omdurman they found appalling squalor and released hundreds of prisoners, some hideously tortured. Private Lison reckoned that 'there is not a sign of civilisation for miles about . . .'[62]

In welcoming the return of Lieutenant-Colonel Gordon L. C. Money (Cameron Highlanders) to Inverness on 15 October 1898, Provost William Macbean spoke as many others did in extolling the imperial triumph. He praised the Camerons for contributing to 'the national work' and helping 'to widen the bounds of this great Empire', an 'empire upon which the sun never set – the largest the world had ever seen – and kept secure with an army, the smallest of any great national Power . . .' This feat he attributed to the 'qualities of a unique fighting force' and 'the just rulers and administrators of the conquered territories'. In replying on behalf of the 'county regiment', Money assured the provost that 'There was nothing the soldiers appreciated more than to feel that their services had been appreciated by their countrymen at home.' He also assured the 'large and influential gathering' in the Town Hall that the 'campaign had brought freedom and civilisation to a large tract of country, which for many years had been oppressed by barbarous savages . . .'[63]

A socially rather different gathering awaited Wauchope on his return to Niddre, Midlothian, where a public holiday was observed in the district and many miners joined the procession to greet the returning laird. In the highly decorated village of Newcraighall, Robert Wilson, a miner, formally welcomed the returning colonel and referred to the collective pride in his military services. Wilson declared that 'the cause of freedom against slavery, of righteousness against tyranny and oppression had been fought and won by our country . . .' Wauchope replied by asserting that the victory has been 'a great gain for civilisation', and that it had been 'our bounden duty' to put an end to a power based 'on murder, rapine and cruelty . . .'[64]

In reviewing the final battle, both Money and Wauchope earned loud applause when they paid tribute to Macdonald's generalship.[65] This son of a Ross-shire crofter, who had risen through the ranks of the Gordon Highlanders and distinguished himself in Afghanistan and in the Egyptian Army, had emerged as 'the hero of the hour'. Kitchener had praised him in dispatches:

Macdonald's Brigade was highly tested, bearing the brunt of two severe attacks delivered at very short intervals from different directions, and I am sure that it must be a source of the greatest satisfaction to Colonel

Macdonald, as it is to myself and the whole Army, that the very great care he has for long devoted to the training of his brigade has proved so effectual, enabling his men to behave with the greatest steadiness under most trying circumstances and repelling most successfully two determined Dervish onslaughts.[66]

The Scottish press printed accounts of his remarkable career and enthused over the commendations by Kitchener, the war correspondents in the Sudan and the commentary in the metropolitan press.[67] While *The Times* asserted that 'the finest episode in the whole day's fighting was the admirable way in which General Macdonald handled his brigade', Burleigh and Steevens provided glowing accounts that would be reprinted by several newspapers and in subsequent accounts. As ever, Steevens captured the essence of Macdonald's achievement:

> the cockpit of the fight was Macdonald's . . . To meet it he turned his front through a complete half-circle, facing successively south, west and north. Every tactician in the army was delirious in his praise . . . 'Cool as on parade,' is an old phrase; Macdonald Bey was very much cooler. Beneath the strong, square-hewn face you could tell that the brain was working as if packed in ice.[68]

Macdonald had become the new Scottish hero. He was awarded a CB for his services, promoted full colonel and appointed as an aide-de-camp to Queen Victoria. He also received the thanks of both houses of parliament and a modest cash award but not a knighthood, so prompting Burleigh to claim that 'Colonel Hector A. Macdonald alone' had received 'scant military recognition of his invaluable services. The post of A. D. C. to Her Majesty is a coveted dignity, but a mere honorary office, carrying neither pay nor emolument.' He claimed that the Scottish people, 'particularly those living in the Highlands', resented this treatment of their hero and suspected that it would damage Highland recruiting.[69] The *Highland News* confirmed 'rightly or wrongly' a belief that 'our countryman received but too scanty acknowledgment from the military authorities . . .'[70]

Burleigh, though, was inclined to make sensational claims. After the Omdurman campaign he had 'scooped' his rivals by returning furtively to Cairo and then breaking the press embargo on the reporting of the Fashoda incident. He had interviewed a Cameron officer, who accompanied Kitchener in his voyage up the Nile into equatorial Sudan and witnessed the successful confrontation with Major Marchand.[71] Yet Burleigh had exaggerated in his reporting on

Macdonald; the Sirdar had not overlooked Macdonald in his dispatches and not all Scots shared a sense of grievance. The *Glasgow Herald* conceded that 'some of our English friends' refer to a 'Macdonald "boom" ', complaining that 'we Scots are at our old trick of monopolising kudos for the men of our own nation'. It admitted that 'We are a little apt . . . to magnify the deeds of our soldiers; the depreciation which English regiments suffered by comparison with the Gordons at Dargai and the Camerons at Atbara was eminently absurd and offensive.'[72]

What was different in Macdonald's case was not merely his central role in a decisive battle but how he conducted himself on his return to Britain in the spring of 1899. On the evening of 6 May he was the guest of honour at a banquet held by the Highland Societies of London in Hotel Cecil. Chaired by the Duke of Atholl, this was a glittering assembly of some six hundred guests, many attired in full Highland costume and speaking in Gaelic. Among the representatives of the Scottish nobility were the Earl of Dunmore, Earl of Kintore, Lord Saltoun, Lord Strathcona and Mount Royal, The Mackintosh of Mackintosh and the Marquis of Tullibardine; Sir Evelyn Wood, VC, the adjutant-general, was the senior officer present; and at least six Conservative and Liberal MPs attended, including the Hon. James Hozier, the Grand Master Mason of Scotland. There were representatives of various Highland associations and the Gaelic Society of London, religious and literary figures including J. M. Barrie, and the agents-general of New South Wales, South Australia, Western Australia, Queensland, Nova Scotia, British Columbia, New Brunswick, Natal and the Cape of Good Hope. Several speeches were made in praise of Macdonald, who replied modestly by commending the original training of the Egyptian Army by Sir Evelyn Wood and the role of the gunners during the battle of Omdurman. Macdonald's health was drunk in a Highland toast, involving guests standing with one foot on the table (as depicted in the *Illustrated London News*), and Macdonald was presented with a splendid sword of honour.[73]

Two days later the Colonel travelled to Glasgow to begin a remarkable tour of Scotland. He lunched with civic dignitaries and then joined regimental colleagues at a smoking concert hosted by the Gordon Highlanders' Association. On the following day he toured the Clydebank Shipbuilding works and the Royal Exchange before receiving another sword of honour from the Clan Macdonald Society and later a dinner from the society for about three hundred people.

Everywhere large crowds gathered to see him and effusive speeches were made about his rise from humble origins and his military service, first as a Volunteer, and then rising by distinguished service through the ranks of the Gordon Highlanders to hold command in the Egyptian Army. Sir David Richmond, the Lord Provost, not only hailed him as an 'inspiring example' to modern youth but also spoke more broadly of the 'brave and heroic deeds of our soldiers on the field of battle in defending and maintaining the privileges, liberties and prerogatives of the British Empire'.[74]

Moving on to the Highlands, Macdonald found himself lionised in the towns of Easter Ross and Inverness-shire. At Dingwall he was hosted by Sir Kenneth MacKenzie of Conan, the Lord Lieutenant of the county, and, on 11 May, he was driven through a flower and flag-bedecked town, where thousands had assembled to welcome him. After the customary short speeches, Macdonald received the freedom of the burgh at a civic luncheon. Enthusiastic receptions followed at Invergordon, Tain and Inverness (where a vast crowd welcomed Macdonald back to the Highland 'capital' where he had first worked as a draper and joined the Volunteers in 1870). He received another hearty reception in his native parish of Mulbuie in the Black Isle,[75] before moving onto Aberdeen where he was greeted by 'a great multitude' at the station and 'a deafening outburst of cheering' that drowned out the bagpipes playing 'Highland Laddie'. Hailed as 'Fighting Mac', he was taken on a tour of the city through 'densely crowded' streets and past 'a continuous roll of cheering'. He met old comrades from the Gordon Highlanders, inspected the Volunteers, visited the University and received another elaborate civic luncheon.[76] Finally, he moved on to Edinburgh (19 May), where the crowds were smaller but the civic luncheon was no less sumptuous and Macdonald had the opportunity of dining with the Gordon Highlanders in the Castle.[77]

During this tour, Scots had every opportunity to reflect not only upon the qualities of Hector Macdonald and the significance of his career but also on the qualities of the Highlander as a soldier. If Macdonald charmed audiences all over the country with his modesty, praise for others and encouragement of local Volunteers, his short, self-effacing speeches only complemented his military achievements. Having risen from the ranks, which was extremely rare in the late-Victorian army, he had done so with awards for bravery (including the Distinguished Service Order) and a proven capacity for leadership in the most difficult of circumstances: all this chimed with the preference for meritocratic promotion north of the border. 'The seeming romance of his career', argued the *Ross-shire Journal*, has gone 'to the heart of the nation', ensuring that the army has a 'still prouder place in the minds of civilians' while serving 'as an encouragement to the humble private'.[78] Macdonald, as described by the *Aberdeen Journal*, was

> A son of the soil, fed on the proverbial oatmeal, entering the army as a private, carving his way to fame by sheer force of character and ability, and drawing forth the unstinted praise of the British nation by his deeds of valour, he is in fact an ideal hero and a soldier of whom any country might be proud.[79]

Highland radicals shared these sentiments but were less impressed when Macdonald advocated conscription to create a 'nation in arms'; the *People's Friend* dismissed such a notion as simply 'a soldier's view'.[80] The *Highland News* reflected instead on the qualities of the Highlander as a soldier, especially as it claimed that only 'good-for-nothing' Highlanders chose to enlist. Such recruits, it asserted, gained distinction not on account of any 'blood-thirstiness' but 'because of their character and high ideal of duty. Highlanders generally feel that they have the character of their race to maintain untarnished.'[81] Sir Kenneth Mackenzie claimed, too, that 'The Scottish Highlander is preeminently a social being. He does not regard himself as an independent unit in the world, but as part of the community in which he was born and reared.'[82] Such Highland stereotyping, expressed by commentators from across the political spectrum, reflected traditional notions of honour and duty as key components of the heroic-warrior ideal, reinforcing the esprit de corps developed within the British regimental system. Good officer-man relations cemented these bonds (the officers not only led from the front but also, as Macdonald argued in connection with the 92nd, encouraged young recruits within the regimental family and 'set an example' by entering into 'the sports and pastimes of the private soldiers'). Finally, discipline and training could build on these foundations to produce excellent fighting men (as Macdonald had demonstrated in training his Sudanese soldiers).[83]

These reflections upon the personal qualities of the Highland soldier, doubtless accentuated by Macdonald's tour, hardly obscured the continuing recruiting problems in Scotland. As neither the Camerons nor the Seaforths were due to return home after their service in the Sudan, the publicity benefits of the campaign proved of short duration. As early as June 1898 the London correspondent of the *Edinburgh Evening News* reported that the War Office was again worried about Scottish recruiting now that 'the Dargai fever has subsided'. It had permitted another recruiting march by the King's Own Scottish Borderers through their district,[84] and, as Sir Evelyn Wood, the adjutant-general, had alluded to Scotland's recruiting difficulties in his speech at the Hotel Cecil, he clearly hoped that Macdonald's tour would revive recruiting, particularly in the Highlands.[85]

The national composition of Scottish regiments was possibly less at risk (as these units, even if bolstered by English and Irish soldiers, would continue to embody the national identity) than the notion of a Scottish soldier rooted in the values derived from Highland communities. If these communities were changing faster than the mythology, the heroic-warrior ideal faced an even more daunting challenge from the evolving nature of modern warfare. Hitherto the British, as Wauchope claimed, had exploited the potential of 'scientific warfare' by virtue of Kitchener's logistical planning, especially the construction of the railway, the 'perfect' transport and commissariat arrangements and the supply and medical support of the forces.[86] All this organisation and planning had enabled the Anglo-Egyptian army to exploit its long-range fire power (from gunboats, artillery, machine guns and smokeless magazine rifles), effectively keeping the enemy, as Macdonald conceded, 'at a safe distance'.[87]

Smokeless, long-range fire power was changing the face of battle. The Mahdists had embodied many aspects of the heroic-warrior ideal: they had earned all manner of plaudits for their bravery and heroism at the battle of Omdurman but their gunners and riflemen had been hopelessly outmatched, and the majority of their warriors, whether on horse or foot, had fought with edged weapons. Some even fought in medieval chain mail, so enabling Major Nason (Egyptian Army) to collect 'two coats of armour mail and helmets' among his battlefield loot, relics replicated in newspaper sketches.[88] This vast disparity in organisation and weaponry had ensured that the Anglo-Egyptian army prevailed in the very different battles of the Atbara and Omdurman. In each battle Scottish battalions and generals had contributed significantly, fully testing their offensive resolve in the former and their fire discipline in the latter, but Colonel Money claimed that the soldiers had much preferred the former, with the opportunity to engage in 'hand to hand fighting'.[89] Whether they would find opportunities for similar fighting, if faced with an enemy armed with modern firearms, and ready to use them effectively, would soon be tested.

Notes

1 G. W. Steevens, *With Kitchener to Khartum* (Edinburgh: Blackwood, 1898), p. 22.

2 Harrington, 'Images and Perceptions', in Spiers (ed.), *Sudan*, pp. 82–3.

3 F. R. Wingate, *Mahdiism and the Egyptian Sudan* (London: Frank Cass, 2nd edition, 1968), pp. 466–7; see also E. M. Spiers, 'Introduction', in Spiers (ed.), *Sudan*, pp. 1–10, and Hill, 'The Gordon Literature', pp. 102–3.

4 'Amusing Letter from a Cameron Highlander', *Edinburgh Evening News*, 22 March 1898, p. 4; 'The Soudan Campaign', *Standard*, 30 March 1898, p. 5; on how the Camerons assisted the Warwicks, see 'A Drummer of the "Sixth" on the Soudan Campaign', *Warwick & Warwickshire Advertiser & Leamington Gazette*, 30 April 1898, p. 6.

5 NAM, Acc. No. 1979-06-139, Grieve Mss, Lance-Sergeant C. Grieve to his mother, 20 January 1898.

6 'Amusing Letter from a Cameron Highlander', p. 4.

7 'The Camerons in the Soudan', *Inverness Courier*, 17 May 1898, p. 5.

8 'Interesting Episodes in the Sudan', *Ross-shire Journal*, 6 May 1898, p. 7; see also 'Letter from a Seaforth', *Northern Weekly*, 19 May 1898, p. 2; 'Letter from a Nairn Man at the Atbara', *Nairnshire Telegraph*, 25 May 1898, p. 3.

9 'A Soldier's Experience of the Battle of Atbara', *Nairnshire Telegraph*, 18 May 1898, p. 3; G. Egerton, *With the 72nd Highlanders* (London: Eden Fisher, 1909), p. 6.

10 Keown-Boyd, *A Good Dusting*, p. 202.

11 *Huntly Express*, 16 April 1898, p. 4; *Aberdeen Journal*, 11 April 1898, p. 4; *North British Daily Mail*, 11 April 1898, p. 4; 'The Battle of Nakeila [sic]', *Inverness Courier*, 15 April 1898, p. 3; 'Great Battle in the Sudan', *Northern Chronicle*, 13 April 1898, p. 6; 'The Late Major Urquhart', *Aberdeen Journal*, 11 April 1898, p. 4; 'The Death of Major Napier', *Highland Times*, 28 May 1898, p. 5.

12 *Scotsman*, 11 April 1898, p. 6; *Kinross-shire Advertiser*, 16 April 1898, p. 2; *Glasgow Evening News*, 11 April 1898, p. 4.

13 *Scotsman*, 11 April 1898, p. 6.

14 'The Soudan', *Ross-shire Journal*, 15 April 1898, p. 4; *Falkirk Herald*, 13 April 1898, p. 4.

15 *Kinross-shire Advertiser*, 16 April 1898, p. 2.

16 NLS, Haig Mss, Acc. 3155, H6b, Captain D. Haig to Henrietta, 5 June 1898; see also 'The Camerons', *Evening News*, 11 April 1898, p. 2; 'Teaching the "2nd Battalion" the Bagpipes' and 'Leaving for the Front', *Navy and Army Illustrated*, 4 March 1898, p. 320.

17 'The Battle of Atbara', *Daily Mail*, 29 April 1898, p. 4.

18 NLS, Haig Mss, Acc. 3155, H6g, Haig to Sir E. Wood, 29 April 1898.

19 'The Atbara', *Evening News*, 16 June 1898, p. 2; see also 'An Oxfordshire Man in the Soudan', *Abingdon Herald*, 28 May 1898, p. 6; 'A Soldier's Experience of the Battle of Atbara', p. 3.

20 'The Camerons in the Soudan', p. 5; see also 'A Soldier's Experience of the Battle of the Atbara', p. 3; 'Highlanders' Experiences at Atbara', *Edinburgh Evening News*, 14 May 1898, p. 2; 'At the Battle of the Atbara', *Northern Scot and Moray & Nairn Express*, 21 May 1898, p. 3.

21 'An Inverness Soldier', *Highland News*, 21 May 1898, p. 2; 'The Battle of Atbara', *Scotsman*, 18 May 1898, p. 11.

22 'At the Battle of Atbara', p. 3; 'Highlanders' Experiences at Atbara', p. 2; 'A Horncastrian at the Battle of Atbara', *Horncastle News and South Lindsay Advertiser*, 28 May 1898, p. 5; ' "Remember Gordon" ', *Grimsby News*, 17 May 1898, p. 5; 'Our Lincolnshire Lads', *Gainsborough Leader*, 21 May 1898, p. 9.

23 'Highlanders' Experiences at Atbara', p. 2; 'At the Battle of Atbara', p. 3.

24 'Letter from a Seaforth', p. 2; 'Letter from a Nairn Man at Atbara', p. 3.

25 'The Camerons in the Soudan', p. 5; 'The Atbara', p. 2.

26 'A Soldier's Experiences at the Battle of Atbara', p. 3; 'At the Battle of Atbara', p. 3.

27 'The Battle of the Atbara', *Aberdeen Journal*, 13 May 1898, p. 4; 'Highlanders' Experiences at Atbara', p. 2; J. W. Stewart, 'A Subaltern in the Sudan, 1898', *The Stewarts*, 17, no. 4 (1987), pp. 223–8.

28 NAM, Acc. No. 1983–05–55, Cameron Mss, Captain N. Cameron to his father, 5 June 1898; 'An Aberdeen Soldier at Atbara', *Aberdeen Journal*, 14 May 1898, p. 4.

29 'An Oxfordshire Man in the Soudan', p. 6.

30 'A Soldier's Experience of the Atbara', p. 3; 'An Inverness Soldier', p. 2.

31 'The Battle of Atbara', *Scotsman*, 18 May 1898, p. 11.

32 'Argyll and Sutherland Highlanders', *Aberdeen Journal*, 4 May 1898, p. 4.

33 Editorial and 'The March of the Cameron Highlanders', *Aberdeen Journal*, 6 May 1898, p. 4.

34 'The Battle of the Atbara', *Aberdeen Journal*, 13 May 1898, p. 4; NAM, Acc. No. 1979-06-139, Grieve Mss, Lance-Sergeant C. Grieve to his father, 14 April 1898.

35 Brigadier-General A. J. McNeill, 'Further Reminiscences of a Subaltern', *Cabar Feidh: The Quarterly Magazine of The Seaforth Highlanders*, 7, no. 49 (1934), pp. 12–15.

36 'The Bravery of the Lincolnshire Regiment', *Grantham Journal*, 28 May 1898, p. 7; 'A Leamington Soldier in the Soudan', *Leamington, Warwick, Rugby and County Chronicle*, 28 May 1898, p. 8; 'After the Battle', *Lincolnshire Chronicle*, 5 November 1898, p. 2.

37 NAM, Acc. No. 1983-05-55, Cameron Mss, Major-General A. Hunter to Sir W. Cameron, 25 April 1898.

38 'In the Soudan Campaign', *Hampshire Observer*, 8 October 1898, p. 3.
39 National Register of Archives for Scotland (NAS), Monro of Williamwood Mss, RH4/84, item 122, Spencer Ewart diary, 4 June 1898.
40 NAM, Acc. No. 1983-05-55, Cameron Mss, Hunter to Sir W. Cameron, 25 April 1898; see also NLS, Haig Mss, Acc. 3155, H6g, Haig to Wood, 29 April 1898, and Egerton, *With the 72nd Highlanders*, pp. 14–15.
41 'British Soldiers in the Soudan', *Edinburgh Evening News*, 9 June 1898, p. 2.
42 NAS, Spencer Ewart diary, 9 August 1898.
43 'An Oxfordshire Man in the Sudan', p. 6 (the identity of this writer is revealed in a subsequent letter 'With the Troops in the Soudan', *Oxford Times*, 1 October 1898, p. 10); 'Letter from a Seaforth', p. 2; 'A Soldier's Experience of the Battle of Atbara', p. 3.
44 NAS, Spencer Ewart diary, 27 June and 31 July 1898.
45 Egerton, *With the 72nd Highlanders*, p. 24.
46 W. Baird, *General Wauchope* (Edinburgh: Oliphant Anderson & Ferrier, 1900), p. 124.
47 Sandes, *Royal Engineers in Egypt and the Sudan*, pp. 250 and 271; Wilkinson-Latham, *From Our Special Correspondent*, p. 236; 'Mr R. B. Haldane at Haddington', *Glasgow Herald*, 20 September 1898, p. 8, and *Parl. Deb.*, fourth series, vol. 67 (24 February 1899), col. 459.
48 *Aberdeen Journal*, 5 September 1898, p. 4; *Ross-shire Journal*, 9 September 1898, p. 4; *Glasgow Herald*, 5 September 1898, p. 6; *North British Daily Mail*, 5 September 1898, p. 4.
49 *Stirling Observer*, 7 September 1898, p. 4; see also *Glasgow Herald*, 5 September 1898, p. 6, *Nairnshire Telegraph*, 7 September 1898, p. 3, and *Kinross-shire Advertiser*, 10 September 1898, p. 2.
50 *Dundee Courier & Argus*, 5 September 1898, p. 4; *Glasgow Evening News*, 5 September 1898, p. 4; *Scotsman*, 6 September 1898, p. 4.
51 *Scotsman*, 7 September 1898, p. 6.
52 'An Account by a Manchester Man', *Manchester Courier*, 28 September 1898, p. 9; 'With the Troops in the Soudan', p. 10.
53 'Letters from the Soudan', *Grimsby News*, 4 October 1898, p. 6.
54 'With the Troops in the Soudan', p. 6.
55 'Letters from the Soudan', p. 6.
56 *Scotsman*, 6 September 1898, p. 4.
57 'An Account by a Manchester Man', p. 9; see also NAM, Acc. No. 1983-05-55, Cameron Mss, Cameron to his father, 4 September 1898.
58 NLS, Haig Mss, Acc. 3155, H6b, Haig to Henrietta, 6 September 1898; *Scotsman*, 5 and 6 September 1898, pp. 6 and 4; Harrington, *British Artists and War*, pp. 265–7.
59 'A Berwick Trooper in the Lancers' Charge', *Edinburgh Evening News*, 14 October 1898, p. 2 (the newspaper misnames him as Trooper 'M.' Byrne).

60 'The Camerons at Omdurman', *Inverness Courier*, 7 October 1898, p. 5.
61 H. Cecil, 'British Correspondents and the Sudan Campaign of 1896–98', in Spiers (ed.), *Sudan: Reconquest Reappraised*, pp. 102–27.
62 'Letters from the Soudan', p. 6; 'An Oxfordshire Man in the Soudan', p. 6; 'The Camerons at Omdurman', p. 5; Spiers, 'Campaigning under Kitchener', in Spiers (ed.), *Sudan: Reconquest Reappraised*, pp. 60, 66, 73.
63 'Presentation of Address to Colonel Money, Cameron Highlanders', *Northern Chronicle*, 19 October 1898, p. 5.
64 'Colonel Wauchope's Homecoming to Niddre', *Scotsman*, 11 October 1898, p. 7.
65 Ibid., and 'Presentation of Address to Colonel Money', p. 5.
66 TNA, PRO, WO 33/148, 'Correspondence on the Nile Expedition' enclosing Sir H. Kitchener to Sir F. Grenfell, 5 September 1898, p. 6.
67 'Success of a Ross-shire Soldier', *Invergordon Times*, 14 September 1898, p. 4; ' "The Hero of the Hour" ', *Ross-shire Journal*, 7 October 1898, p. 4; *Scotsman*, 6 September 1898, p. 4.
68 'The Battle of Omdurman', *The Times*, 16 September 1898, p. 10; 'Full Account of the Sirdar's Great Victory', *Western Morning News*, 24 September 1898, p. 8; Steevens, *With Kitchener to Khartum*, p. 278.
69 B. Burleigh, *Khartoum Campaign: or the Reconquest of the Soudan* (London: Chapman & Hall, 1899), pp. 289–90.
70 *Highland News*, 13 May 1899, p.4; see also a review of the controversy in T. Royle, *Fighting Mac: The Downfall of Major-General Sir Hector Macdonald* (Edinburgh: Mainstream Publishing, 2003), pp. 96–7.
71 'Full Account of the Sirdar's Expedition to Fashoda', *Daily Telegraph*, 4 October 1898, p. 7.
72 *Glasgow Herald*, 9 May 1899, p. 6.
73 'The Hero of Omdurman Entertained in London', *Highland News*, 13 May 1899, p. 5; ' "With Highland Honours": Banquet to Colonel H. A. Macdonald on May 6', *Illustrated London News*, 13 May 1899, p. 674.
74 'Colonel H. A. Macdonald in Glasgow' and 'Colonel Macdonald in Glasgow', *Glasgow Herald*, 9 and 10 May 1899, pp. 9 and 9.
75 'The Hero of Omdurman', *Ross-shire Journal*, 12 May 1899, pp. 6–8; 'The Hero of Omdurman in Inverness', *Highland News*, 20 May 1899, p. 2; 'Colonel Macdonald's Tour in the North' and 'Colonel Macdonald in the Black Isle', *Aberdeen Journal*, 13 and 16 May 1899, pp. 6 and 5.
76 'Colonel Macdonald in Aberdeen' and 'Colonel Macdonald in Aberdeen', *Aberdeen Journal*, 18 and 19 May 1899, pp. 5 and 5.
77 'Colonel Hector Macdonald', *Scotsman*, 20 May 1899, p. 10.
78 *Ross-shire Journal*, 12 May 1899, p. 4.
79 'Interesting Sketch of his Brilliant Career', *Aberdeen Journal*, 12 May 1899, p. 8.
80 *People's Friend*, 13 May 1899, p. 6.

81 *Highland News*, 13 May 1899, p. 4.

82 'Colonel Macdonald's Home-Coming', *Ross-shire Journal*, 12 May 1899, p. 7.

83 'Colonel H. A. Macdonald in Glasgow', *Glasgow Herald*, 9 May 1899, p. 9.

84 'Scottish Recruiting a Failure', *Edinburgh Evening News*, 9 June 1898, p. 2, and 'March of the Scottish Borderers', *Glasgow Herald*, 28 September 1898, p. 9.

85 'Banquetted [sic] in London', *People's Friend*, 13 May 1899, p. 6.

86 *Scotsman*, 6 September 1898, p. 4; 'Colonel Wauchope on the Soudan Campaign', *Edinburgh Evening News*, 1 October 1898, p. 3.

87 'Colonel H. A. Macdonald', *Glasgow Herald*, 9 May 1899, p. 9.

88 'The Great Battle in the Soudan', *Strathearn Herald*, 1 October 1898, p. 2; 'Omdurman Relics', *People's Friend*, 13 May 1899, p. 6.

89 'Presentation of Address to Colonel Money, Cameron Highlanders', p. 5.

8

MAGERSFONTEIN AND ITS AFTERMATH

കൃ

The South African War (1899–1902) proved the ultimate imperial challenge of the late nineteenth century. It erupted after prolonged negotiations between the Boers and British government failed to resolve the dispute over the rights of the *Uitlanders*, or settlers, in the Transvaal. The ensuing conflict would involve every Scottish infantry regiment (including both battalions of the Gordons and the Black Watch), the Scots Greys, Scots serving in the artillery and the support arms, and later many Scots auxiliary forces (Militia, Volunteers and Imperial Yeomanry). It represented Britain's first major imperial war against a well-armed enemy able to use modern firearms with devastating effect. As the war proved unexpectedly protracted, it received extensive coverage from the British and foreign media and produced a voluminous, uncensored correspondence from soldiers at the front. The war linked, too, the home and military fronts in a way that an imperial war had never done before, producing heated debates and political controversy at home, a surge of recruiting, and, periodically, remarkable scenes of patriotic celebration in Scotland as elsewhere in the United Kingdom. As the campaign experience of the Scots has been examined in other works,[1] the next two chapters will focus on the linkage between the war at the front and at home, exemplifying as it does, the depth and significance of the military commitment in Scotland and the passions aroused by this major imperial conflict. Whereas this chapter will review how the Scots came to terms with the disaster of Magersfontein and its aftermath, the next chapter will analyse how Scotland responded to a prolonged guerrilla war, with the extensive involvement of its citizen soldiers.

When the war began after the expiry of a Boer ultimatum on 11 October 1899, the Boers invaded Cape Colony and Natal and invested the strategic border towns of Kimberley and Mafeking (14 October). The vast majority of Scotland's newspapers (with the odd exception such as the *Edinburgh Evening News*) expressed outrage at the turns of events. The fact that the Boers had precipitated the war

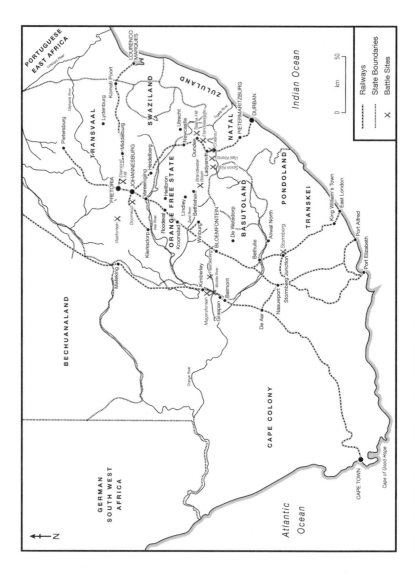

Map 9   *The South African War, 1899–1902*

ensured that many Liberal newspapers rallied in support of a vigorous military response. 'Whatever errors of diplomacy the Government and the Colonial Office have made', argued the *Kinross-shire Advertiser*, 'it is now our duty to stand solid for the imperial power'; 'the country', exhorted the *Kilmarnock Standard*, 'ought now to show a united front'; 'there must be no Majubas', urged the *Greenock Herald*, 'our full military strength must be committed at once'; and 'the Boer cup of iniquity is now full', claimed the *Highland News*, 'they must be humbled and taught subordination to British authority'.[2] The Unionist *Scotsman* added that 'we should hear no more excuses for the Boers, no more pleas that war with a people so minded is avoidable, or could from the first be avoided'.[3]

While Conservatives and Liberal Unionists rallied behind the war effort, the Scottish Liberals split. Seventeen of Scotland's forty-one Liberal MPs voted in favour of a parliamentary amendment on 19 October 1899, deploring the conduct of the pre-war diplomacy: all but one of them (T. C. H. Hedderwick of Wick)[4] became known as pro-Boers by virtue of their subsequent parliamentary voting and public speeches.[5] Sir Henry Campbell-Bannerman, the Scottish leader of the Liberal party, sought to preserve party unity but sympathised with the critique of the pre-war diplomacy. He earned thereby both editorial rebuke and the opposition of the Liberal Imperialist camp, headed by Lord Rosebery and several MPs representing Scottish constituencies, namely Herbert H. Asquith, Richard B. Haldane and Ronald Munro-Ferguson (the Scottish Liberal whip). The Liberal Imperialists defended the rights of *Uitlanders* in the Transvaal, the honour and integrity of the empire generally, and the cause of national efficiency to hold the nation and colonies together.[6]

This did not mean that Scotland was split between imperialism and anti-imperialism. Although antipathy towards the empire had its adherents in Scotland, not least in some radical and socialist circles, and, as Manny Shinwell recalled, among the southern Irish Catholics in the east end of Glasgow,[7] this was not the driving impulse behind the pro-Boer movement. Gladstonian Liberals, such as Thomas Shaw (Hawick) and John Morley (Montrose), denounced the war as avoidable and therefore unjust, immoral and potentially costly, diverting resources from social reforms at home, but they were neither hostile to the empire (Shaw even believed that 'advanced Liberalism' saved the empire)[8] nor critical of the soldiers who had to implement the government's policy.

This was eminently sensible as martial enthusiasm gripped much of Scotland as it did the rest of the United Kingdom. Reservists returned to the colours in huge numbers, bringing battalions up to or close to their war establishments (394 reservists served in the Cameron Highlanders out of 1,091 officers and men),[9] and reinforced the links between the soldiers on active service and their families at home. Rapturous crowds cheered the battalions as they left for South Africa. Whether it was the 2nd Battalion, Seaforth Highlanders marching through Ardeseir, where the villagers illuminated their windows in the same way that Londoners had illuminated windows during the 'Glorious Revolution', 'bidding the Seaforths go forth and do battle for the same great principles of freedom and civil right', or the 1st Battalion, Gordon Highlanders (the 'Dargai' Battalion) marching from Edinburgh Castle through crowded and barricaded streets to Waverley Station, or the 1st Battalion, Royal Scots enjoying a tumultuous send-off at the Empire Theatre, Belfast, Scottish soldiers were fêted everywhere.[10] In sailing down the Clyde, the Seaforths received an ecstatic send-off amid bands playing 'loyal and patriotic airs':

> Passing harbour ferries and other vessels were crowded with sight-seers, who also joined in the ovation, which was continued till after the vessel had passed Govan. All down the river people lined the banks, clambered on half-built ships, and cheered to their hearts' content, thus helping to increase the heartiness of the Seaforths' send-off . . .[11]

The illustrated press followed the tartan, printing numerous photographs of Highland units leaving England and India and later arriving in South Africa: the *Illustrated London News* devoted a front page to the 2nd Battalion, Gordon Highlanders en route to their first battle at Elandslaagte.[12]

An unprecedented number of British and foreign correspondents reported on the war – over seventy authorised correspondents at its outset – and many more followed, with *The Times* having twenty-four correspondents in the field by the end of the war.[13] They provided extensive coverage of the Scots as they served in all theatres of the conflict and several correspondents, including Steevens, Prior and W. T. Maude of the *Graphic*, found themselves besieged in Ladysmith with the 2nd Gordons by 2 November 1899. This investment, coupled with the sieges of Mafeking and Kimberley, prompted Sir Redvers Buller, who had just arrived in Cape Town, to change his strategy and divide his army corps into three divisions. Scots served in each division, namely the Natal relief force, Gatacre's division dispatched to the eastern Cape, and in the Highland Brigade as part of Lord Methuen's division dispatched towards Kimberley.

In writing from the front, Scottish soldiers exuded confidence initially, clearly expecting a quick, decisive outcome. They wrote of the warmth of their welcome from fellow countrymen and the English-speaking communities generally in the Cape and Natal,[14] and described how they adapted to the rigours of the South African climate, a test for regulars and reservists alike.[15] More importantly, they learned lessons from the early battles in Natal, characterised by the inability to see a concealed enemy firing smokeless rifles at long range, the vulnerability of officers wearing badges of rank and wielding claymores, and the difficulty of mounting offensives and crossing fire zones swept by magazine rifles. Elandslaagte (21 October 1899) may have been a victory, reflecting the value of open-order deployments practised in India, but it was a costly one for the Gordons, especially in officers with five killed and eight wounded (70 per cent of those engaged).[16] Although the Argylls covered their kilts with khaki aprons and their officers dressed like the men, they also encountered a ferocious fire zone from a 'hidden' enemy at the Modder River (28 November 1899). Pinned to the ground for much of the day, many Argylls suffered from severe blisters to the backs of their knees but some managed to cross the river and helped to turn the Boers' flank. Despite incurring 122 casualties out of 478 officers and men engaged, they occupied the Boer camp as the enemy withdrew.[17] Fresh soldiers joined the Argylls to form the Highland Brigade under the command of Major-General Andrew Wauchope. As a Seaforth corporal wrote from the Modder River camp:

> You would not know the regiment now if you saw it, the changes being khaki aprons, no sporrans, stripes or ribbons. Everything that would make a mark for the Boers has to be taken off. The troops have all big whiskers, and they look pure warriors . . . The regiment is in excellent health, there being scarcely any sickness . . . We pass the nights very well with our chums of the Highland Light Infantry, Black Watch, and Argylls . . . We are all longing to have another 'bash' at the Boers.[18]

Complementing this confidence was a deepening hostility towards the enemy. Scottish and English soldiers serving in the Seaforths wrote of their disgust at the ransacking of farms and the slaughtering of cattle as the Boers retreated northwards.[19] Others deplored the Boer tactics, notably their readiness to withdraw from positions under artillery fire, or when threatened by a bayonet charge, and their abuse of the white flag: 'some of them', wrote Major T. Mowbray Berkeley (Black Watch), 'are awful hounds'.[20] The more perceptive victims of Boer fire power had a rather different perspective: as Corporal Philip Littler, a Gordon Highlander invalided home from Elandslaagte, remarked, 'it is a mistake to look upon the Boers as poor ignorant farmers . . . They will take some beating, and we shall want a lot more men over there, because we have such a wide area to cover.'[21]

As letters took several weeks to reach Scotland, relatively few arrived before the shock of Magersfontein (11 December 1899), one of three disastrous defeats in what became known as the 'Black Week' of 10 to 15 December. Unlike the battles of Stormberg (10 December, where 561 British soldiers were captured) and Colenso (15 December, where 1,139 were killed, wounded or missing), Scots incurred the vast majority of the 948 killed, wounded and missing at Magersfontein.[22] After a night march over difficult terrain with the darkness compounded by a thunderstorm, the much-vaunted Highland Brigade, then in the act of deploying from its quarter-column formation, encountered 'terrific fire' from unseen Boer trenches just before daybreak. Wauchope fell mortally wounded and many in the advanced companies of the Black Watch were killed, wounded or retreated into the supporting units. The mixed units lay pinned to the ground for hours; some rushes were made and the 1st Gordons came up in support but the Boer fire power prevailed. When 'retire' was shouted in early afternoon, a rush to the rear ensued and the bulk of the casualties occurred.[23]

The first cryptic reports on the battle caused consternation in Scotland. The *Scotsman* desperately described the battle as 'drawn', even if the losses were 'naturally' very heavy and the 'most grievous loss of all is that of the gallant and well-loved commander of the Brigade, General Wauchope'.[24] Shock and incomprehension were as evident in other editorials, and political meetings were cancelled as a mark of respect. In cancelling such a meeting in Oddfellows Hall, Edinburgh, Arthur Dewar, the pro-Boer MP of Edinburgh South, paid tribute to Wauchope whom he had defeated in a by-election in the previous June: Wauchope, he declared, 'has died, as he lived, serving his Queen and country, and I am very certain of this, that had he chosen his own end he would not have had it otherwise'.[25] In Perth, the heart of the Black Watch regimental district, the *Perthshire Advertiser* claimed that an 'air of subdued sorrow and sympathy . . . overhung the city like a pall . . . It touched all classes, and for the moment, welded them into one . . .' Yet the *Advertiser* assured its readers that the sacrifice of the Black Watch (later calculated as seven officers, including Lieutenant-Colonel J. H. C. Coode, and eighty-eight men killed and eleven officers and 207 men wounded, the heaviest loss of any battalion in the battle) had not been in vain. 'Their cause', it stated, 'was the cause of the nation and the Empire: their cause was the cause of the missionary and civilisation: of freedom and justice against tyranny and aggression.'[26]

A flood tide of messages and gifts for the Highland Brigade soon followed not only from Scotland but more immediately from Cape Town, especially from the ex-patriot Scottish community. The latter sent gifts to the wounded and tobacco, cigarettes and beer to the Highlanders on New Year's Day. Gifts of money and clothing also poured into relief funds for the wives, families and dependants of regulars and reservists; by mid-January 1900 the Perth relief fund had received £3,946 and over a thousand articles of clothing for the 162 families on its register.[27] All reservists were called up, and Scotland responded, as did most of Britain, to the requests of the War Office in December 1899 for Volunteers and then Imperial Yeomanry to undertake active service. Sir J. H. A. Macdonald, who had command of a Scottish Infantry Brigade, soon had 4,000 Volunteers in camp for a month and sent three active service companies to the war: 'For once they were paid soldiers of the Queen.'[28] Scottish recruiting flourished at this time; the nation sent eleven Volunteer special service companies to South Africa and raised four companies of Imperial Yeomanry – the 17th (Ayr and Lanark), 18th (Glasgow), 19th (Lothians and Berwick) and 20th (Fife and Forfar).[29] Local authorities, often accompanied by ministers of the Kirk, hosted receptions and presented gifts or awarded the freedom of their burghs to local Volunteers. At the departure of the 4th Volunteer Battalion, Royal Highlanders (Black Watch) from Perth, the Reverend P. A. Gordon Clark declared: 'when the trumpet sounded the Empire thrilled with a deep sense of kinship, in every dependency men awoke in the consciousness of their unity in a mighty brotherhood . . .'[30]

Magersfontein, though, remained a tragic backdrop to Scottish reflections on the war. At a dinner in Stirling, where departing Volunteers received the freedom of the burgh, the Earl of Mar and Kellie exhorted each man to 'do his utmost to maintain the glorious traditions of the Highland Brigade'.[31] Yet these traditions seemed at issue after the brigade's first clash with the enemy, one that contrasted so dramatically with Tel-el-Kebir and the battles of the Crimean and Napoleonic wars. The images in the illustrated press were

Figure 8 *'All That Was Left of Them'* (R. Caton Woodville, Illustrated London News, *20 January 1900*)

overwhelmingly those of defeat and of wounded men, the burial of Wauchope, and poignant gatherings of survivors, not least Caton Woodville's stark depiction, 'All That Was Left of Them', a photogravure given away with the first number of *The Sphere*.[32] Reports in the metropolitan press, which were reproduced in Scottish newspapers, ranged from vivid accounts of the Highlanders rushing onwards to 'death or disaster' (*Daily News*) to more prosaic claims that the retreat had contravened Methuen's orders (*The Times*) or more emphatically that the 'Highlanders broke and ran; there is no other word for it' (*Morning Post*).[33]

Consequently the interest in first-hand accounts from the front was considerable, matched only by the readiness of the survivors, whether wounded or not, to recount their versions of the disaster. Many wrote simple, if often graphic, narratives; some focused on their own experiences and remarkable escapes, others laced their accounts with camp gossip or sought to apportion blame or responded to criticisms and oversights, real or imagined, in the press reports. Soldiers of the Black Watch, who had led the advance, were all too aware of the hazards of the night march in quarter-column formation, guided by a line held by a scout. It was 'cold and wet', wrote Private G. Cooper; 'a very tiresome march', recalled Private James Nicoll, 'in the darkness and over very uneven ground, rain falling heavily'; and in this darkness, 'for about ten minutes', as Piper A. Wynter remembered, 'the searchlight from Kimberley showed us quite plainly to those on the side of the hill'.[34] Unaware that the Boers had entrenched at ground level, the brigade, as Sergeant William Hamilton (HLI) described, 'simply marched on to their position . . . Instead of us making the surprise, we were surprised. They knew all about our movements all along. I shall never forget the sight. It was like the mouth of hell opening up to swallow us.'[35]

Fortunately much of the early shooting was far too high as the brigade was so close to the enemy trenches, with estimates of the distance ranging from about one hundred to three hundred yards (some trenches were closer to the column than others). The task of extending the formation under 'a perfect hail of bullets', as recalled by Colour-Sergeant Alex Matheson (Seaforths), resulted in 'perfect disorder' with units, often lacking officers, becoming hopelessly intermingled.[36] Some broke to the right or left or retired, whereupon Colour-Sergeant A. J. Gray (Black Watch) and one of his officers, Captain A. R. Cameron, discovered 'a mob of excited soldiers of all regiments . . . and tried to get them together but they had lost their head', and, when several Boers began to move round their flank and started to fire from that direction, 'they became disorganised'.[37] Men were pinned to the ground and when the day dawned, added Matheson, 'what was worst of all, we could not see anything to fire at, as the Boers were so securely entrenched'.[38] Soldiers were now brutally frank about the state of the brigade. When a rush was made, wrote Private John Heard (Seaforths), 'It was not a general advance, it was a rabble, everybody acting on his own hook.'[39] The Gordons reinforced the brigade in early morning, attacking, as Sergeant Baxter recalled, in three lines with five paces between each man, 'a magnificent sight [from the support line] . . . of green and yellow tartan and khaki clad warriors'; they advanced, as Private E. Hall noted, by 'rushing and lying down in turns'. Encountering a 'heavy cross fire', their firing and support lines soon merged and they were duly pinned to the ground under a scorching sun, suffering like the other Highlanders from a lack of water and burns to the backs of their knees.[40] Finally, when somebody shouted 'retire', 'we did', claimed an HLI soldier, 'well, not a retire, but a stampede: 4000 men like a flock of sheep running for dear life'.[41] Private A. Mair (Gordons) doubted that the Highland Brigade had ever received 'such a cutting up before', and Private Allan Ross (HLI) reckoned that 'some of the men would have run to Scotland if they had found a road'.[42]

These were not accounts that anyone wanted to tell and differed markedly from the traditional image of Scottish soldiery. Captain Cameron (Black Watch) maintained that the battle had to be placed in context:

> I do not consider any account I have seen of Magersfontein does justice to the Highland Brigade: they never mention that any attempts to get up the kopje were frustrated by our own artillery fire and they never mention how we were fighting the whole day in the bushes on our right to prevent our right flank being turned & where our heaviest loss took place . . .[43]

Others sought to explain the defeat by grossly exaggerating the Boer numbers, possibly reflecting camp gossip that the brigade had been outnumbered by at least three to one and by seeking consolation in vastly inflated claims of Boer casualties.[44] The brigade was outnumbered by some 8,000 Boers but Methuen's division had a numerical advantage overall and some claimed that Wauchope should have extended his formation sooner.[45] Most Highlanders, though, bemoaned the loss of their venerated commander: Private G. Archer (Black Watch) deprecated any aspersions cast on 'poor old Wauchope', and Private J. Ruddick (Black Watch) claimed that 'if the Press only knew how the men of the Highland Brigade resent any slurs thrown at our brave General . . . I think all hints would stop immediately . . .'[46] Some thought that Wauchope had had doubts about Methuen's plan of attack (which was launched without any reconnaissance of the Boer positions, despite the availability of an observation balloon). Captain Charles E. Stewart (Black Watch) learned from Colonel Spencer Ewart that 'General Andy had not the slightest idea of the brigade charging. He thought the Boers were on top of the hill and meant to make a regular attack at day break. No wonder he thought it madness.'[47] Of more immediate significance was the claim repeated by soldiers from every unit in the brigade that the general had died disclaiming responsibility: 'It is no fault of mine, men; I have to take my orders the same as you.'[48]

Whether these were his final words or were words twisted in camp gossip remained a matter of conjecture (and many more claimed to have heard these remarks than could possibly have done so). Wauchope's widow discounted any possibility that he could have made such remarks and the more responsible Scottish newspapers urged their readers to treat these comments with caution: the *Fife Herald* happily printed a more honourable utterance, 'go on men, never mind me', which Private Ronald Ferguson (HLI) claimed that he had heard Wauchope say as he fell riddled with bullets.[49] Whether this was any more accurate was also doubtful (as the HLI were originally in reserve while Wauchope died at the head of his men), but it upheld the honour of the fallen Scottish general, while not deflecting attention from the bane of the brigade, Lord Methuen himself.

Many Highlanders expressed frank and forceful criticisms of Methuen. They ranged from moderate condemnation of 'These frontal attacks, with no tactics, on impossible positions do no good; the loss is awful'[50] to claims that Methuen was 'guilty of almost criminal negligence', suicidal tactics, a 'blunder', and was responsible for 'a lot of lives [lost] that day'.[51] Many deeply resented his post-battle speech, sympathising with 'their *terrible loss*', a speech dubbed by Captain Cameron as 'most impolitic and insulting'.[52] Argylls, who had suffered in successive battles under Methuen's generalship, and lost Lieutenant- Colonel G. L. J. Goff at Magersfontein, were particularly bitter. Corporal Bevan denounced the advance in quarter-column formation, Private A. Thomson claimed that the men had 'lost all confidence in General Methuen', another that 'the men grumble every hour of the day about the way he treats the Highland Brigade', and a corporal even alleged that there was 'a wild spirit of mutiny among the men'.[53] If other sources failed to corroborate the last assertion, they endorsed the widespread loss of confidence in Methuen which Hector Macdonald, the new brigade commander, passed on to Lord Roberts, the incoming commander-in-chief.[54] Roberts removed the brigade from Methuen's division, and Lord Methuen accepted that 'the Highland Brigade will never wish to serve under me again'.[55]

News of Macdonald's appointment, and then the removal of the brigade from Methuen's division, lanced one boil of recriminations at the front and gave fresh hope to Scots at home. The *Ross-shire Journal* commended the 'admirable choice' of the War Office 'in placing "Fighting Mac" at the head of his gallant countrymen'.[56] Many Scots, whether in the press, pulpit or political leadership, responded to the disaster with professions of resolve and support for the imperial cause. Following Magersfontein, the Reverend John Addie reassured his Perthshire congregation that 'our flag does mean freedom, political and religious. We do believe that our cause in South Africa is the cause of social, moral, and spiritual progress.'[57] In Alness Parish Church, the Reverend Wallace Brown declared that 'the war was a war of the British race in defence of their ideal of civilisation', and at St Leonard's Free Church, the Reverend Dr D. Bannerman described 'how the nation and Empire has risen to face the seriousness of the crisis, how party strife has been silenced, and men of all ranks have been drawn together in a common patriotism . . .'[58] Those Liberals who criticised the origins of the war, generally supported the soldiers at the front: as Campbell-Bannerman, a former Secretary of State for War, affirmed, 'We have a united people in this country and in every part of the Empire. And with these forces on our side, moral and material, success is certain.'[59] The Scottish press not only printed many of these sermons and speeches but also recorded the enthusiastic scenes whenever local reservists or Volunteers left for the front. At the departure of the Ayrshire Yeomanry, Corporal John Paterson recalled how a crowd gathered 'all the way down the Clyde to bid us farewell, the ship-building yards turned out every man to give us a cheer'.[60]

There was much less sympathy at home for the other major source of recrimination at the front, namely the praise accorded in the press to the supporting units of the Guards and Gordons at Magersfontein. Cameron reckoned that what hurt the feelings of the Black Watch 'more than anything else is the excessive praise given to the Gordons in contradistinction to the other regiments . . .'[61] Soldiers from across the brigade endorsed these complaints, remarking bitterly in the case of Lance-Corporal W. Macfarlane (Seaforths), 'As for the Gordons and Guards they did nothing – in fact, none of them passed our second line. That was about 500 yards from the enemy's position.'[62] In defending themselves, the Gordons claimed that they got much closer to the Boer trenches than their critics alleged, and could not understand, as one corporal remarked, 'the green spirit which actuates some fellows to write disparagingly of our regiment'.[63] Outside of regimental circles, or communities with close regimental ties,[64] these debates were unlikely to resonate in Scotland because the Gordons had clearly done their duty and would continue to do so. The 1st Battalion had lost its colonel, G. T. F. Downman, among nine officers and men killed or died of their wounds and twenty-one officers and men wounded, at Magersfontein but earned another VC in the battle. Its soldiers served in the trenches at the battle of Paardeberg (18–27 February 1900) but not in the costly offensive launched by Kitchener on the 18th, when the Seaforths lost fifty-three officers and men killed and one hundred wounded. Meanwhile, the 2nd Battalion, Gordon Highlanders displayed commendable stoicism throughout the siege of Ladysmith. They endured the daily round of fatigues often in dreadful weather, worsening privations as food became scarce, a mounting toll of sick (but only thirty deaths from disease or 5 per cent of those engaged), and desperate fighting at Caesar's Camp (6 January) where they helped to repel a Boer attack.[65]

The 'gay and gallant Gordons' remained a highly positive image, both in Scotland and throughout the United Kingdom. The image was utilised in the illustrated press, in wartime advertising, and was reinforced by the commendations of war correspondents and occasionally by English and colonial soldiers.[66] If some of these reports lavishing attention on the Gordons were, as Ernest N. Bennett alleged, the product of correspondents 'without any previous knowledge of military matters',[67] they were, nonetheless, a reassuring antidote to the pervasive images of defeat, dying and wounded after Magersfontein. In Scotland, too, they may have been considered as a counterpoise (however partial in effect) to the lionisation of the Irish war effort.

Whatever divisions the outbreak of war had caused in Scotland, these paled by comparison with the upsurge of nationalist passions in Ireland. The anti-recruiting drives, led by Maud Gonne and her pro-Boer ladies, made recruiting more difficult in parts of Ireland but recruiting still increased marginally in 1900, and regiments such as the 2nd Royal Irish Rifles and 1st Battalion, Royal Inniskilling Fusiliers left Ireland amid scenes of great enthusiasm. This response seemed even more significant as fellow Irishmen had joined the Boers and in several battles fought against their countrymen and the Rand-Irish who supported the British cause. The pro-Boer contingent had a symbolism that far outweighed its numerical strength (never exceeding three hundred in the two so-called 'Irish Transvaal Brigades', compared with over 30,000 Irishmen fighting for the Crown),[68] and so after the role of the 2nd Battalion, Royal Dublin Fusiliers in the victory at Talana Hill (20 October 1899), Irish loyalty, heroism and purported love of fighting became a favourite theme of music-hall songs and sketches. Leo Dryden's 'Bravo, Dublin Fusiliers' (1899) was one of several popular songs that served to rehabilitate the Irish by virtue of their war effort.[69]

Like the Scots, the Irish had suffered from appalling generalship and incompetent staff work. During the retreat from Stormberg four officers and 216 men of the Royal Irish Rifles were left behind, and Hart's Irish Brigade (the 1st Battalions, Dublin Fusiliers, Inniskilling Fusiliers and Connaught Rangers) incurred heavy casualties at Colenso and again at Hart's Hill (23–4 February 1900) in the final advance on Ladysmith. Queen Victoria expressed her sympathy and admiration for the fighting qualities of 'my brave Irish soldiers',[70] and in March 1900 she issued a royal order that henceforth on St Patrick's

Day all Irish regiments would wear a sprig of shamrock in their head-dress. In the following month, she gave her assent to the creation of a new regiment of Foot Guards, the Irish Guards, and, at eighty years of age and in delicate health, paid her last and longest visit to Ireland, so boosting the unionist/loyalist forces in the country, and possibly countering pro-Boer influences both internally and in South Africa.[71]

This political strategy aroused mixed feelings in Scotland. The merest rumour that the Irish Guards might wear the kilt prompted an editorial in the *North British Daily Mail* denouncing the idea, and a Banffshire man wrote a lengthy letter to the *People's Friend*, calcu-lating the respective wartime contributions of Ireland and Scotland (on dubious assumptions about the national compositions of Irish and Scottish regiments): he did so because the 'flattery of Pat is . . . just a trifle overdone at present'.[72] Any Scottish sensitivity on such issues seemed misplaced to the *Edinburgh Evening News* (it com-mended the 'courage and devotion' of the Irish soldier) and to M. H. Grant, one of the more perceptive English commentators on the war, who reckoned that there was an 'Irish-cum-Highland monopoly of public attention' throughout much of the conflict.[73]

Magersfontein, nonetheless, had left its mark in Scotland, if not in doubts about the rectitude of the cause, still less in the prospect of ulti-mate victory (now that Roberts was in overall command), then in anxiety about the tide of defeats and Scotland's role in the ensuing hos-tilities. While the Royal Scots languished in a support role for Gatacre's column and the Scots Greys recovered from the flanking operation that ultimately relieved Kimberley (but cost them heavily in horses),[74] the Royal Scots Fusiliers and the Cameronians served under Buller in Natal. Despite the defeats in this theatre (Colenso, Spion Kop and Vaal Krantz), Scottish soldiers recognised Buller's genuine concern for his men, his reluctance to sacrifice lives unnecessarily, and his tactical adaptability in the breakthrough to Ladysmith where he had to cross particularly difficult terrain. However much the press criticised Buller, most of his soldiers, including the Scots, lauded their commander. Buller, wrote Corporal George Logan (2nd Cameronians), 'is just what he is represented to be, a great general'.[75] Yet the main focus of Scottish hopes remained the Highland Brigade, battling Cronjé's forces, and supported at Paardeberg by the King's Own Scottish Borderers. The surrender of 4,000 Boers under Cronjé on Majuba Day (27 February 1900) was a great relief but, after Magersfontein and Paardeberg, the brigade, as Macdonald conceded, had 'left fit for work 24 officers and about 1600 men out of 87 officers and over 3000 men. Such is war.'[76]

Following the news of Paardeberg and the coincident relief of Ladysmith, extraordinary demonstrations erupted across Scotland, replicating similar scenes south of the border. Richard Price has described these scenes of jubilation, and similar demonstrations after the relief of Mafeking and the capture of Pretoria, as 'celebratory' occasions similar to 'those of Armistice Night and VE Night'. He distinguished between these crowds and the 'jingo mobs', reportedly involving prominent bodies of middle-class youth intent on breaking up the pro-Boer rallies. By claiming that the celebratory crowds were simply 'rejoicing: England had regained her honour. And that is what these crowds were about,' Price sought thereby to absolve the working class from any taint of imperialism.[77] However, the unprecedented scenes of jubilation in Scotland, involving men and women of every class, warrant further analysis. The spontaneous outbreak of enthusiasm from mid-morning on 1 March 1900 spread across the towns and villages of the country – from Ayr to Aberdeen, Kirkwall to Kirkcudbright, St Andrews to Stornoway – culminating in civic receptions, vast processions through streets bedecked with flags and bunting, and followed by bonfires and fireworks displays at night.

Doubtless people participated for all manner of reasons but, if the press reports were accurate, there was more than patriotic enthusiasm that galvanised students and striking Clyde riveters to celebrate together within Glasgow's Royal Exchange or prompted workmen in Motherwell's public works to down tools for the day or stimulated scenes of 'wild enthusiasm' in Aberdeen's fish market and among Aberdonian joiners on strike. First and foremost, after all the military disappointments, the crowds were celebrating an imperial triumph: as a banner carried round Galston, Ayrshire, proclaimed, 'Bravo Buller: Success at last'.[78] The crowds were displaying a genuine sense of relief after all the disappointments of the war. Moreover, those involved were praising the achievements of their own soldiers, not only the Gordons who had served under Sir George White, VC, another Gordon Highlander, in Ladysmith, but also Scots – sometimes from their own communities – who had served in the relief force and those who had fought at Paardeberg (although knowledge of the Seaforths' long casualty list, and the regiment's connections with Lewis, dampened celebrations in Stornoway). Finally, many of the crowds were seeking in their own way to confound the queen's enemies, and the Boer cause, by burning in effigy all over Scotland their military and political leaders: Cronjé, Marthinus Steyn, the President of the Orange Free State, and, above all, Paul Kruger, the

President of the Transvaal. Even in Kirkcaldy, a bastion of Liberalism with a pro-Boer MP, 'great rejoicing' occurred in the public works, girls in the factories joined in the singing of 'Rule Britannia', flags, banners and emblems appeared from every window of the Victoria Cabinetmaking works and crowds cheered for Buller, White and 'Bobs' (Lord Roberts). 'Everything passed over peacefully', added the *Fife Herald*, 'there being few pro-Boers in Kirkcaldy'.[79]

Although rowdyism was rare during the Ladysmith celebrations,[80] it seems somewhat contrived to separate the passions and enthusiasm released on that day from the jingoistic protests that erupted barely a week later. The subsequent protests occurred at pro-Boer rallies held in connection with the speaking tour of S. C. Cronwright-Schreiner, a South African anti-war activist. Just as students from Glasgow, Edinburgh and St Andrews Universities were prominent in the Ladysmith celebrations, so students were reportedly to the fore in barracking the speakers in Glasgow on 6 March, in breaking up the meeting in Edinburgh on the following night, and in the mob violence that occurred in Dundee on 8 March. In Dundee the meeting was broken up and the manse of the minister, who had tried to host the meeting, attacked.[81] Where the jingo mobs differed from the Ladysmith celebrations was in their organisation, especially in Edinburgh and Dundee where they carried placards and clubs, and in their intent to protest at and, if possible, to disrupt the pro-Boer proceedings. They used force to intimidate people and in some cases to attack individuals and premises. If Scottish Liberals recoiled at this display of jingoism, supported by leading Unionist newspapers and undertaken in Edinburgh with the apparent collusion of the police, they were not converted to the pro-Boer cause. The *North British Daily Mail*, though outraged over the 'Hooliganism' in Edinburgh and the attack on free speech, still wondered at the judgement of the pro-Boers 'being so strangely warped'.[82]

Support for the pro-Boers was unlikely to grow in Scotland as the tide of the war seemed to be turning decisively. The large army assembled by Lord Roberts pressed on to seize Bloemfontein, the capital of the Orange Free State, on 13 March, whereupon Corporal Charles McKimmie (Royal Horse Artillery) was able to recount the hearty welcome from the British people, especially the Scots, in the town. He described how the Free Staters were 'coming in here by the hundreds laying down arms'.[83] Scottish soldiers had not fought any more major battles but they had marched prodigious distances on half rations, scarce supplies of water and often without tents. These privations, surmised a King's Own Scottish Borderer, had not been reported as the censored war correspondents 'are not allowed to tell the truth'.[84] Once encamped at Bloemfontein for six weeks, many of those who had drunk polluted water from the Modder River began to suffer from enteric (typhoid) fever and the toll of sick and the deaths from disease mounted rapidly.[85] These experiences merely exacerbated the feelings of enmity towards the Boers, whom Private James Irvine (1st Battalion, Scots Guards), reckoned had 'been preparing for war for a long time . . . [and] certainly meant to make it a Dutch South Africa'.[86] Private George C. Fraser (1st Battalion, Royal Scots Mounted Infantry) was equally incensed by the destruction and cruelty perpetrated by the Boers: he wished to 'take a British pro-Boer by the ear and show him some of the outrageous work committed by his Dutch friends . . .'[87]

When Roberts resumed his advance towards Pretoria, Scots soon had further cause for celebration in the relief of Mafeking (17 May 1900). Scots, like most of Britain and large parts of the empire, celebrated the relief of this small, remote outpost, especially after the earlier disasters in the war. Amid all the press accounts of popular rejoicings, processions and bonfires burning effigies of Kruger, the story of how Major-General R. S. S. Baden-Powell and his small garrison had held out for 217 days was told repeatedly. Testifying to the pervasive appeal of Baden-Powell's own publicity (often expressed laconically and with scant reference to the support of armed blacks) were the speeches in Stornoway, hailing Baden-Powell as a 'gallant and worthy son of the Empire', and in Ayr, describing him as 'a noble example . . . beyond all Greek and Roman fame'.[88] In reflecting on 'the tumultuous rejoicings' about the 'modern Thermopylae', the *Kilmarnock Standard*, hardly an organ of jingoism, maintained that 'Every Briton in Mafeking was a volunteer in defence of Queen and country, and it is because the glory is shared by soldier and civilian alike that all creeds and classes of British men and women indulged in such a frenzy of joy last Saturday.'[89] Even at the pro-Boer rally in Aberdeen on 20 May, which only took place because of the intervention of the police and sixty Gordon Highlanders, Cronwright-Schreiner praised the 'heroic Baden-Powell'.[90]

The celebrations that followed the eagerly anticipated entry into Pretoria (5 June 1900) were reportedly even more ecstatic than their predecessors, largely because the end of the war now seemed imminent. Some municipal authorities provided funds for the bunting and illuminations (an entire side of George Square, Glasgow, was illuminated with the word Pretoria emblazoned in letters a yard deep), and others organised receptions or declared public holidays. Vast crowds celebrated in Glasgow throughout the day and up till midnight, prompting the claim of the *Glasgow Herald* that 'The working classes required no one to tell them that the occasion was one for widespread jubilation' (which hardly accords with the claim that there was little imperialist sentiment in Glasgow during the war).[91] Once again, all across Scotland church bells were rung, processions followed Volunteer bands, and bonfires were lit, burning Kruger in effigy. Among the many tributes to the military success of Lord Roberts, some like Sir Felix Mackenzie in Forres and Bailie Harley in Dunfermline reflected upon the unprecedented imperial achievement of sending 'upwards of 200,000 men four [sic, nearer six] thousand miles over the sea' and then provisioning them and providing support over 'very long lines of communication'. As Mackenzie observed, 'No other nation could have accomplished so much', and, in comparing the South African undertaking with 'the pitiable Madagascar expedition' mounted by France in 1895 (when France had to rent shipping from Britain), Harley claimed that Britain had confounded its critics: 'Instead of showing weakness . . . the British Empire had given an object lesson to the whole of the nations of the world.'[92]

Doubtless a degree of hubris had developed as events began to improve in South Africa, reflecting the intensity of the reaction in Scotland after the profound shock of Magersfontein. Pride in the imperial recovery, and in Scotland's response to adversity, particularly in the response of its Volunteers, was a feature of many of the speeches in the wake of Pretoria's surrender. James Bryce, the pro-Boer MP for Aberdeen South, had anticipated this theme when he addressed local Liberals on 4 June 1900. He began by applauding the alacrity with which the Volunteers in Aberdeen and the north of Scotland had offered their services and the prowess they had displayed at the front. Assuming that the war was 'practically over', he looked forward to a future in which the Liberals could unite on the basis of Liberal Imperialism as he did not know of any Liberal who wished to 'renounce that empire which, under the providence of God, had come to their hands'. He insisted, though, that the empire must be preserved in light of Gladstone's 'spirit', upholding the principles of justice, humanity, peace and self-government.[93] In other words, by early June 1900 most of Scotland looked forward to another imperial triumph. If imperialism meant different things to different Scots, the martial dimension, if only part of the phenomenon, had widespread appeal at this time. The wave of military victories, in the wake of Magersfontein, had occasioned scenes of unprecedented jubilation all across Scotland.

Notes

1 Spiers, 'The Scottish Soldier in the Boer War', in Gooch (ed.), *The Boer War*, pp. 152–65, 273–7, and *The Victorian soldier in Africa*, ch. 9.

2 *Kinross-shire Advertiser*, 14 October 1899, p. 2; *Kilmarnock Standard*, 7 October 1899, p. 4; *Greenock Herald*, 14 October 1899, p. 2; *Highland News*, 14 October 1899, p. 2.

3 *Scotsman*, 11 October 1899, p. 6.

4 Hedderwick, though critical of the pre-war diplomacy, found opposition to the war very unpopular in the northern burghs. He trimmed his opinions over the coming year and was even described as a 'Liberal Imperialist' at the time of his electoral defeat in October 1900. 'Mr Hedderwick on Tour' and 'The General Election', *Ross-shire Journal*, 13 October 1899, p. 4, and 19 October 1900, p. 6.

5 *Parl. Deb.*, fourth series, vol. lxxvii (19 October 1899), cols 367–72; see also Brown, ' "Echoes of Midlothian" ', pp. 164, 171.

6 'The Liberal leader and the War', *Perthshire Advertiser*, 20 November 1899, p. 2; NLS, Rosebery Mss, Ms. 10019, ff. 125–6, R. Munro-Ferguson to Lord Rosebery, 30 October 1899, and Haldane Mss, Ms. 5965, ff. 229–30, R. B. Haldane to his mother, 23 June 1901; see also P. B. Jacobson, 'Rosebery and Liberal Imperialism 1899–1902', *Journal of British Studies*, 13 (1973), pp. 83–107; G. L. Bernstein, 'Sir Henry Campbell-Bannerman and the Liberal Imperialists', *Journal of British Studies*, 23 (1983), pp. 105–24; and H. C. G. Matthew, *The Liberal Imperialists: The ideas and politics of a post-Gladstonian elite* (Oxford: Oxford University Press, 1973), pp. 167, 171–80.

7 R. Price, *An Imperial War and the British Working Class: Working-Class Attitudes and Reactions to the Boer War 1899–1902* (London: Routledge & Kegan Paul, 1972), pp. 82–7; M. Shinwell, *Lead with the Left: My First Ninety-six Years* (London: Cassell, 1981), pp. 22–3; *Edinburgh Evening News*, 21 December 1899, p. 2.

8 T. Shaw, *Letters to Isabel* (London: Cassell, 1921), pp. 194–5; D. A. Hamer, *John Morley: Liberal Intellectual in Politics* (Oxford: Oxford University Press, 1968), pp. 311–28; S. Koss (ed.), *The Pro-Boers: The Anatomy of an Antiwar Movement* (Chicago: University of Chicago Press, 1973), p. xxxviii.

9 *South African War Record of the 1st Battalion Queen's Own Cameron Highlanders 1900-1-2* (Inverness: Northern Counties Printing Company, 1903), p. 11.

10 'Departure of the Seaforth Highlanders', *Inverness Courier*, 24 October 1899, p. 6; GH Museum, PB 92, Private Ford, diary, 8 November 1899;

NAM, Acc. No. 1977-04-56, Preston Mss, 2nd Lieutenant J. Preston to his mother and Alison, 4 November 1899; 'The Gordon Highlanders' Leave of Edinburgh', *Scotsman*, 9 November 1899, p. 8.

11 'The 2nd Seaforths off to the Front', *Ross-shire Journal*, 27 October 1899, p. 7.

12 *Illustrated London News*, 21, 28 October, 11 and 18 November 1899, pp. 575, 635, 680 and 711.

13 S. Badsey, 'War Correspondents in the Boer War', in Gooch (ed.), *The Boer War*, pp. 187–202, 279–83; Wilkinson-Latham, *From Our Special Correspondent*, p. 252.

14 'Letter from an Ayr Fusilier at the Front', *Ayr Advertiser*, 28 December 1899, p. 5; 'Letters from a Glasgow Man with Gatacre's Column', *Glasgow Herald*, 26 December 1899, p. 6; 'Letter from a Black Watch Sergeant', *Perthshire Constitutional & Journal*, 8 January 1900, p. 3.

15 'Letter from a Seaforth Highlander', *Inverness Courier*, 22 December 1899, p. 3; 'Scarcity of Water', *Western Morning News*, 16 January 1900, p. 8; 'A Soldier's Letter', *Ayr Advertiser*, 18 January 1900, p. 7.

16 GH Museum, PB 175, Lieutenant-Colonel Sir N. Macready, diary, pp. 3–6; 'Whisky in the Boer Camp. A Lively Letter', *Inverness Courier*, 1 December 1899, p. 5; 'Old Blairbridge Boys at the Front', *Falkirk Herald*, 11 August 1900, p. 6; Greenhill Gardyne, *Life of a Regiment*, vol. 3, pp. 25–6.

17 'The Battle of Modder River', *Glasgow Evening News*, 2 January 1900, p. 2; 'The Modder River Battle', *Glasgow Herald*, 26 December 1899, p. 6; 'Letter from a Stirling Soldier Killed at Magersfontein', *Stirling Observer*, 3 January 1900, p. 6; R. P. Dunn-Pattison, *The History of the 91st Argyllshire Highlanders* (Edinburgh: W. Blackwood & Sons, 1910), p. 270.

18 'Letter from a Seaforth Highlander at Modder', *Ross-shire Journal*, 5 January 1900, p. 6.

19 'Letters from the Front', *Manchester Evening News*, 9 January 1900, p. 3, and the letter from Private Wallace Maxwell in the *Falkirk Herald*, 3 February 1900, p. 6.

20 BWRA, 0396/2, Mowbray Berkeley Mss, Major T. Mowbray Berkeley to his mother, 27 November 1899; see also 'A Perthshire Soldier and the Modder Fight', *Strathearn Herald*, 13 January 1900, p. 2.

21 'Back from the Front. A Wounded Halifax Reservist', *Bradford Daily Argus*, 12 January 1900, p. 4.

22 Major-General Sir F. B. Maurice and M. H. Grant, *History of the War in South Africa 1899–1902*, 4 vols (London: Hurst & Blackett, 1906), vol. 1, pp. 301, 329, 374.

23 TNA, PRO, WO 32/7870, Lieutenant-Colonel T. W. Hughes-Hallett to the Chief Staff Officer, 1st Division, 13 December 1899, and Lord

Methuen to General Officer Commanding, 13 December 1899, and WO 32/7966, 15 February 1900.

24 *Scotsman*, 14 December 1899, p. 6.

25 'Reception of the News in Edinburgh', *Perthshire Advertiser*, 15 December 1899, p. 3; see also *Ross-shire Journal*, 15 December 1899, p. 4.

26 *Perthshire Advertiser*, 18 December 1899, p. 2; see also J. Stirling, *British Regiments in South Africa 1899–1902* (Polstead, Suffolk: J. B. Hayward & Son, 1903), p. 244.

27 'The Battle of Magersfontein', *Invergordon Times*, 24 January 1900, p. 3; 'Letter from the Front', *Argyllshire Herald*, 10 February 1900, p. 3; E. & A. Linklater, *The Black Watch*, pp. 131–2; 'Administration of Perth Relief Fund', *Perthshire Constitutional and Journal*, 22 January 1900, p. 3.

28 J. H. A. Macdonald, *Fifty Years of It: The Experiences and Struggles of a Volunteer of 1859* (Edinburgh: Blackwood, 1909), pp. 486–7.

29 'The Wave of Patriotism', *John O'Groat Journal*, 19 January 1900, p. 2; *Perthshire Advertiser*, 10 January 1900, p. 4; Grierson, *Records of the Scottish Volunteer Force*, p. 93; T. F. Dewar, *With the Scottish Yeomanry* (Arbroath: T. Buncle, 1901), p. 7.

30 'War Service in City Hall', *Perthshire Advertiser*, 12 February 1900, p. 2; see also 'The Glasgow Volunteers', *Glasgow Evening News*, 3 February 1900, p. 6; 'Presentation to Hamilton Yeomen and Volunteers', *Hamilton Advertiser*, 10 February 1900, p. 4; 'Ayrshire Imperial Yeomanry', *Ayr Observer*, 22 February 1900, p. 5.

31 'Argyll and Sutherland Highlanders', *Falkirk Herald*, 7 February 1900, p. 4.

32 'Burial of General Wauchope, the Fallen Chief of the Highland Brigade' and 'All That Was Left of Them', *Illustrated London News*, 20 January 1900, pp. 86–7, 102; 'The graves of the fallen Highlanders on the battlefield of Magersfontein', *Daily Graphic*, 18 January 1900, p. 4; 'A Friend in Need is a Friend Indeed', *Shurey's Illustrated*, 3 February 1900, p. 12.

33 'The War', *Elgin Courant*, 12 January 1900, p. 3; 'The Battle of Magersfontein', *Inverness Courier*, 12 January 1900, p. 8.

34 'A Salford Man's Experience', *Manchester Evening News*, 28 February 1900, p. 5; 'Letters from St Andrews Soldiers at the Front', *Fife News*, 3 February 1900, p. 8; 'A Doune Man at Magersfontein', *Stirling Observer*, 17 January 1900, p. 8.

35 'The War', *Argyllshire Herald*, 13 January 1900, p. 3.

36 'Letter from a Ross-shire Soldier at the Front', *Ross-shire Journal*, 26 January 1900, p. 7; on the Boer shooting, the distances and mixed-up units, see 'Birnie Lads at the Front' and 'Letter from a Nairn Man at the Front', *Elgin Courant*, 16 January 1900, p. 3; 'Magersfontein', *The*

Times, 12 January 1900, p. 3; 'Experiences of Lieutenant the Hon. Maurice Drummond at the Battle of Magersfontein', *Strathearn Herald*, 13 January 1900, p. 3.

37 'A Colour-Sergeant of the Black Watch on the Battle', *Scotsman*, 9 January 1900, p. 2.

38 'Letter from a Ross-shire Soldier at the Front', p. 7.

39 'A Wounded Seaforth's Experiences', *Western Morning News*, 12 January 1900, p. 8; see also 'Interesting Letter from a Crieff Soldier at the Front', *Strathearn Herald*, 20 January 1900, p. 2.

40 'A Gordon Highlander's Version of the Battle of Magersfontein', *Manchester Evening News*, 27 February 1900, p. 5; 'Letters from the Front', *Kinross-shire Advertiser*, 27 January 1900, p. 3; see also 'The Seaforths at Magersfontein', *Ross-shire Journal*, 19 January 1900, p. 7, and 'Letter from a Crieff Soldier at the Front', *Strathearn Herald*, 24 February 1900, p. 3.

41 'Magersfontein', *Elgin Courant*, 12 January 1900, p. 5.

42 'The Cutting Up of the Highland Brigade', *Inverness Courier*, 23 January 1900, p. 3; 'The Truth about Magersfontein', *Aberdeen Journal*, 12 January 1900, p. 6.

43 BWRA, 0186, Cameron Mss, Captain A. R. Cameron to Nellie, 16 January 1900; see also NAM, Acc. No. 1973-10-85, Private H. Bly, diary, 10 December 1899.

44 'The Battle of Magersfontein', *Invergordon Times*, 24 January 1900, p. 3; 'The War in South Africa', *Dunfermline Journal*, 20 January 1900, p. 6; 'The War', *Argyllshire Herald*, 13 January 1900, p. 3; 'Letter from an Uddingston Man', *Hamilton Advertiser*, 13 January 1900, p. 3.

45 'The Truth about Magersfontein', p. 6; 'A Bolton Soldier Tells of Magersfontein' and 'A Broughton Soldier at Magersfontein', *Manchester Evening News*, 18 January 1900, p. 5; 'Another Account of the Modder River Disaster', *Perthshire Advertiser*, 10 January 1900, p. 5; TNA, PRO, WO 32/7870, Hughes-Hallett to the Chief Staff Officer, 13 December 1899; and T. Pakenham, *The Boer War* (London: Weidenfeld & Nicolson, 1979), pp. 189, 203, 205.

46 'The Magersfontein Battle', *Aberdeen Journal*, 13 January 1900, p. 6; 'A Crieff Soldier's Opinion of the Boers', *Strathearn Herald*, 3 March 1900, p. 2; see also 'The Modder River Battle', *Fife News*, 20 January 1900, p. 3.

47 BWRA 0196, Captain C. E. Stewart, diary, 7 January 1900.

48 'A Colour-Sergeant of the Black Watch on the Battle', p. 6; 'Letter from a Baillieston Man', *Hamilton Advertiser*, 27 January 1900, p. 3; 'Kilmarnock Soldiers at the Front', *Kilmarnock Standard*, 24 February 1900, p. 3; 'The Decimation of the Highland Brigade', *Western Morning News*, 11 January 1900, p. 8; 'The "Death Trap" at Magersfontein', *Perthshire Advertiser*, 10 January 1900, p. 5.

49 'The Wauchope Methuen Reports' and 'The True Version of General Wauchope's Notable Utterance at Magersfontein', *Fife Herald*, 24 January 1900, p. 3; see also *Ross-shire Journal*, 12 January 1900, p. 4.

50 'Magersfontein', *The Times*, 11 January 1900, p. 2, reprinted in the *Scotsman*, 12 January 1900, p. 6.

51 'The Order to Retire' and 'Written on the Battlefield', *Glasgow Evening News*, 9 and 11 January 1900, pp. 2 and 5; 'A Tain Man at the Front', *Invergordon Times*, 7 February 1900, p. 2; 'Soldiers' Accounts of Magersfontein', *Glasgow Herald*, 10 January 1900, p. 9.

52 NAM, Acc. No. 1973-10-85, Bly, diary, 14 December 1899; BWRA, 0186, Cameron Mss, Cameron to his mother, 25 December 1899.

53 'Written on the Battlefield', p. 5; 'Kilmarnock Soldiers at the Front', *Kilmarnock Standard*, 24 February 1900, p. 3; 'Stirling Soldiers' Impressions of Campaign', *Bridge of Allan Reporter*, 13 January 1900, p. 5; 'Mutinous Spirit in Highland Brigade', *John O'Groat Journal*, 19 January 1900, p. 2.

54 'A Perth Soldier's Experience at Magersfontein', *Perthshire Advertiser*, 17 January 1900, p. 4; 'The Order to Retire', p. 2; NAM, Acc. No. 1971-01-23-177-1, Roberts Mss, Lord Roberts to Lord Lansdowne, 30 January 1900.

55 Wiltshire and Swindon Record Office, Methuen Mss, Lord Methuen to his wife, 4 February 1900.

56 'All Eyes on "Fighting Mac" ', *Ross-shire Journal*, 26 January 1900, p. 6.

57 'The Local Pulpit and the War', *Supplement to Perthshire Advertiser*, 20 December 1899.

58 'The Pulpit and the War', *Ross-shire Journal*, 26 January 1900, p. 6; 'Rev. Dr. Bannerman and the War', *Perthshire Advertiser*, 8 January 1900, p. 3.

59 'Sir H. C. Bannerman in Aberdeen', *Aberdeen Journal*, 20 December 1899, p. 6.

60 NAM, Acc. No. 1972-08-8, Paterson Mss, Corporal J. Paterson to Tom, 28 February 1900; see also 'Borderers for the Front', *Galashiels Telegraph*, 30 January 1900, p. 3; 'The Argyll and Sutherland Highlanders Volunteer Company. Departure for the Front – Enthusiastic Send-off', *Falkirk Herald*, 17 February 1900, p. 5; '3rd. V.B. Seaforths' and 'The Grantown Volunteers for the Front', *Elgin Courant*, 19 January and 9 February 1900, pp. 3 and 3.

61 BWRA, 0186, Cameron Mss, Cameron to Nellie, 16 January 1900.

62 'A Nairn Man at Magersfontein', *Elgin Courant*, 16 February 1900, p. 3; see also 'Soldiers' Letters', *Manchester Evening Chronicle*, 15 February 1900, p. 3; 'A Salford Highlander's Picture of the Magersfontein Fight', *Manchester Evening News*, 25 January 1900, p. 5; 'A Soldier's Letter from Modder River', *Edinburgh Evening News*, 15 February 1900, p. 4;

The Highlanders' Museum (THM), Williamson TS Mss, Private A. Williamson to Nell, 15 January 1900.

63 'An Indignant Gordon', *Edinburgh Evening News*, 17 February 1900, p. 4; 'A Gordon Colour-Sergeant's Letters', *Edinburgh Evening News*, 25 January 1900, p. 4; 'A Gordon Highlander's Version of the Battle of Magersfontein', p. 5.

64 'Highland Regiments', *Ross-shire Journal*, 2 March 1900, p. 4.

65 On Paardeberg, 'A Graphic Narrative', *Manchester Evening Chronicle*, 12 April 1900, p. 3; 'Hard Times in the Free State' and 'A Gordon on the Capture of Cronje', *Manchester Evening News*, 28 March 1900, p. 5, and 19 April 1905, p. 5; on Ladysmith, 'Letters from Ladysmith', *Strathearn Herald*, 21 April 1900, p. 3; 'Letters from the Front', *Highland News*, 21 April 1900, p. 6; 'Letter from the Front', *Ayr Advertiser*, 16 August 1900, p. 4; Greenhill Gardyne, *Life of a Regiment*, vol. 3, p. 72 and appendix 24.

66 'The Battle of Magersfontein: Gordons Covering the Retreat of the Highland Brigade', *Illustrated London News*, 13 January 1900, p. 37; advertisement for vi-cocoa, *Daily News*, 23 January 1900, p. 10; 'West Australian Sergeant's Impression', *Manchester Evening Chronicle*, 29 March 1900, p. 3; 'Letter from the Front', *Somerset Standard*, 31 August 1900, p. 7.

67 E. N. Bennett, *With Methuen's Column on an Ambulance Train* (London: Swan Sonnenschein, 1900), pp. 58–9.

68 Spiers, 'Army organisation and society in the nineteenth century' and D. Fitzpatrick, 'Militarism in Ireland, 1900–1922', in Bartlett and Jeffery (eds), *A Military History of Ireland*, pp. 335–57, 493–6 and pp. 379–406, 498–502; D. P. McCracken, *MacBride's Brigade: Irish Commandos in the Anglo-Boer War* (Dublin: Four Courts Press, 1999).

69 L. Senelick, 'Politics as Entertainment: Victorian Music-Hall Songs', *Victorian Studies*, 19 (1975), pp. 149–80; Russell, *Popular music in England*, p. 149; Richards, *Imperialism and music*, p. 331.

70 A. E. C. Bredin, *A History of the Irish Soldier* (Belfast: Century Books, 1987), p. 377.

71 K. Jeffery, 'The Irish Soldier in the Boer War', in Gooch (ed.), *The Boer War*, pp. 141–51, 271–3.

72 'The Kilt for Irish Soldiers', *North British Daily Mail*, 21 April 1900, p. 4; 'The Fighting Scots and Irish', *People's Friend*, 28 April 1900, p. 2.

73 *Edinburgh Evening News*, 2 March 1900, p. 2; 'Linesman', *Words by an Eyewitness* (Edinburgh: Blackwood, 1902), p. 142.

74 'What the Scots Greys have been doing', *Edinburgh Evening News*, 12 April 1900, p. 4; 'Scotland Aye to the Front', *Fife Herald*, 18 April 1900, p. 2; letter from Sergeant-Major T. M. Ross in *Elgin Courant*, 20 April 1900, p. 5; Pakenham, *The Boer War*, pp. 327–8.

75 'The Relief of Ladysmith', *Aberdeen Journal*, 4 April 1900, p. 6; see also 'A Marple Man at the Tugela Disaster', *Manchester Evening News*, 25 January 1900, p. 5, and 'A Perth Man in the Ladysmith Relief Column', *Strathearn Herald*, 3 March 1900, p. 2.

76 'The Brigade Cut Down to Half', *Ross-shire Journal*, 30 March 1900, p. 6.

77 Price, *An Imperial War*, ch. 4 and pp. 133, 241; for a critique of this thesis, see M. D. Blanch, 'British Society and the War', in P. Warwick (ed.), *The South African War: The Anglo-Boer War 1899–1902* (London: Longman, 1980), pp. 210–38.

78 *Aberdeen Journal*, 2 March 1900, p. 6; *Glasgow Herald*, 2 March 1900, p. 9; *Dumfries and Galloway Courier*, 3 March 1900, p. 4; *North British Daily Mail*, 2 March 1900, p. 2.

79 *Fife Herald*, 7 March 1900, p. 6.

80 *Elgin Courant*, 2 March 1900, p. 5; *Aberdeen Journal*, 2 March 1900, p. 6.

81 *Dundee Courier & Argus*, 9 March 1900, p. 6; see also Price, *An Imperial War and the British Working Class*, pp. 150–1; Brown, ' "Echoes of Midlothian", Scottish Liberalism and the South African War', pp. 168–9; *Edinburgh Evening News*, 8 March 1900, p. 2.

82 *North British Daily Mail*, 13 April 1900, p. 4.

83 'A Son of Huntly at Bloemfontein', *Huntly Express*, 27 April 1900, p. 6.

84 'Hardships of the Campaign', *Glasgow Evening News*, 14 April 1900, p. 2; see also THM, Williamson Mss, Williamson to Nell, 20 February and 25 March 1900, and ASHM, N-D1.NOB, Corporal J. H. Noble, diary, 14 March 1900.

85 THM, Williamson Mss, Williamson to Nell, 10 April 1900.

86 'Letters from the Front', *Aberdeen Journal*, 3 April 1900, p. 6.

87 'Twixt Veldt and Kopje', *Inverness Courier*, 22 May 1900, p. 3.

88 *Highland News*, 26 May 1900, p. 6; *Ayr Observer*, 22 May 1900, p. 5; and T. Jeal, *Baden-Powell* (London: Hutchinson, 1989), pp. 277–85, 303–4.

89 *Kilmarnock Standard*, 26 May 1900, p. 4.

90 *Aberdeen Journal*, 21 May 1900, pp. 5–6.

91 Compare *Glasgow Herald*, 6 June 1900, p. 8, and 'Rejoicings', *Dundee Advertiser*, 6 June 1900, p. 6, with I. G. C. Hutchison, 'Glasgow's Working-Class Politics', in R. A. Cage (ed.), *The Working Class in Glasgow 1750–1914* (London: Croom Helm, 1987), pp. 98–141, especially p. 126.

92 *Elgin Courant*, 8 June 1900, p. 7; *Dunfermline Journal*, 9 June 1900, p. 5; see also J. Stone and E. Schmidl, *The Boer War and Military Reforms* (Lanham, MD: University Press of America, 1988), p. 25.

93 *Aberdeen Journal*, 5 June 1900, p. 6.

9

CITIZEN SOLDIERS IN AN IMPERIAL WAR

⌒

The celebrations that convulsed Scotland after the capture of Pretoria found reflection in South Africa, where the Ayrshire Yeomanry, as Corporal John Paterson described, 'were all in high spirits at the prospect of soon getting home again'.[1] Even without a formal Boer surrender, the optimism seemed infectious: 'The Boers', claimed Private George C. Fraser (Royal Scots Mounted Infantry), 'are now seeing the errors of their ways' and, after a period of desultory skirmishing, a Gordon Highlander wrote from Komati Poort, that 'the Transvaal is evidently settling down to the new order of things'.[2] When these hopes began to wane with the onset of guerrilla warfare, reporting from the front declined significantly but the role of the citizen soldiers still consumed attention. Scots felt intensely proud of the men from their own localities who had volunteered to serve in the war. As Provost Macrae explained to the first draft of Seaforth Volunteers on their return to Dingwall,

> Ever since you landed in South Africa we daily scanned the war news in our newspapers to learn of your movements . . . We felt depressed by [your] very severe hardships and the very severe privations . . . We felt elated at the stamina, the powers of endurance you exhibited . . . [and] at the bravery and gallantry you ever displayed. You have, indeed, proved that you are worthy successors of . . . the saviours of our Indian Empire, the bravest of the brave.[3]

Although the war proved unexpectedly protracted and increasingly controversial, Scottish newspapers, irrespective of their political sympathies, sustained this interest in the citizen soldier. They printed portraits of the men, reported on their travels and service experience, reproduced their letters and diaries, and chronicled the celebrations whenever they returned. Even the rabidly pro-Boer *Edinburgh Evening News* emulated the Unionist *Scotsman* in covering the active service of citizen soldiers from Edinburgh and the Lothians.[4]

In seeking Volunteers for active service, the War Office required that the men should be not under twenty years or over thirty-five, first-class (Volunteer) shots, efficient in the years 1898 and 1899, of good character, medically fit and, by preference, unmarried. They were to be paid, rationed, clothed and equipped like regular soldiers, but on completion of their term of service would be granted a bounty of £5 as a gratuity. Scots responded fully to the first two calls for Volunteers in 1900 and 1901, but not so enthusiastically in 1902 (when only 2,413 men responded across Britain to the call for 10,500 Volunteers).[5] Yet the precise number of Volunteers remains difficult to determine as so many left their corps to enlist in the regular army, the Militia, Imperial Yeomanry or the colonial forces. In his official history of the Scottish Volunteers, Major-General J. M. Grierson reckoned that the men serving in South Africa, including the London and Liverpool Scottish, numbered at least 5,000, or about 10 per cent of the enrolled force.[6]

They responded to the wave of patriotic fervour for various reasons. It was 'clearly my duty', reflected Jack Gilmour, a staunch Unionist who served with the Fife and Forfar Imperial Yeomanry; others, in the opinion of Thomas Dewar (Ayrshire Yeomanry), enrolled to seek their livelihood or foreign adventure or escape from some mishap at home, with about half of his company having 'a blend of motives, in which patriotism, ambition, and love of adventure had each a share'. [7] Many volunteered with their mates, reflecting the profound sense of local involvement; William Home (a KOSB Volunteer) asserted that 'nowhere was this patriotic spirit more apparent than in the Borderland'.[8] These motives doubtless fluctuated in scope and intensity over time; improved rates of pay attracted recruits for the second and third contingents of Imperial Yeomanry (and, at five shillings a day, induced the transfer of many Volunteers), while fear of unemployment, as Richard Price claims, may have stimulated the surge of recruitment from the Fife coal field in February 1902 (although this motive hardly proves that the miners lacked any patriotic impulse).[9] Local factors often distorted the process: whereas 245 members of the Inverness Volunteers served in the war, primarily with the 1st Camerons and the Lovat Scouts, reportedly 'the highest proportion . . . of any battalion in Scotland', the Inverness Militia refused to serve overseas. It was only one of four Militia battalions out of seventy-two to do so (the other three were Irish), a reflection allegedly of the unpopularity of the unit's commanding officer, Colonel The Mackintosh of Mackintosh, and of the high proportion of fishermen in the ranks.[10]

Those citizen soldiers who left Scotland in 1900 soon earned largely positive reports from the front despite encountering some scepticism at first. Captain Cameron, on meeting 266 Militia Reservists for the Black Watch, admitted that he would be 'very glad to get them away from the temptations of Capetown', but, within a week of their arrival at the training camp, conceded that 'they are doing excellently and getting back to their old soldiery ways very quickly'.[11] As several Scottish regular units were severely depleted, they generally welcomed the assistance of auxiliary forces once the latter were trained in South African conditions. Captain C. E. Stewart (Black Watch) praised the support proffered by mounted Yeomanry and Sergeant William Hamilton (HLI), like many others, commended the scouts raised by Lord Lovat, who 'proved themselves to be the most daring and efficient scouts that had yet been attached to the Highland Brigade'. [12]

The auxiliaries discharged a wide range of duties, including garrison duty, manning convoys and protecting lines of communication – 'a very needful job', wrote Corporal Paterson, 'but not exactly what we expected. It is a job you get plenty of work at and very little honour and glory.'[13] Undertaking such support tasks, added Colour-Sergeant Hector Gray (Royal Scots Volunteers), meant that they were not 'fortunate enough to get into a respectable fight'.[14]Some were more fortunate, with the Gordon Volunteers serving in the second line at the battle of Doornkop (29 May 1900) and the Ayrshire Yeomanry completing a daring night march, in appalling conditions, to relieve Potchefstroom and receive an ecstatic welcome from the British inhabitants.[15] Serving in the front-line columns meant that the auxiliaries experienced all the privations of regular soldiers on 'extremely wearisome' marches amid 'choking dust' and under a 'scorching sun', enduring extremes of temperature (with bitterly cold nights) and scant provisions (sometimes a daily allowance of four biscuits, a tin of bully beef and tea with sugar). It was even worse, wrote Dr Findlay, when the columns crossed miles of burned grassland, especially into the wind: 'You might as well be in a coal pit, or on board a steamer taking in coals. It is awful, and the eyes smart terribly.'[16] Occasionally they occupied small Boer towns, like Heilbron, finding themselves isolated and with little to do for several weeks; sometimes they skirmished with parties of Boers. At Spitz Kop, wrote Chaplain Robert McClelland, 'The Cameron Volunteers particularly distinguished themselves, advancing at the double up the face of almost inaccessible cliffs.'[17] They were involved, too, in the 'very distressing' work of burning Boer farms and removing or destroying their livestock.[18]

Yet these operations, particularly those involved in hunting mobile commandos under Christiaan de Wet and the other Boer commanders, were becoming immensely frustrating. Repeatedly de Wet eluded capture (notably at Brandwater Basin (30 July 1900), where General Martinus Prinsloo surrendered with 2,000 men) and counterattacked. De Wet's brother, Piet, forced the surrender of the Irish Yeomanry at Lindley, Christiaan captured a convoy bound for the Highland Brigade, and Boer commandos regularly destroyed parts of the railway. By the summer and autumn of 1900, Scottish infantry were complaining about the 'sickening work' of trekking after de Wet, while mounted forces on inferior horses found the task 'very trying', and readily applauded 'the marvellous energies and skilful tactics of Christian De Wet'.[19] By 29 October 1900 the Ayrshire Yeomanry had covered some 2,210 miles on horseback and travelled 750 miles by rail. It retained only two of its original 106 horses and could only muster between forty and fifty men in an engagement with de Wet's forces on 27 October, where they captured a gun and harried the retreating convoy. Yet the rivalry between the Yeomanry units remained intense, as Sergeant Brownlie wryly observed: 'the Glasgow Company started with us [on the 27th] but did not finish with us. Nothing unusual.'[20]

None of these reports portended a decisive encounter battle nor even the likelihood of another reverse on the scale of Magersfontein. Despite all its trekking, the Highland Brigade earned an unenviable reputation for 'misfortunes' after the failure to trap de Wet at Brandwater Basin, or, as part of the 9th Division, to relieve the Irish Yeomanry at Lindley. A company of Highlanders (152 men) also lost the convoy of fifty-seven wagons ambushed by de Wet en route to Heilbron (4 June 1900). The *Dundee Courier* summarised the loss by claiming that 'the Highlanders made a hopeless resistance, and had to surrender', a view fiercely resented by the men involved although they could not dispute the capitulation.[21] Some complained, too, about Macdonald as a commanding officer, disparaging his partiality for the Gordons (whom he inserted into the Brigade at the expense of the HLI), his desire that the men should wear distinguishing tartan patches (only to be shot himself when doing so), his limited intellectual powers, and his disciplinary zeal as a former NCO. Lance-Corporal James Thomson (Lanarkshire Yeomanry) asserted that he was the 'most hated officer' in South Africa.[22] None of these complaints, though, approached the crescendo of criticism over Methuen, and Dewar, in scanning the newspapers and magazines that reached him in late September 1900, observed correctly 'that the British public is losing interest in the war. This is very natural', he added, as 'we who are on the spot are tending to do the same'.[23]

Much of this correspondence overlapped with the general election in Britain (September–October 1900), where the Conservatives entered the contest with a majority of 130 seats (having lost several by-elections since 1895) but defied any 'swing of the pendulum' to win another landslide victory with a majority of 134 seats. Having fought the 'khaki' election primarily on the war, the Conservatives and Liberal Unionists had every reason to be pleased with the outcome in Scotland where they gained seven seats overall, becoming the largest party for the first time since before the Reform Act of 1832. Even more significantly, the Liberals lost their last two seats in Glasgow, giving all seven to the Unionists, and won only six of the twenty-nine county and burgh seats in the west of Scotland. 'Scotland', admitted Campbell-Bannerman, 'has not done nearly so well as we hoped', but he was loathe to admit that the imperial war had had an effect. He attributed the debacle, including the scything of his own majority, to the defection of some Irish Catholics over education issues: 'There were of course a few influenced by the war, but not many.'[24] In another letter he blamed the 'wretched result in Scotland' upon 'our own factions, which have taken some of the heart out of us'.[25] Several scholars have amplified these points, casting doubt on the salience of the war and emphasising the electoral impact of divisions within the Liberal party, Unionist legislation on social reform and the significance of local issues in specific constituencies. In giving 'the lie to the belief that 1900 was a "khaki" election dominated by patriotic concern', Price emphasises that there was a low turn-out (albeit on a relatively old register) and that many pro-Boers held their seats. Of the sixteen Scottish pro-Boer MPs, two withdrew, five lost their seats and one more was elected, leaving ten in Scotland. Discounting losses in marginal Liberal constituencies, he claims that Aberdeenshire East and Sutherlandshire 'were the only seats which the Conservatives captured solely as a result of the war'.[26]

Undoubtedly local issues played their part in this election and some pro-Boers, like many Liberal Imperialists, retained their seats comfortably (Scotland began and ended the election with twelve Liberal Imperialist MPs). Moreover, the swing against the Liberals in Scotland was less than 2 per cent, leaving them with a bare majority of the popular vote (50.2 per cent). Nevertheless, the Liberals found it disastrous to contest an election against the backdrop of an imperial war; it was not merely that jingoism was rampant on the Clyde (where the war expenditure was welcomed), and the Orange vote backed the Unionists,[27] but also that the Liberal dissension derived from their divisions and hapless leadership during the war. Irrespective of how people voted, the war had undermined the Liberal party before the election began. Many Liberals failed to understand how the war had such strong support in parts of Scotland and how the 'new' imperialism appealed across both parties. Liberals failed to attract strong candidates in several seats, or any in three (part of the 143 Unionist seats uncontested in this election compared with 109 in 1895), and the splits within the party (the pro-Boer, Dr G. B. Clark lost his Caithness seat to a Liberal Imperialist), were all symptoms of the party's malaise: as Munro-Ferguson, the party's Scottish whip, bemoaned, 'The west went to pieces partly for the want of outstanding men . . .' [28] The war had disrupted politics in Scotland far more than south of the border, and the traditional Liberal slogans of peace, retrenchment and reform had limited appeal at a time when Scots were fighting a war. As John F. McCaffrey argues, 'This fusion of Scottish pride within a British sense of identity made Liberal particularism and squabbling seem parochial and petty.'[29]

However, the electoral success of the government was not being matched by military achievements in South Africa. To the dismay of the Highlanders, the Highland Brigade was broken up into small detachments to protect the towns near Bloemfontein. As a Seaforth explained, his regiment now had two companies at Jagersfontein, two at Fauresmith, two at Phillipolis, two at Springfontein and one at Bloemfontein: 'So you can see how we are squandered.'[30] If the splitting up of regiments would become a recurrent complaint in future months,[31] so too would be the loss through sickness, disease and wounds. Home reported an 'appalling' amount of sickness among the troops during the first month of their arrival at Pretoria: 'men died like flies'. [32] By January 1901 Captain Gilmour reminded his mother that the Fife and Forfar Imperial Yeomanry had 'left Cupar as a fine body of men in health and in proficiency . . . Of the 116 men seventy-four are now away killed, died of disease, in Hospital out here or invalided home, or have got civil employment. The list of sick is a heavy one . . .'[33]

Nevertheless, after one year's campaigning, Scotland's war service was remarkable. Statistics published by the War Office revealed that

Scotland had 'a greater proportion of killed and wounded and a lower proportion of prisoners and deaths from disease' than any other national grouping in the imperial war effort. The Black Watch had the highest total of killed and wounded, while the 2nd Seaforth had lost the highest number of killed in action. Of the twenty-three Victoria Crosses awarded at this time, the Scots won six (including five by Gordon Highlanders).[34] Such sacrifices and achievements earned plaudits from commanders like Roberts and Buller, commending the 'unflinching bravery of the Highland Brigade at Magersfontein and Paardeberg'.[35] Even so, many soldiers admitted being 'fed up' with the war and wanted to go home: 'It is nearly a year since I left home', wrote a Seaforth Volunteer, 'but I would not put in such another year for £100.'[36] Yet this grumbling did not imply that Scots had become less hostile towards the enemy or less willing to engage in punitive action. The Reverend James Robertson, when chaplain to the Highland Brigade, was not alone in favouring the use of more draconian methods: 'I wish to make war, dreadful though it is, more dreadful . . . it is the only way to stop it'. [37] They believed that the policies of Lord Roberts, whereby burghers, if they laid down their arms and took the oath of neutrality, could return to their farms, were far too lenient (as many Boers, sometimes under pressure, rejoined the commando). Although Roberts introduced more punitive measures – collective fines (and cancelled receipts for requisitioned goods in districts where damage had been inflicted on the railway and telegraph lines), civilian travel on trains (virtually as hostages) and the seizure of supplies and livestock from districts that had risen in revolt again – Scots continued to criticise. 'The job would have been done months ago', insisted one Seaforth, 'if Roberts had cleared them out at first. I firmly believe that we would have been on our way home if this mob had not broken out.'[38] When Kitchener replaced Roberts, he sustained his policy but laid greater emphasis (in his proclamation of 7 December 1900) upon clearing the country of supplies and livestock to undermine the enemy's military operations.

How Liberals should respond to developments in the war worried Campbell-Bannerman. He warned Bryce that 'we must be very careful not to take any line which might seem to be anti British, for our countrymen, though sick at heart are all the more touchy and obstinate . . .'[39] This was timely advice in January 1901 as many parts of Scotland were now celebrating the return of their citizen soldiers with displays of local pride and patriotic fervour. Unlike previous imperial wars when regular units returned, if they did, after the conflict, and proceeded to march though garrison towns, past crowds used to military processions led by pipe bands and entered their barracks, the return of the Volunteers, whether in entire service companies, sections or as individuals, during the South African War was completely different. Units did not merely march to depots past crowded streets and displays of flags and bunting, but they also dispersed in sections or smaller groups back to their own communities, so that the scenes of welcome, patriotic celebrations and rousing speeches rippled across the country. The recurrence of such scenes all across Scotland sustained the passions evoked by the war in a way that had never been possible in previous imperial conflicts.

For example, when the KOSB Volunteers returned to the regimental depot in Berwick in December 1900, the first to depart were the Dumfries and Galloway section, then the Roxburgh and Selkirk men, later the Berwickshire men and finally sections to the principal Border towns. At Galashiels six soldiers were greeted by civic officials and paraded through the town in a torchlight procession past huge crowds and illuminated buildings, with the town's band playing 'Braw, Braw Lads'. The provost and the minister of Galashiels Parish Church delivered stirring speeches, applauding the self-sacrifice of the men, defending the 'very severe measures' employed in the war and excoriating the pro-Boers for encouraging the enemy to prolong the hostilities.[40]

Similar scenes greeted returning Volunteers, Yeomen and time-expired regulars all over Scotland. Frequently the receptions attracted vast crowds (reportedly 'many thousands' at Musselburgh to greet six returning Volunteers).[41] They were followed by civic luncheons, church services and subsequently ceremonies, often graced by lord lieutenants and county elites, to present the returning soldiers with medals and gratuities, sometimes with the freedom of their local burghs. As the Reverend Dr Nimmo Smith assured the officers and men of the 7th Royal Scots, 'especially have we been interested in our own townsmen, and those of our community and county . . .'[42] The local press, clergymen and civic dignitaries waxed eloquently on 'the wave of patriotism which has brought all ranks and orders together, and bound them as in a bond of brotherhood', and, more specifically, on a response which had helped to 'maintain the Empire'. The 'home and colonial Volunteers', claimed the Reverend Dr MacGregor, 'had not only united but saved the Empire'.[43]

The military services of the Volunteers were recognised too. Local provosts praised their Volunteers for enduring the dangers, hardships and privations of war, and claimed that they had now eroded the

Figure 9 Trooper J. R. P. Haig mounted, of the Fife and Forfar Yeomanry, South Africa c. 1900 *(William Skeoch Cumming, reproduced by permission of the National Museums of Scotland)*

former distinctions between the regular and auxiliary forces. In addressing the Fife and Forfar Imperial Yeomanry, who had trekked for 2,573 miles and engaged the enemy on eighty-five occasions, Provost Watson of Cupar asserted that the 'reserve forces' could now be regarded as 'the backbone of the nation'. [44] Captain Millar (Black Watch Volunteers) was equally ready to acknowledge how much the 'citizen soldier' had learned from seeing the comradeship and self-sacrifice of the regular soldier in the field.[45] Yet no aspect of a citizen soldier's service was regarded with greater affection than the act of volunteering itself, particularly in the wake of Magersfontein. Provost Keith assured the returning 4th Battalion, Cameronians, that the townsfolk of Hamilton

> remembered well that the battalion did not go out on active service at the beginning of the war, when the general impression was it would be a military procession, but that they had rendered their service at a time when everyone knew the war was no light matter. They were in the strictest sense of the word, Volunteers . . .[46]

Similarly, at Inverness, Provost Macbean greeted the Service Company of the 1st Volunteer Battalion, Cameron Highlanders, by recalling that they had 'volunteered for the front when the military situation was critical, when the fortunes of war seemed to be against this country and when the world stood wondering what was to be the final issue of the great sanguinary struggle. It spoke well for their patriotism . . .'[47] Characteristically the Lovat Scouts received a distinctive and warm welcome in Inverness, where tributes were paid to the 'power of the Highland chief . . . [to] touch a chord in the Celtic heart at the call of duty'.[48]

If this rhetoric reinforced the patriotic message and the support at local and county levels for an imperial war, its impact was magnified by the sense of occasion that these events aroused and by the outpouring of local enthusiasm. The receptions and the hearty send-offs for the second wave of Volunteers, which often followed formal civic functions and attracted vast crowds (far beyond immediate families and friends),[49] testified to the support for the citizen soldier and the appreciation of his services. The sense of personal sacrifice in a great imperial cause was reinforced by the widely reported eulogies at some of the earliest memorials erected to the war dead. At the unveiling of the granite cross at Niddre, the first Wauchope memorial, in May 1901, Dr Norman MacLeod maintained that 'General Wauchope died where he would have wished to die . . . at the head of his Highland Brigade'. Two months later, at the dedication of the Alyth War Memorial (an Egyptian obelisk standing twenty-three feet high in honour of the late Earl of Airlie, Nigel Neis Ramsay of Banff and Charles Wedderburn Ogilvy of Ruthven), Lord Breadalbane paid tribute to the regular and Volunteer soldiers who had come forward 'to uphold the dignity of the Empire'.[50]

Scots realised that their military service was highly valued, not least by the War Office desperate to replenish the ranks of the mounted infantry. It was now willing to pay the second contingent of Imperial Yeomanry at colonial rates of pay (five shillings a day), and accept men without the two to three months' training in Britain undertaken by the first contingent. Many of these untrained recruits arrived in South Africa unable to ride, shoot or care for their horses, and earned widespread criticism from regulars at the front (hence the insistence upon three months' preliminary instruction for the third contingent). The Scottish Horse was an exception. Conceived as an idea by its future commanding officer, the Marquis of Tullibardine, and appro-ved by Kitchener in December 1900, the nucleus consisted of Scots who were resident in South Africa. Within a month the marquis had raised, equipped and taught to ride and shoot 500 men, 'but it was not play', he informed his father, the Duke of Atholl. He raised further squadrons of scouts and cyclists in South Africa and sought support from Caledonian societies in Australia and London, as well as from contingents raised in Scotland by his father. So popular was the notion of Scots from across the empire serving together that the corps eventually consisted of two regiments, numbering 3,252 NCOs and men, of whom 1,250 enlisted in Britain. The Scottish Horse earned an excellent reputation for its gallantry and tenacity in several hard-fought engagements, losing thirty-nine officers killed or wounded and 237 men in its first year (of whom only one officer and twenty-two men were taken prisoner). The success of this unique imperial volun-tary unit based on the 'spirit of Scottish nationality' persuaded the marquis to advocate its retention after the war.[51]

In the interim, Scots persevered in fruitless de Wet hunts and the destruction of Boer farmsteads. The harrying of the various com-mandos remained immensely frustrating. In January 1901 Trooper John J. Macmorland (Ayrshire Yeomanry) conceded that 'the whole Company is awfully sick of this harassing and trekking'. [52] Yet Sergeant William McLanachan maintained that the Ayrshire company was 'pretty well up to this sort of game now, and will hold their own with any in the service'. [53] Sergeant J. Easton (Royal Scots Mounted Infantry) agreed; he observed that by April 1901, the 'Scottish Yeomanry . . . have been continually on the trek after De Wet this last six months, with never a single day's rest. They have a splendid way of working, and seem to be better disciplined than the majority.'[54] In addition, Scots were engaged in the burning of farms, the destruction of crops and livestock, and the rounding up of Boer families. Many soldiers found this work distasteful but recognised its utility: slaughtering hundreds of cattle, sheep and goats, noted

William Grant (Ayrshire Yeomanry), was 'horrible work' but it kept them 'from falling into the hands of the Boers'; similarly, Sergeant William Hamilton (HLI) claimed that 'One thing in our favour is the clearing off the people. This move has destroyed their principal means of intelligence.'[55]

Lord Roberts had complemented this policy by establishing concentration camps to protect the surrendered burghers and accommodate the displaced families. By March 1901 there were twenty-seven camps; by September 1901 they held about 110,000 white inmates and some 65,000 blacks. Although conditions varied from camp to camp, diseases such as pneumonia, measles, dysentery and enteric fever swept through the camps, with the death toll in the burgher camps rising from 250 in the first three months of 1901 to 395 in April, 2,666 in August and 3,205 in October 1901. When Emily Hobhouse, the humanitarian and pacifist, produced reports on the camps, describing the risks to inmates, including children under sixteen years of age, she caused outrage among the pro-Boers in Britain. On 14 June 1901 Campbell-Bannerman joined the protests, asking 'When is war not a war? When it is carried on by methods of barbarism in South Africa.'[56]

The Unionist press was horrified. 'Sir Henry Campbell-Bannerman', claimed the *Scotsman*, 'has become rabid' and the Liberal leader was forced to clarify his speech in the House of Commons and later in Southampton, asserting that the 'system' was barbarous and not the officers or the men. He insisted that no one felt 'that barbarity more than the unfortunate men whose duty it is to enforce that system'.[57] This failed to mollify many Scottish Liberals (only seventeen out of thirty-four supported him in the Commons), let alone the Unionists, who later seized upon official reports on the camps chronicling the insanitary habits, the prejudices of many Boer mothers and their reluctance to heed medical advice (which had contributed to the spread of disease, although the families had never lived in such numbers and in close proximity to each other before).[58]

Irrespective of their own views on the war, many Scottish soldiers deprecated the expression of pro-Boer opinions in Britain, a resentment that festered throughout the war. The Reverend C. E. Greenfield, acting chaplain with the Scots Greys, denounced the 'humane' policy as 'the more bloody, the more expensive and the more breaking to the enemy. I am convinced that the longer the Boer resists, the more utterly will he be ruined. There is blood on the hands of the sentimental politician.'[59] Lieutenant-Colonel Hamilton-Campbell

(Ayrshire Yeomanry), speaking at his reception after being invalided home, deplored anyone who accused 'our soldiers of committing barbarities in South Africa'. [60] Some defended the camps: a Gordon Highlander insisted that many Boers were being 'treated as well, if not better, than Tommy Atkins', while a Ross-shire soldier claimed that the Boer families were 'very much better attended to than our men in the field and probably better than many of our men's wives at home'.[61] Many simply deplored the pro-Boers for giving encouragement to the enemy and thereby prolonging the hostilities: as Sergeant Hamilton (HLI) asserted, 'We have to thank a few people at home for the war being continued so long.'[62]

Several soldiers denounced the pro-Boers for their blinkered perspectives and their reluctance to acknowledge Boer atrocities. Trooper William McKenzie, like many others, castigated the use of explosive bullets by the Boers; Private Skinner (KOSB) testified to the Boers shooting and clubbing British wounded on the ground at Vlakfontein (29 May 1901), and numerous Scots protested about the murder of black scouts. A Black Watch soldier even claimed, 'We have freed the natives – i.e., Basutos and Kaffirs – from a state of almost slavery.'[63] The role of blacks had remained a peculiarly sensitive issue throughout a supposedly 'white man's' war: as Sergeant McLanachan recognised, 'The blacks play a very prominent part on both sides as scouts and carrying the news. They do it for us for gold. They do it for the Boers for the sjambok (as their backs show by marks).'[64] Corporal J. Henderson (Galloway Rifles) perceived a deeper bond of affection for the British, depicting the blacks as

> wonderfully quick, active, and obliging, being gifted with marvellous powers of endurance. . . . They seem to stand in awe of us, for we can make them do anything we want, and that without being abusive, and they are respectfulness personified, calling us Boss, Massa, Sir, etc., and doffing their hats or saluting us when passing. [65]

During the Yeomanry's encampment at Stellenbosch, the relations were so cordial, wrote Corporal Paterson, that patrols were sent out every night 'to keep the soldiers from speaking to the black ladies for fear it should lower "the dignity of the British soldier in the eyes of the Dutch" '.[66] Scots appreciated that the blacks provided more direct military support, too, whether in driving bullock-drawn wagons across country, labouring, carrying messages, or serving as scouts and sometimes providing armed assistance. In expressing their outrage whenever they saw the corpses of captured black scouts,[67] Scottish soldiers were addressing another dimension of the conflict and one that received rather less attention at home.

Although the native assistance was extremely helpful, the systematic tactics of Kitchener proved decisive in bringing the Boers to the peace negotiations at Vereeniging (preliminary discussions began in April 1902, with formal meetings in the following month). Kitchener had harried the enemy effectively by dividing the countryside into sectors, using some 3,700 miles of barbed wire guarded by 8,000 blockhouses, and thereupon swept the sectors with flying columns. Trooper J. MacKenzie (Lovat Scouts) described the new tactics:

> We have no waggons carrying our stores now, as in the earlier stages of the war . . . we carry all our stores on pack mules, which is much handier . . . in the mountains. When we shift from one place to another, we very often do it in the night time . . . very often we have to climb very high mountains . . . But although the work is a bit rough at times, I like it well enough.[68]

Fighting 'slim', as described by Trooper McNaught (Ayrshire Yeomanry), [69] had its advantages over fatigue duty at a time when most of Kitchener's forces were serving in garrisons, on lines of communication or in the small, isolated blockhouses. Blockhouse life, as described by Drummer A. Fraser (3rd Seaforth Volunteer Service Company), was dull and monotonous, if by no means idle with rounds of picquet duty and labouring in the trenches: 'We are getting quite experts with the pike [sic, probably pick] and shovel.' [70] In rear areas or garrisons, soldiers could enjoy hunting, sport and social events, although reports of the Stirlingshire Militia playing cricket while Boers were in the vicinity appalled the *Stirling Observer*. [71]

Nevertheless, in the spring of 1902, as the peace talks were underway, Scots assembled in their thousands to greet the returning Volunteers of the second contingent, even if some units had seen little fighting. The 2nd Volunteer Service Company, Cameronians, was described as 'none the worse of their hard work amidst the blockhouses and their 1,300 miles trek', while the 2nd Volunteer Service Company of the Argyll and Sutherland Highlanders was greeted in Stirling by Provost Thompson as 'the heralds of peace . . . [and] the forerunners of our returning victorious army'. As in 1901, sections then dispersed to rapturous receptions in Greenock, Dumbarton, Dunoon and Alexandria (but not in Paisley where the town had not been warned of their arrival and so the reception was strangely indifferent). [72]

When the 'momentous and most welcome news' of peace arrived in Scotland – on the Sabbath, so somewhat diluting the celebrations (although flags were flown, church bells rung and the National Anthem sung at the end of some evening services) – there was a huge sense of relief. Reports of the public response indicated that the patriotic demonstrations were less rapturous than two years' previously, but flags and bunting appeared in some localities, with processions led by pipe bands, and bonfires in which effigies of the Boer leaders were burned again.[73] Staunch supporters of the war welcomed the surrender and abolition of the Boer republics; the *Kilmarnock Standard* asserted that the price paid in 'blood and treasure' for 'the consolidation of our Empire in South Africa . . . [was] certainly not too much when we consider the momentous issues at stake . . .'[74] The *Glasgow Herald* commended the 'wise generosity' of the terms by which the burghers in exchange for an oath of allegiance could return to their homes with an amnesty, the repatriation of prisoners-of-war, promises of financial compensation and payment of Boer debts, equal standing of the two languages, Dutch and English, and no change in the franchise as regards blacks.[75] Some Liberal newspapers noted that these were not the terms that had often been 'spoken of on Unionist platforms', and that had the 'same wise policy' been displayed before the war 'millions of money and thousands of lives might have been saved'.[76]

Scots recognised that their citizen soldiers had contributed towards the outcome and greeted the returning Volunteers in vast numbers after the peace. [77] Throughout the conflict Scots applauded the act of volunteering, followed the wartime services of the Volunteers and revered the citizen soldiers as representatives of their own communities. Whereas the regular soldiers seemed to embody a national identity, whether using 'Scots' or 'Scottish' in their titles or in their readiness, especially if based in the Highlands, to recruit across Scotland as a whole (and find a proportion of men from England and Ireland), [78] the Volunteers had recruited locally and seemed more representative of specific communities or county areas. Irrespective of their personal motives, the citizen soldiers had enrolled (or volunteered to serve overseas in the case of the Militia) at a time of imperial crisis, thereby reinforcing the bonds between Scotland and the defence of the empire. In anticipating the peace settlement, Sir Robert Reid, the redoubtable pro-Boer MP for Dumfries burghs, reaffirmed his belief in the virtues of Gladstonian imperialism. Defending 'the greatness of the British Empire', he asserted that 'our work of colonisation had been a great gain to humanity . . . [and] our justice was incorruptible'. If this work was 'worthy of a great nation', he regretted nonetheless that the 'new' imperialism had produced 'unnecessary wars', and that its costs had thwarted social improvements at home.[79] Less apologetically, the *Perthshire Advertiser* extolled the response of 'the nation and the Empire' to the test of war, especially to the 'disasters and disappointments . . . in the early stages'. The challenge, it affirmed, had stiffened resolve and called 'into exercise the best qualities, as well as the brotherhood of race'. [80] In short, after a long and controversial war, imperialism aroused widely differing perspectives, values and emotions, and in some people doubtless shades of indifference or outright hostility, but the response of the citizen soldiers at a time of imperial crisis remained a source of pride in many Scottish communities. It added a further dimension to the role of the Scottish soldier in defending the empire.

Notes

1 NAM, Acc. No. 1972-08-8, Paterson Mss, Paterson to Tom, 6 June 1900.

2 'The Queen's Birthday at Bloemfontein', *Inverness Courier*, 6 July 1900, p. 5; 'The 1st and 2D Gordons fight side by side', *Edinburgh Evening News*, 12 November 1900, p. 2.

3 'Arrival at the Town Buildings', *Ross-shire Journal*, 3 May 1901, p. 5.

4 For example, *Edinburgh Evening News*, 16 January 1901, p. 4; 18 March 1901, p. 4; 6, 10 and 15 April 1901, pp. 6, 4 and 4; 25 May 1901, p. 2; *Scotsman*, 21 May 1900, p. 8; 5 June 1900, p. 6; 5 September 1900, p. 8; 17 January 1901, p. 8.

5 *Dundee Courier & Argus*, 21 January 1902, p. 6; *Scotsman*, 15 February 1902, p. 9; Grierson, *Records of the Scottish Volunteer Force*, pp. 92–4; J. K. Dunlop, *The Development of the British Army, 1899–1914* (London: Methuen, 1938), p. 103.

6 Grierson, *Records of the Scottish Volunteer Force*, p. 95.

7 P. Mileham (ed.), *Clearly My Duty: The Letters of Sir John Gilmour from the Boer War 1900–1901* (East Linton: Tuckwell Press, 1996), p. 6; Dewar, *With the Scottish Yeomanry*, pp. 28–9.

8 Lieutenant William Home, *With the Border Volunteers to Pretoria* (Hawick: W. & J. Kennedy, 1901), p. 2.

9 D. Judd and K. Surridge, *The Boer War* (London: John Murray, 2002), p. 74; Price, *An Imperial War*, pp. 215–16.

10 Fairrie, *'Cuidich 'N Righ'*, p. 55; 'The Inverness-shire Militia', *Highland News*, 8 March 1902, p. 4; Dunlop, *The Development of the British Army*, p. 90.

11 BWRA, 0186, Cameron Mss, Cameron to his father, 10 March 1900, and to Nellie, 18 March 1900.

12 'Letters from the Front', *Argyllshire Herald*, 20 October 1900, p. 3; BWRA, 196, Captain C. E. Stewart, diary, 16 June 1900; see also BWRA, 186, Cameron Mss, Cameron to Tina, 10 July 1900; M. L. Melville, *The Story of the Lovat Scouts 1900–1980* (Librario Publishing Ltd, 2004).

13 Home, *With the Border Volunteers*, p. 94; Dewar, *With the Scottish Yeomanry*, p. 44; NAM, Acc. No. 1972-08-8, Paterson Mss, Paterson to Tom, 27 April 1900.

14 'With the Royal Scots Service Company', *Haddingtonshire Advertiser*, 6 July 1900, p. 2.

15 Gordon-Duff, *With the Gordon Highlanders*, pp. 99–101; P. J. R. Mileham, *The Yeomanry Regiments: A Pictorial History* (Tunbridge Wells: Spellmount, 1985), p. 28; NAM, Acc. No. 1972-08-8, Paterson Mss, Paterson to Tom, 15 June 1900.

16 'Letters from the Front', *Kilmarnock Standard*, 4 August 1900, p. 5; see also 'Letter from Sergeant Cattanach, Volunteer Service Company, South Africa', *Bridge of Allan Reporter*, 28 July 1900, p. 2; 'With Lord Lovat's Scouts', *Nairnshire Telegraph*, 4 July 1900, p. 4; 'The Taking of Pretoria', *Stirling Observer*, 1 August 1900, p. 8.

17 'The Cameron Highlanders', *Inverness Courier*, 2 October 1900, p. 3; 'Letters from the Front', *Argyllshire Herald*, 4 August 1900, p. 3.

18 Dewar, *With the Scottish Yeomanry*, p. 68.

19 BWRA, 0186, Cameron Mss, Cameron to his father, 30 June 1900; 'The Marauding Boers', *Ross-shire Journal*, 30 November 1900, p. 8; 'A Letter from the Front' and 'Twixt Veldt and Kopje', *Inverness Courier*, 7 September and 9 November 1900, pp. 3 and 3; 'Letter from the Front', *Argyllshire Herald*, 29 September 1900, p. 3.

20 'The Ayrshire Yeomanry's Fight with de Wet', *Ayr Observer*, 7 December 1900, p. 3.

21 Compare 'The Highland Brigade', *Dundee Courier & Argus*, 26 June 1900, p. 4, with 'Private A. Hetherington', *Falkirk Herald*, 20 October 1900, p. 6. On Brandwater Basin, see A. Hunter, *Kitchener's Sword-Arm:The Life and Campaigns of General Sir Archibald Hunter* (Staplehurst: Spellmount, 1996), ch. 15.

22 'With the Highland Brigade', *Haddingtonshire Advertiser*, 19 October 1900, p. 2; see also BWRA, 0186, Cameron Mss, Cameron to Tina, 27 February 1900, to his mother, 4 March 1900, and to Nellie, 11 May 1900, and BWRA, 0396/2, Mowbray Berkeley Mss, Mowbray Berkeley to Maud, 16 February 1900.

23 Dewar, *With the Scottish Yeomanry*, p. 129.

24 BL, Add. Mss, 41,216, f. 22, Campbell-Bannerman Mss, Sir H. Campbell-Bannerman to H. Gladstone, 12 October 1900; see also

Blanch, 'British Society and the War', in Warwick (ed.), *The South African War*, p. 222; Brown, ' "Echoes of Midlothian" ', pp. 170–1.

25 BL, Add. Mss, 41,216, f. 27, Campbell-Bannerman Mss, Campbell-Bannerman to H. Gladstone, 22 October 1900.

26 Price, *An Imperial War*, pp. 97–9, 102–5, 110–11; see also Hutchison, *A Political History of Scotland*, pp. 177, 204, and 'The Triumph of Scottish Unionism in 1900', *Aberdeen Journal*, 4 March 1901, p. 5.

27 Hutchison, *A Political History of Scotland*, p. 176; McFarland, 'Outposts of the Loyalists of Ireland', in Macdonald (ed.), *Unionist Scotland 1800–1997*, p. 47; Brown, ' "Echoes of Midlothian" ', p. 171.

28 BL, Add. Mss, 41,222, f. 330, Campbell-Bannerman Mss, R. Munro-Ferguson to Campbell-Bannerman, 24 October 1900.

29 McCaffrey, *Scotland in the Nineteenth Century*, p. 106; see also Fry, *Patronage and Principle*, p. 117.

30 'A Soldier's War Story', *Edinburgh Evening News*, 19 December 1900, p. 2; see also 'Letter from the Front', *Argyllshire Herald*, 5 January 1901, p. 2, and 'The Highland Brigade Grievances', *Stirling Observer*, 8 September 1900, p. 8.

31 'Letter from the Front', *Argyllshire Herald*, 6 April 1901, p. 3; BWRA, 0127, Lieutenant C. W. E. Gordon, diary, 23 November 1901.

32 Home, *With the Border Volunteers*, pp. 100–1; see also 'Moffat Volunteer's Letter from the Front', *Dumfries and Galloway Courier*, 25 July 1900, p. 6; G. H. Smith, *With the Scottish Rifle Volunteers at the Front* (Glasgow: W. Hodge & Co., 1901), p. 12.

33 Mileham (ed.), *Clearly My Duty*, p. 115; see also 'Fife & Forfar Yeomanry in South Africa', *Fife Herald and Journal*, 10 April 1901, p. 4.

34 'Casualties in Scottish Regiments', *Aberdeen Journal*, 12 October 1900, p. 7.

35 'The Scotch Regiments', *Aberdeen Journal*, 26 January 1901, p. 7; see also 'Letters from the Front' and 'The Highland Regiments', *Aberdeen Journal*, 27 November 1900, p. 5, and 9 February 1901, p. 6.

36 'A Soldier's War Story', p. 2; 'Seaforth Volunteers Wanting Home', *Ross-shire Journal*, 22 March 1901, p. 5.

37 'Chaplain of the Highland Brigade on how to deal with the Boers', *Perthshire Constitutional and Journal*, 9 July 1900, p. 3.

38 'A Soldier's War Story', p. 2; see also 'Letters from the Front', *Falkirk Herald*, 20 October 1900, p. 6; E. M. Spiers, 'The British Army in South Africa: Military Government and Occupation, 1877–1914', in P. B. Boyden, A. J. Guy and M. Harding (eds), *ashes and blood: The British Army in South Africa 1795–1914* (London: National Army Museum, 1999), pp. 72–84.

39 BL, Add. Mss, 41, 211, f. 150, Campbell-Bannerman Mss, Campbell-Bannerman to Bryce, 18 January 1901.

40 'The Return of the Border Volunteers', *Galashiels Telegraph*, 4 December 1900, p. 3.

41 'Musselburgh's Welcome', *Scotsman*, 18 June 1901, p. 6; see also 'Welcome Home Volunteers', *Dumbarton Herald*, 22 May 1901, p. 5.

42 'The Home-Coming of the Volunteers', *Haddingtonshire Advertiser*, 24 May 1901, p. 2.

43 'The Montrave Welcome Home', *Fife Herald and Journal*, 31 July 1901, p. 4; 'Musselburgh's Welcome', p. 6; 'The Rev. Dr MacGregor on the War', *Scotsman*, 8 July 1901, p. 7; 'Presentation of War Medals at Dingwall', *Ross-shire Journal*, 18 October 1901, p. 6.

44 'The Yeomanry's Welcome Home', *Fife Herald and Journal*, 3 July 1901, p. 5; J. Sturrock, *The Fifes in South Africa* (Cupar: A. Westwood & Sons, 1903), pp. 191–7; see also 'The Black Watch Volunteers', *Scotsman*, 18 May 1901, p. 9, and 'The Volunteers and the War', *Stirling Observer*, 25 September 1901, p. 5.

45 'Captain Millar and the Black Watch', *Perthshire Advertiser*, 20 May 1901, p. 3; see also Sturrock, *The Fifes in South Africa*, p. 43.

46 'Return of the Hamilton Militia from South Africa', *Hamilton Advertiser*, 29 June 1901, p. 4.

47 'Home-Coming of Cameron Service Company', *Highland News*, 4 May 1901, p. 2.

48 'The Lovat Scouts', *Highland News*, 17 August 1901, p. 5.

49 'Departure of Ross-shire Volunteers for the Front', *Ross-shire Journal*, 15 February 1901, p. 8; 'The Lovat Scouts', *Highland News*, 15 June 1901, p. 4; 'Argyll and Sutherland Active Service Volunteer Company', *Stirling Observer*, 20 March 1901, p. 3; 'The Volunteers. Public Farewell', *Perthshire Advertiser*, 13 March 1901, p. 8.

50 'The Wauchope Memorial at Niddre' and 'Alyth War Memorial', *Scotsman*, 27 May 1901, p. 8, and 5 August 1901, p. 5.

51 PP, *Report of Her Majesty's Commissioners Appointed to Inquire into Military Preparations and other matters connected with the War in South Africa*, C 1789 (1904), XL, pp. 72–6; 'Stirling Men for the Scottish Horse', *Stirling Observer*, 8 January 1902, p. 5; 'The Scottish Horse', *Perthshire Advertiser*, 10 February 1902, p. 3.

52 'Letter from an Ayrshire Imperial Yeoman', *Ayr Observer*, 26 February 1901, p. 7.

53 'Ayrshire Yeomanry in South Africa', *Ayr Observer*, 15 February 1901, p. 3.

54 'Interesting Letter from South Africa', *Ayr Observer*, 14 May 1901, p. 4.

55 NAM, Acc. 1983-05-97, W. Grant, diary, 23 July 1901, and 'Letter from the Front', *Argyllshire Herald*, 6 April 1901, p. 3.

56 'National Reform Union', *Scotsman*, 15 June 1900, p. 10; see also S. B. Spies, *Methods of Barbarism? Roberts and Kitchener and Civilians in the Boer Republics: January 1900–May 1902* (Cape Town: Hunan

& Rousseau, 1977), pp. 214–6, and P. Warwick, *Black People and the South African War, 1899–1902* (Cambridge: Cambridge University Press, 1983), p. 151.

57 *Scotsman*, 15 June 1901, p. 8; *Parl. Deb.*, fourth series, vol. 95 (17 June 1901), col. 599; BL, Add. Mss, 41,243A, f. 39, Campbell-Bannerman Mss, Southampton, 2 July 1901.

58 Brown, ' "Echoes of Midlothian" ', p. 175; *Fife Herald and Journal*, 10 July 1901, p. 4; 'The Concentration Camps', *Ross-shire Journal*, 22 November 1901, p. 4; Spiers, 'The British Army in South Africa', in Boyden, Guy and Harding (eds), *ashes and blood*, p. 82.

59 'A Boer Stronghold', *Ayr Advertiser*, 5 September 1901, p. 7; see also 'Interesting Letters from the Front', *Kilmarnock Standard*, 3 August 1901, p. 5.

60 'Lieutenant-Colonel Hamilton-Campbell', *Scotsman*, 27 January 1902, p. 8.

61 'A Soldier's Reply to the Pro-Boers', *Inverness Courier*, 11 June 1901, p. 3; 'A Notable Letter from the Front', *Ross-shire Journal*, 21 March 1902, p. 5; Sturrock, *The Fifes in South Africa*, p. 120.

62 'At the Front', *Argyllshire Herald*, 9 November 1901, p. 3; see also 'Slandering British Troops', *[Dundee] Weekly News*, 26 April 1902, p. 8; 'A Notable Letter from the Front', p. 5.

63 'Experiences of a Brechin Soldier', *Dundee Courier & Argus*, 30 January 1902, p. 5; 'The Vlakfontein Murders', *Aberdeen Journal*, 15 July 1901, p. 5; Judd and Surridge, *The Boer War*, pp. 233–4; 'Soldier on Pro-Boers', *Ayr Advertiser*, 5 September 1901, p. 7; NAM, Acc. No. 1972-08-8, Paterson Mss, Paterson to Tom, 8 December 1900.

64 'Ayrshire Yeomanry in South Africa', p. 3.

65 'Humours and Privations of the Campaign', *Dumfries and Galloway Courier and Herald*, 25 July 1900, p. 6; see also 'With the Royal Scots at Wepener', *Scotsman*, 29 June 1900, p. 6; 'Letters from Lance-Corporal McCririck', *Kilmarnock Standard*, 5 May 1900, p. 6; 'An Aberdeen Man at Pretoria', *Aberdeen Journal*, 1 August 1900, p. 6.

66 NAM, Acc. No. 1972-08-8, Paterson Mss, Paterson to Tom, 20 April 1900.

67 'Letter from a Lovat Scout at the Front', *Ross-shire Journal*, 28 March 1902, p. 8; 'Letter from a Black Watch Man', *Perthshire Advertiser*, 27 March 1901, p. 5; 'Ayrshire Men and the War', *Ayr Observer*, 7 January 1902, p. 3.

68 'With the Lovat Scouts at the Front', *North Star and Farmers' Chronicle*, 27 March 1902, p. 5; see also Spiers, 'The British Army in South Africa', in Boyden, Guy and Harding (eds), *ashes and blood*, p. 82.

69 'Letter from an Ayrshire Man at the Front', *Ayr Observer*, 20 August 1901, p. 3.

70 'Life in a Blockhouse', *North Star and Farmers' Chronicle*, 22 May 1902, p. 5; see also 'What the Seaforths are Doing', *Ross-shire Journal*, 13 September 1901, p. 7; 'Letters from the Front', *Northern Scot and Moray & Nairn Express*, 6 July 1901, p. 3; 'Letter from Sergt. Edgar', *Kilmarnock Standard*, 5 July 1902, p. 3.

71 'Stirlingshire Militia in South Africa', *Stirling Observer*, 19 April 1902, p. 8.

72 'Arrival of the Scottish Rifles Service Volunteers', *Hamilton Advertiser*, 24 May 1902, p. 4; 'Return of the Volunteers. Argyll and Sutherland Regiment', *Kinross-shire Advertiser*, 3 May 1902, p. 2; 'Return of Second Active Service Company Argyll and Sutherland Volunteers', *Scotsman*, 28 April 1902, p. 7.

73 *North Star and Farmers' Chronicle*, 5 June 1902, p. 6; *Ayr Observer*, 3 June 1902, p. 3; *Scotsman*, 2 June 1902, p. 5.

74 *Kilmarnock Standard*, 7 June 1902, p. 4.

75 *Glasgow Herald*, 3 June 1902, p. 6.

76 *Dunfermline Journal*, 7 June 1902, p. 4; *Stirling Observer*, 4 June 1902, p. 4.

77 'Homecoming of Gordon Volunteers', *Aberdeen Daily Journal*, 7 June 1902, p. 7.

78 H. Streets, 'Identity in the Highland Regiments in the Nineteenth Century: Soldier, Region, Nation', in S. Murdoch and A. Mackillop (eds), *Fighting for Identity: Scottish Military Experience c. 1550–1900* (Leiden: Brill, 2002), pp. 213–36, especially pp. 222–5.

79 'Sir Robert Reid at Sanquhar', *Scotsman*, 5 April 1902, p. 10.

80 *Perthshire Advertiser*, 2 June 1902, p. 2.

EPILOGUE

The South African War marked the apogee of the Scottish soldier's imperial involvement, involving a tragic denouement in Magersfontein at the front coupled with acute political divisions at home. After the war, Scottish regiments undertook additional garrison duties in South Africa, with the 2nd Camerons protecting Pietermaritzburg during the Zulu rebellion of 1906, and, on the North-West Frontier, the 1st Seaforth served in the Zakka Khel and Mohmand expeditions of 1908,[1] but Scottish soldiers never had an opportunity to secure another imperial triumph before 1914. Meanwhile, the Scottish Liberals resolved their wartime divisions. The end of the war undermined the distinctive case for Liberal Imperialism, and, as soon as Joseph Chamberlain raised the issue of tariff reform in 1903, he split the Conservatives and reunited the Liberals under the banner of free trade.[2] Yet Scotland's martial service in an imperial context hardly faded away; it became the theme of post-war receptions for returning units and featured in the writings of Scottish soldiers, particularly the citizen soldiers. It was commemorated, too, in a remarkable array of post-war memorials,[3] with the unveiling ceremonies becoming further occasions for the display of local and regimental pride in recent military service and sacrifice. The funerals of legendary imperial generals Hector Macdonald and Archibald Alison brought thousands of Scots onto the streets of Edinburgh (and into Dean Cemetery), and the imperial theme resonated in the rhetoric of the army reforms developed by a Scottish Secretary of State for War, Richard B. Haldane. In many respects the traditional image of the Scottish soldier survived the South African War and underpinned the response of Scots to the onset of the First World War.

As regular units did not always return to Scotland after the war, or sometimes only did so after several years,[4] the more immediate receptions for the returning Volunteers were particularly effusive. As in the war, civic dignitaries greeted these Volunteers, who often followed pipe bands through crowded streets, bedecked with flags and bunting, to

formal receptions, civic lunches and the presentation of medals in subsequent ceremonies. The vast number of spectators from all classes,
including mill girls, engineering apprentices and laundry workers as
well as students in Aberdeen, were not simply attracted by the spectacle or entertainment as the late Colin Matthew supposed.[5] Many were
demonstrating pride in the military service of Volunteers from their
own communities; they cheered speeches commending the display of
imperial unity during the war and the achievements of particular units,
whether Gordon Volunteers in Aberdeen or Lovat Scouts in Inverness.[6]

Imperial themes also dominated the writings of citizen soldiers.
Lieutenant Home was delighted that the citizen army of '100,000 volunteers' had kept the Union Jack – 'the guarantee of freedom, of political equality, and of just government' – flying over Pretoria, and that
the Volunteer had proved himself 'in the hour of national danger' as
able to 'take his place shoulder to shoulder with the soldier of
the line . . .'[7] Lance-Corporal James Baker (Argyll and Sutherland
Volunteers) reckoned that volunteering at home would henceforth
be undertaken in a more 'realistic spirit' on account of the war,[8] while
others recalled the impressive spectacle of British imperial power
during the war and the readiness of colonies to rise 'in defence of the
Mother Country'.[9] Another lasting memory for Surgeon-Captain
Dewar was the pervasive Scottish presence within South Africa, not
merely 'serving in a military capacity' but also 'engaged in all sorts of
occupations, railway porters, storekeepers, pressmen, doctors, stock-
brokers'. As he affirmed,

> Truly our little nation has well played its part in the extension of
> Empire. . . . If England had not fallen, by the laws of inheritance, into the
> hands of our Scots King James, we should never have had adequate scope
> for our great energies, never have been able to manifest our colonising and
> empire-enlarging genius![10]

More visible as a reminder of the war, and of the sacrifices and
sentiments it evoked, were the multitude of memorials erected in
Edwardian Scotland. Whether in the form of mural tablets and
windows in churches and schools, or public works of art in the form of
statues, obelisks, towers and crosses, these appeared in the major
cities, county towns, villages and loch sides, wherever there was local
or regimental support. Public subscriptions, led by King Edward VII,
honoured 242 Gordon Highlanders who died in the war with a
window in Holburn Parish Church, Aberdeen; local citizens and
friends of General Wauchope raised £200 to erect an obelisk in his

memory in Yetholm, Kelso; and the fellow Academicals of Lieutenant Lewis Balfour Bradbury commemorated his services by commissioning the Bradbury Shield that would hang in the hall of Edinburgh Academy. Many memorials took the form of mural tablets and stained-glass windows, commemorating the services of specific regiments (notably the tablets to the Royal Scots, Cameron Highlanders and Royal Scots Fusiliers in the High Kirk of St Giles), the gallantry of individual soldiers (the memorial to Lieutenant Digby Jones, VC in St Mary's Cathedral, Edinburgh) and the ideal of the Christian soldier (the Wauchope window in Liberton Parish Church). Several sculptures depicted soldiers with rifles 'at the ready', or, more poignantly, soldiers protecting wounded comrades,[11] in defiant scenes, representing a resolute defence of empire rather than the 'never again' spirit that characterised the many memorials erected after the First World War.

Some memorials were functional, including the Memorial Institute, Aberdeen (in memory of Lieutenant-Colonel Dick-Cunyngham, VC) and the Memorial Library of Trinity College, Glenalmond, but public works of art predominated. Although some were located in traditional military settings, including the esplanades of Edinburgh and Stirling Castles (the Celtic cross to the Scottish Horse in Edinburgh and the Highland soldier in memory of the Argyll and Sutherland Highlanders in Stirling), many more occupied prominent positions in cities, towns (Alloa, Falkirk, Dingwall, Dunbar and Ayr), villages (Beauly and Yetholm) and municipal parks (Dumbarton, Hawick and Glasgow), symbolising the deepening links between Scottish communities and their soldiery. Several Scottish sculptors designed these works but their doyen was W. Birnie Rhind, who sculpted the three prestigious works in Edinburgh (honouring the Scots Greys in Princes Street, the King's Own Scottish Borderers on the North Bridge and the Black Watch on the Mound) as well as the memorials to the HLI in Kelvingrove Park, the 'Men of Clackmannan' in Alloa and a mural tablet to the Royal Scots in St Giles.[12]

These memorials aroused their share of controversy, not least the claim that the money raised could have been spent on homes, hospitals and other charitable institutions. Colonel E. C. Browne answered this criticism when he spoke as chairman of the committee that raised the funding for a memorial to the Royal Scots Fusiliers at Ayr. Works of art, he claimed:

> educated and enriched the minds of youth, engendering a spirit of veneration for, and a desire to emulate, noble deeds and personal sacrifices

undergone by their countrymen in times of stress and danger. Thus, the dead in the service of their country were made alive again on the canvas of the painter, in marble and bronze of the sculptor.[13]

In unveiling this statue (1 November 1902) before 'an immense throng of people', the Earl of Eglinton claimed that the memorial would console families and friends of the bereaved with the knowledge that these men would not be forgotten in the future. Provost Templeton, in accepting 'this magnificent statue' (sited in Burns Station Square in front of the railway station), declared that it would be 'a fitting and lasting adornment to this ancient and historic town'.[14]

Similar scenes occurred across Scotland throughout the decade as large crowds gathered whenever monuments were unveiled. At Dingwall, on 6 August 1904, where a twenty-foot-high, Ionic cross in pale pink granite was unveiled to the Seaforth Highlanders, Provost Macrae once again linked the history of the regiment as 'saviours of our Indian Empire' with the readiness of local Volunteers to serve in South Africa. The Ross-shire people, he declared, had every reason to be proud of their 'county' soldiers.[15] Over a year later local pride fused with Highland passion at Beauly when the fifty-foot-high memorial, costing £500, was unveiled to the Lovat Scouts. As Lord Lovat emphasised, the scouts were 'a movement in which Highlanders alone were occupied. It was the development of a particular form of duty for which Highlanders were specially adapted, and the men and officers were entirely Highland.'[16]

If Scots readily commemorated battlefield deaths, they responded in remarkable fashion to the suicide of Sir Hector Macdonald, recently knighted for his services in South Africa. The controversy attending this death has been examined by Trevor Royle, namely the allegations of sexual misconduct with young boys in Ceylon, Macdonald's suicide in Paris (25 March 1903) when the charges were made public by an American newspaper and the family's attempt to have a discreet funeral in Edinburgh.[17] Apart from a cryptic reference to the 'grave, very grave charges' against Macdonald, the Scottish press barely commented on the circumstances prompting the suicide but printed eulogies about his career and commented on the depth of anguish in many parts of Scotland.[18] The public response was astonishing. When the coffin was brought from Paris through London en route to Edinburgh, hundreds of Scots gathered at King's Cross Station, including representatives of all the Highland societies and many clan associations in the metropolis, with two pipers playing

'Flowers of the Forest'. At Waverley Station, despite the early and unadvertised arrival of the train on a dull, wintry Monday morning, a couple of hundred 'workpeople' gathered at the scene, but as soon as the news of the private interment at the Dean Cemetery began to circulate, thousands of people 'of all classes' came to pay their respects. In unprecedented scenes at least a thousand men, women and children passed the grave side each hour on every day until the weekend, whereupon the numbers rose to 5,000 an hour, with 'fully 30,000 people' visiting the grave on Sunday, 5 April. Among the multitude of floral tributes were several magnificent wreaths, one in the form of a claymore from the Edinburgh Skye Association and another from Queensland on behalf of Macdonald's 'fellow countrymen beyond the seas'.[19]

Nowhere was the grief more deeply felt than in the Highlands. At Dingwall Parish Church, the Reverend J. R. Macpherson asked his congregation to set aside 'the buried facts and the unknown thoughts of [Macdonald's] mind' and remember him

> at Charasiab, at Majuba Hill, at Omdurman; we see in him the soldier who represented to the world the triumph of a man over every hindrance and difficulty; the ideal British soldier; the true Highland warrior, as he rose from the ranks to the highest commands; the man whom this country honoured for his bravery, his indomitable energy, his tactical skill.[20]

Dingwall's town council even sent a letter to Macdonald's widow, complaining that the body should have been buried in Dingwall and indicating their desire to erect a memorial in honour of Sir Hector. Lady Macdonald rightly rebuked the council over its crass insensitivity, which she could only explain by the depth of feelings that the town had for her husband.[21] She merely wanted a simple monument over the grave, but the council pressed on with its plans and executive committees were formed in Edinburgh and Glasgow to raise donations 'from almost every quarter of the globe'. The monies proved sufficient to erect a monument over the grave and construct a huge memorial tower (one hundred feet high) on Mitchell Hill, overlooking Dingwall, which the Marquis of Tullibardine would open on 23 May 1907. The marquis described Macdonald as 'a modest, simple straightforward Highlander' and urged critics to be charitable in their judgements and recognise the monument as 'a tribute to his splendid achievements as a soldier'.[22]

The Macdonald memorial was erected only months after a much more conventional military funeral, namely that of Sir Archibald

Alison. The death of this distinguished imperial soldier occasioned lengthy tributes prior to his funeral service first in London and then in St John's Episcopal Church, Edinburgh, before his burial in Dean Cemetery (9 February 1907). The final procession was accorded full military honours. Seaforth Highlanders carried the coffin of their former colonel from the church, Seaforth pipers played 'Flowers of the Forest', and a troop of Scots Greys led the gun carriage, draped in the Union flag, past 'a huge crowd of sympathetic spectators, who thickly lined the route all the way from the church to the cemetery'. The number of wreaths was so large that three carriages conveyed them to the cemetery.[23]

If these funerals testified to Edinburgh's longstanding ties with the military, so too did the unveiling of memorials to the King's Own Scottish Borderers on 4 October 1906 (a regiment formed to defend the capital in 1689 and the only one allowed to march through the streets with fixed bayonets), to the Scots Greys on 16 November 1906 (a regiment first raised in the Lothians), and again, on 27 June 1910, when the Black Watch statue was handed over to the lord provost. At all these occasions, vast crowds gathered (reportedly some 5,000 to observe the Black Watch ceremony) at prime sites in the centre of the capital and there were justifiable plaudits for the elegance of Birnie Rhind's sculptures.[24] Locating the Black Watch sculpture in Edinburgh testified to the depth of national feeling over the losses of the Highland Brigade, and in particular the Black Watch, at Magersfontein, and national feelings were equally apparent in the unveiling of the Scots Greys' memorial. The sculpture was unveiled at a time when the regiment was due to be moved from its Scottish barracks at Piershill under economies imposed by Haldane, the new Liberal Secretary of State for War. At the subsequent luncheon in the North British Hotel, Lord Rosebery declared:

> it does seem hard that, with all our pride in this illustrious regiment, which is bound to us not merely in the history but in the very nationality of Scotland – that we are not allowed to retain that or any other cavalry regiment within the borders of this ancient realm.[25]

The *Scotsman* endorsed this well-received speech, arguing that Haldane's assurance about preserving the 'nationality' of the Scots Greys would mean little more than 'metaphysical subtleties' if the regiment lost its centre, training and recruiting ground 'within the realm of Scotland'.[26]

Haldane, who believed that he had to cut defence costs before he could reform the army, responded privately:

> Seriously I think I mind abuse less than most people. Here is Scotland clamouring for the retention in Edin. of the Scots Greys. But I cannot leave the officers & men at Piershill, & I have not £200,000 to build new barracks. If the public want economy they must put up with things.[27]

Determined upon the reform of the regular and auxiliary forces, Haldane would claim in his post-war memoirs that the reforms were designed to deploy a well-trained and fully equipped fighting force alongside the armies of France in August 1914. This was not what he proposed at the time, either privately or publicly, and much of the defence planning up to 1910 at least had a traditional imperial purpose.[28] When speaking at the opening of new headquarters of the Scottish Horse at Blair Atholl on 14 September 1907, Haldane explained that the reforms were intended to create a two-line army: 'the expeditionary force – which has its outposts in the distant parts of the Empire, but which is the nucleus and heart and core of the regular troops in these islands, and the second line – the home or territorial troops – whose primary function shall be home defence'. While he envisaged the Militia replacing the immediate wastage of war, he wished to create fourteen territorial divisions for home defence out of the existing Volunteers and Yeomanry, and to exploit the 'national sentiment in Scotland' by creating 'Highland and Lowland' Divisions. By organising and equipping these divisions properly, he claimed that 'in a great Imperial emergency' they would 'come together as the forces came together in 1900' and show 'the world that although a peaceful Empire we were an Empire with immense military resources at our back'.[29]

Neither the reference to national sentiment (both British and Scottish intertwined) nor the designated imperial mission were passing rhetoric. Privately Haldane described his 'new plans' as 'an "Army of the Empire" ',[30] and, as he toured the country beating the drum for Territorial recruits, he urged men to come forth for their 'nation and the country to which they belonged'. Even in his last year as war minister, when he appeared before a regimental gathering of the HLI in Glasgow on 10 January 1912, Haldane appealed for the formation of a citizen army for home defence:

> They all knew that we were the centre of a great Empire, and that to hold that Empire together we required a great Navy and a great provisional overseas Army. We had got that, but we required something more. To be

free, we required our citizen army, our citizens forming something like a
nation in arms, and we were beginning to get that . . .[31]

Although the struggle of Haldane to find sufficient recruits for the
Territorial Force is not strictly relevant to this study (and has been
examined elsewhere),[32] his efforts to draw on the support of county
elites (as at Blair Atholl) and regimental units (like the HLI in
Glasgow), as well as his appeal to the sentiments of nationality and
imperial purpose, reflected both the strengths and weaknesses of his
approach. He built on the existing support for the military in
Scotland, and the links between the regulars and auxiliary forces bolstered by service in the South African War, to establish his new army.
He also created county associations to raise the new Territorial units
but never broadened the appeal of this army sufficiently to overcome
the profound resistance to military service. In spite of Haldane's commendable efforts, voluntary recruiting remained an endemic problem
in Scotland (as it did in most of the United Kingdom) and the number
of Scots in the regular army fell to 17,282 by the eve of the First World
War (or 7.5 per cent of the army as a whole, well below the 21,852
or 8.1 per cent in 1904).[33] Military service had a distinctly limited
appeal, not least on account of the rates of pay, terms of service and
limited prospects of post-service employment, but even part-time
service in the Territorials, as Lord Reith recalled, could meet with
jeers and derision in parts of Glasgow.[34]

So was the image of the Scottish soldier, and his predominantly
imperial mission, largely a romantic notion of pipes and kilts, set in
exotic locations far removed from much of ordinary, everyday life in
Scotland? To an extent it was, especially during the *pax Britannica* of
the Edwardian era, but the recent services of the citizen soldier had
broadened the base of support for the army as an instrument of imperialism, if not as a career. To some extent, too, the new conditions of
war seemed to blunt the traditional role of the heroic-warrior, armed
with claymore or bayonet, but the qualities of courage, heroism,
inspirational leadership, esprit de corps and offensive zeal would
always find an outlet in battle. The army had adapted operationally
and tactically in South Africa, and the Edwardian army learned from
this experience (and from studying the Russo-Japanese War of
1904–5). It introduced more regular and systematic training in accordance with a doctrine of fire and movement, enabling its expeditionary force to enter the First World War, as the official historian
Brigadier J. E. Edmonds claimed, 'incomparably the best trained, best

organised, and best equipped British Army which ever went forth to war'.[35] Nevertheless, the traditional imagery endured, utilised by Haldane and others, partly because it reminded Scots of their distinctive national role within an imperial setting, a role that had by no means lost its popular appeal.

Imperialism remained a potent force in Edwardian Scotland, not least in schools and youth movements. Apart from the celebration of Empire Day in schools, there was a growing cult of the Union Jack. Schools exchanged flags with other schools in the colonies, and, on 21 February 1908, when 1,500 schoolchildren gathered in the McEwan Hall, Edinburgh for 'Children's Day', the Edinburgh branch of the Victoria League (founded in 1901 in memory of the late queen) presented flags to each school. Lord Rosebery delivered an address on imperial unity and citizenship, commending the empire as representing 'justice, good government, liberty and Christianity', and exhorted Scottish boys to be ready to fight for their flag and defend their country.[36] By November 1909 the *Educational News*, the journal of the Educational Institute of Scotland, complained that 'what between Boys' Brigades, Boy Scouts, Girl Guides, Navy Leagues, Union Jack Leagues, and other organisations, there is ground for fear that there is just a little too much "flag-waving" business in our schools'.[37]

There were also cadet corps in some Scottish schools; John (later Lord) Reith was an original member of the cadet corps formed in Glasgow Academy in 1901 and later joined the Officers' Training Corps when it was formed in Glasgow University in 1908.[38] The Queen Victoria School and Memorial at Dunblane, Stirlingshire was also opened in 1908, following a long fundraising campaign to raise subscriptions from individual Scots, counties and burghs. Another national memorial to the Scottish dead of the South African War, it provided elementary education, with a distinctive military ethos (miniature kilted uniforms and a pipe band), for the sons of Scots in the naval or army service and for the sons of soldiers of any nationality serving in Scottish regiments.[39] Highland soldiers retained their prominence in school textbooks and juvenile literature, and in various imagery whether in popular art, picture postcards (which sustained the wartime boom with numerous regimental series produced in the Edwardian years), or in advertising where once again the kilted Highlander with drawn claymore promoted jingoistic brands of whisky such as 'Supremacy Scotch'.[40]

Highland regiments remained conspicuous in performing an array of ceremonial duties, both in the colonies and at home. The 1st

Argylls took part in the parade in Johannesburg to commemorate the coronation of King Edward VII and attended the unveiling of the memorial to the Highland Brigade on a hill at Magersfontein – an Ionic cross bearing the inscription 'Scotland is poorer in Men but richer in Heroes'.[41] The 2nd Seaforth, on their return from South Africa, participated in the Royal Review in Phoenix Park, Dublin (July 1903) and furnished a guard of honour for the King's Levee. The 1st Camerons paraded in London for the funeral of Edward VII in 1910 and for the coronation of King George V.[42]

These ceremonies were not only prized by the regiments concerned but also sustained the distinctive image of the Highland soldier, reflecting the contribution of Scots within the army as a whole. Unlike the more numerous Irish soldiery (whose numbers were also falling, primarily through the effects of depopulation),[43] Scots did not feel any need to demonstrate their loyalty to the Union. Whereas Scottish memorials simply commemorated the service of particular regiments or individual soldiers, the famous arch, thirty-two feet high and twenty-seven feet wide, erected to the Royal Dublin Fusiliers at the Grafton Street corner of St Stephen's Green, Dublin, was a conspicuous display of unionist sentiment. Unveiled in August 1907, it soon earned the popular nickname, 'Traitors' Gate'.[44]

Spared such controversy, the Scottish soldier retained an image and an imperial role that enjoyed a broad base of support across Scotland, irrespective of class, region or political affiliation (apart from the more extreme fringe elements in Scottish politics). There was a strain of pacifist, anti-military opinion in Scotland as reflected in the views of James Ramsay MacDonald, who first entered Parliament in 1906 representing Leicester. During the debates on the Territorial and Reserve Forces Bill, MacDonald led the opposition to Haldane's attempt to fund school cadet corps through the county associations. He aroused great support on the Liberal and Labour back benches by denouncing the proposal as liable to 'poison the springs of politics at the very source'. Haldane bowed before this opposition and withdrew the measure, so leaving the proposed school and university cadet corps unable to supply an adequate reserve of officers.[45] Yet the South African War had reflected the pervasive appeal of martial values within Scotland, and the readiness of Scots, including editors of pro-Boer or radical newspapers, to praise the services of regular and Volunteer soldiers. If the imperial mission had the staunch support of Unionists and Liberal Imperialists alike, its implementation by Scottish soldiers earned few criticisms from Campbell-Bannerman or his pro-Boer colleagues. In condemning recourse to 'methods of barbarism' in South Africa, the Liberal leader had insisted quickly that he 'never thought of blaming' the soldiers who were only doing their duty.[46] The press also noted that Thomas Shaw, a pro-Boer MP who had secured re-election for Hawick burghs, laid one of the more conspicuous wreaths at the grave side of Sir Hector Macdonald.[47]

Inevitably the martial values associated with contemporary notions of the Scottish soldier, infused with patriotic feelings and a sense of imperial purpose, aroused more passions in war than in peace. During the late-Victorian conflicts, the exploits of Scottish soldiers captured attention in Scotland (and periodically in parts of the United Kingdom and empire), testifying to the longstanding assumptions about the Scots as warriors in service of their queen and country in an imperial context. By the writings of the soldiers and war correspondents, and by the images they evoked, Scottish soldiers gained periodically a celebratory status that earned widespread, if not universal, support. This support, fanned by the coverage of the Scottish press, spread across the regions and classes in Scotland and found reflection in the willingness of communities, both large and small, urban and rural, to celebrate military achievements both at the time and in retrospect.

It seems rather odd that otherwise excellent histories of Scotland, or of Scottish cities, of the late nineteenth century can overlook these outbursts of patriotic and imperial fervour, not merely over the relief of Ladysmith and Mafeking, and then the capture of Pretoria, but also the recurrent demonstrations that celebrated the departure and return of local Volunteers.[48] Even if these outbursts occurred sporadically, they reflected pride in Scottish regiments and their imperial role, a support sustained by popular imagery and widely held assumptions about Britain's imperial purpose. What distinguished the support of the Scottish soldier from that of his Celtic or English county comrades was the role of the Scot in arms as representing a distinctive national identity, not least on account of his costume and musical accompaniment. After the 1881 reforms had ordered Lowland regiments to wear trews and Highland-style doublets, 'the resulting iconographic status of the Scottish soldier', as J. M. McKenzie argues, 'contributed to a sense of an integrated Scottish culture, even if marked out by supposedly distinctive Highland forms of dress'.[49]

Nor did this cultural identity emerge spontaneously. In all these colonial campaigns Scottish soldiers evinced concern about the assessment of their actions by professional superiors, and about the reporting and depiction of their achievements in Scotland and beyond. Like their counterparts south of the border, they cultivated links with war correspondents and war-artists (so following Campbell's example in India),[50] and assisted battle-painters (thereby enhancing the work of Lady Butler, Vereker Hamilton and Allan Stewart). Some individuals sought political office (Wauchope) or exploited their celebratory status (Piper Findlater) or undertook speaking tours (notably Macdonald after Omdurman). Many more expressed themselves by writing from the front; they added detail, if not always accurately, to official dispatches and editorial commentary, addressed the issues of the moment, and chronicled the challenges and hazards of imperial campaigning. If the writing was limited in outlook (with some writers admitting that the recipient might know more about the war than they did) or hastily composed after a battle, with views distorted by camp gossip and regimental rivalry, it provided a personal perspective that editors relished.[51] As Alexander Somerville remarked of the pre-Crimean army: 'it was the *writing* quite as much as the *fighting* of the Scotch regiments which distinguished them'.[52] This was still true in a voluminous correspondence that had range and substance, upholding traditional values and patriotic commitments in the main,[53] and testifying to the bonds that sustained the Scottish military effort. In short, the Scottish soldier played a critical role in embedding an understanding of his values within the public consciousness both within Scotland and beyond.

The war correspondent, special artist, battle-painter, sculptor and producer of all manner of imperial iconography enhanced and spread this image further. The Scottish soldier, especially if wearing the kilt, provided excellent 'copy' for written and illustrative works. He was more colourful than the ordinary British soldier, especially when khaki clothing became the norm, and could be portrayed in the centre of dramatic actions in exotic locations. The image survived in the imperial films of the inter-war years, with Scottish regiments prominent in *The Black Watch* (1929), *Wee Willie Winkie* (1937), *The Drum* (1938) and *Gunga Din* (1939). These films, as Jeffrey Richards argues, dealt in 'drama, dreams and myths',[54] but they built upon the deeply rooted imagery of the Scottish soldier and a core of credibility, namely his effective role as an instrument of imperialism.

The imagery, of course, did not always reflect reality. As in other British units, a few Scottish soldiers deserted (where it was feasible or tempting to do so)[55], and many more succumbed to sunstroke, disease and drink (when available) or engaged in looting and reprisals (as in the Mutiny).[56] Some incurred floggings or fell out on the line of march, or, exceptionally, committed suicide (see chapters three, four and seven). Even units, if severely pressed as at Majuba and Magersfontein, sometimes broke and fled. Nevertheless, the tide of Scottish martial triumphs rolled on from Balaclava, Lucknow, Kumase, Tel-el-Kebir, Kirbekan, Dargai and the Atbara; they dwarfed the episodic lapses, if not the remorse over Magersfontein, and sustained the imperial legacy.

Linked inextricably with this imperial mission were the heroic-warrior virtues – duty, honour, loyalty, courage, self-sacrifice and the noble death – that became almost clichés in Victorian writing. Evaluating the influence of this work, even of the memorable prose of George Warrington Steevens in the largest circulation daily, the *Daily Mail*, remains a matter of conjecture. As Roger Stearn argues, the writing may have 'reached an extensive, largely middle-class, already imperialist readership and confirmed rather than converted'[57] but the Scottish soldier in action enjoyed a broader base of public support. Admittedly, as memories of recent wars began to fade, the soldier hardly remained in the forefront of public consciousness and the military career never had much appeal in peacetime. Yet the assumptions about how Scots performed in battle, and the national pride in their military efforts, resurfaced whenever an imperial war erupted. Irrespective of debates about the origins of these wars, most Scots lauded their soldiers in action and were rarely disappointed in doing so. This depth of support would help to explain how Scotland responded with such passion and alacrity when the First World War erupted, and how the wells of patriotic and national fervour would again be tapped to raise vast numbers of Scots to fight and serve their country.

Notes

1 Fairrie, '*Cuidich'N Righ*', pp. 44, 51.
2 Jacobson, 'Rosebery and Liberal Imperialism', pp. 106–7.
3 Colonel Sir J. Gildea, *For Remembrance and In Honour of Those Who Lost Their Lives in the South African War 1899–1902* (London: Eyre & Spottiswoode, 1911), pp. 264–94.
4 Whereas the 1st Cameronians came home within months of the peace, the 2nd Cameronians did not leave Cape Town until 6 May 1904 and the 2nd Seaforth were sent to Dublin on their return in February 1903. 'Arrival of Cameron Highlanders at Fort George', *Inverness Courier*, 14 October 1902, p. 5; Johnston, *The History of The Cameronians*, 1, p. 298; Fairrie, '*Cuidich'N Righ*', pp. 47, 50.

5 H. C. G. Matthew, 'The Liberal Age (1851–1914)', in K. O. Morgan (ed.), *The Oxford Illustrated History of Britain* (Oxford: Oxford University Press, 1984), p. 522; 'Homecoming of Gordon Volunteers', *Aberdeen Daily Journal*, 7 June 1902, p. 7.

6 'The Return of the Lovat Scouts', *Inverness Courier*, 22 August 1902, p. 6; 'Returned Warriors Honoured', *North Star and Farmers' Chronicle*, 27 November 1902, p. 6; 'Presentation of South African Medals to Lovat Scouts' and 'Presentation of Medals to Seaforth Highlanders', *Inverness Courier*, 16 September 1902, p. 6.

7 Home, *With the Border Volunteers*, pp. 176–7; see also Sturrock, *The Fifes in South Africa*, p. 159.

8 'From the Front', *Stirling Observer*, 22 September 1900, p. 2.

9 Smith, *With the Scottish Rifle Volunteers*, p. 134; NAM, Acc. No. 1972-08-8, Paterson Mss, Paterson to Tom, 23 March 1900.

10 Dewar, *With the Scottish Yeomanry*, pp. 184–5.

11 Gildea, *For Remembrance*, pp. 265, 269, 271, 273, 276–8, 285, 288–9; 'The Wauchope Memorial at Yetholm', *Scotsman*, 25 September 1902, p. 4, and 'Liberton Memorial of General Wauchope', *Scotsman*, 9 June 1905, p. 5.

12 Gildea, *For Remembrance*, pp. 264–8, 272, 274–80; 'Ceremony at Beauly', *Inverness Courier*, 22 December 1905, p. 6.

13 'Royal Scots Fusiliers Memorial', *Kilmarnock Standard*, 8 November 1902, p. 3.

14 Ibid.

15 'Memorial to Seaforth Highlanders', *Ross-shire Journal*, 12 August 1904, p. 6.

16 'Ceremony at Beauly', p. 6.

17 Royle, *Fighting Mac*, pp. 124–41.

18 'Sir Hector Macdonald', *Scotsman*, 25 March 1903, p. 9; 'General Macdonald's Career' and 'The Charges Against Sir Hector Macdonald', *Scotsman*, 26 March 1903, pp. 4–5; see also 'The Late Gen, Sir Hector Macdonald', *Ross-shire Journal*, 27 March 1903, p. 5, and 'Death of Sir Hector Macdonald', *Northern Chronicle*, 1 April 1903, p. 6.

19 'The Late Major-General Sir Hector Macdonald', 'Visitors to the Grave' and 'The Late Sir Hector Macdonald', *Scotsman*, 31 March 1903, p. 5, and 6 April 1903, p. 7.

20 'Pulpit Reference', *Ross-shire Journal*, 3 April 1903, p. 5.

21 'Lady Macdonald and Dingwall Town Council', *Ross-shire Journal*, 10 April 1903, p. 5.

22 'The Macdonald Memorial', *Ross-shire Journal*, 14 May 1907, p. 5.

23 'Death of Sir Archibald Alison', *The Times*, 6 February 1907, p. 4; 'Death of Sir Archibald Alison' and 'Funeral of Sir Archibald Alison', *Scotsman*, 6 February 1907, p. 8, and 11 February 1907, p. 7.

24 'The Memorial to the King's Own Scottish Borderers', 'The Scots Greys Memorial' and 'Black Watch Memorial', *Scotsman*, 5 October 1906, p. 9, 17 November 1906, p. 12, and 28 June 1910, p. 9.
25 'The Removal of the Scots Greys', *Scotsman*, 17 November 1906, p. 12.
26 Ibid., p. 8.
27 NLS, Haldane Mss, Ms.5976, ff. 173–4, Haldane to his mother, 17 November 1906; see also E. M. Spiers, *Haldane: An Army Reformer* (Edinburgh: Edinburgh University Press, 1980), ch. 3.
28 H. Strachan, 'The Boer War and Its Impact on the British Army, 1902–14', in Boyden, Guy and Harding (eds), *ashes and blood*, pp. 87–9.
29 'The New Army Act', *Dundee Advertiser*, 16 September 1907, p. 7.
30 NLS, Haldane Mss, Ms. 5976, f. 68, Haldane to his mother, 22 February 1909.
31 'Territorial Force', *Glasgow Herald*, 11 January 1912, p. 9.
32 Spiers, *Haldane: An Army Reformer*, ch. 8.
33 These were only the Scots born in Scotland, and there were undoubtedly more born elsewhere in the United Kingdom and colonies. PP, *The General Annual Report on The British Army for the year ending 30th September 1913*, Cd. 7252 (1914), LII, p. 92.
34 Lord Reith, *Wearing Spurs* (London: Hutchinson, 1966), p. 25; on the recruiting problems, see E. M. Spiers, *The Army and Society 1815–1914* (London: Longman, 1980), ch. 2.
35 J. E. Edmonds, *Military Operations, France and Belgium, 1914*, 2 vols (London: Macmillan, 1925), 1, pp. 10–11.
36 'Lord Rosebery and Edinburgh School Children', *Scotsman*, 22 February 1908, p. 9.
37 'Patriotism in School', *Educational News*, 26 November 1909, p. 1248.
38 Reith, *Wearing Spurs*, p. 14.
39 Allan and Carswell, *The Thin Red Line*, p. 38.
40 J. M. McKenzie, *Propaganda and Empire: The Manipulation of British Public Opinion, 1880–1960* (Manchester: Manchester University Press, 1984), pp. 27, 173, 198; H. Charles Moore, *Brave Sons of the Empire* (London: Religious Tracts Society, 1911); Holt, *Picture Postcards of the Golden Age*, pp. 81–2; Cane, *For Queen and Country*, p. 54; Murray, *Art of Whisky*, p. 56.
41 Mileham, *Fighting Highlanders*, p. 77; Gildea, *For Remembrance*, p. 362.
42 Fairrie, *'Cuidich'N Righ'*, pp. 47, 51.
43 Fitzpatrick, 'Militarism in Ireland, 1900–1922', in Bartlett and Jeffery (eds), *A Military History of Ireland*, pp. 380–1.
44 Gildea, *For Remembrance*, p. 295; Jeffery, 'The Irish Soldier in the Boer War', in Gooch (ed.), *The Boer War*, pp. 150–1.
45 *Parl. Deb.*, fourth series, vol. 172 (23 April 1907), col. 1,600; Spiers, *Haldane: An Army Reformer*, pp. 112–13, 138, 140–1.

46 'Liberal Leader's Protest', *Dundee Advertiser*, 22 June 1901, p. 7.

47 'Tributes and Sympathy', *Northern Chronicle*, 1 April 1903, p. 6.

48 There is hardly any coverage of military connections, or of the reaction to the South African War, in recent histories of Aberdeen and Dundee; see W. Hamish Fraser and C. H. Lee (eds), *Aberdeen 1800–2000*, and L. Miskell, C. A. Whatley and B. Harris (eds), *Victorian Dundee: Image and Realities* (East Linton: Tuckwell Press, 2000).

49 MacKenzie, 'Empire and National Identities', p. 226; see also T. M. Devine, *The Scottish Nation 1700–2000* (London: Allen Lane, Penguin Press, 1999), pp. 240–1.

50 Johnson, *Front Line Artists*, p. 127.

51 For examples of correspondents who reckoned that their recipients knew more about the war at home or who apologised for writing 'in a haze three or four days' after being shot, see 'Letter from the Highland Brigade Chaplain', *Aberdeen Journal*, 5 June 1900, p. 5, and 'Letters from the Front', *Helensburgh News*, 1 February 1900, p. 3.

52 A. Somerville, *The Autobiography of a Working Man* (London: Charles Gilpin, 1848), p. 188.

53 Some soldiers simply bemoaned their lot; see 'A Wail from a Gordon Highlander', *Manchester Evening News*, 24 April 1900, p. 6.

54 J. Richards, *Films and British national identity: From Dickens to Dad's Army* (Manchester: Manchester University Press, 1997), pp. 41, 210.

55 Robins (ed.), *Romaine's Crimean War*, p. 118.

56 B. Robson (ed.), *Sir Hugh Rose and the Central India Campaign 1858* (Midsomer Norton, Somerset: Sutton Publishing for the Army Records Society, 2000), pp. 178, 248; Forbes-Mitchell, *Reminiscences of the Great Mutiny*, p. 223.

57 Stearn, 'G. W. Steevens and the Message of Empire', p. 226.

BIBLIOGRAPHY

PRIMARY SOURCES

Argyll and Sutherland Highlanders (ASH) Museum

Cameron, diary transcribed by T. Moles (August 1986)	N-B93.MOL
Crauford correspondence	N-C91.1
Greig, diary	N-C93.GRE
H., Robert, letter from the Crimea, 13 November 1854	N-C93.H
Noble, diary	N-D1.NOB
'Reminiscences of Charlie Gray Carlisle Express One of the Thin Red Line'	N-C93.GRA
'Some Quotes about Robert Gibb (1845–1932) & THE THIN RED LINE'	N-B93.PEA
Stotherd correspondence	N-C93.STO
Taylor, diary	N-C93.TAY
Wiseman Clarke, Lieutenant-General S., 'A short personal narrative of the doings of the 93rd, Sutherland Highlanders from 1857 to 1st March 1859' (London, 1898)	N-C93.WIS

Black Watch Regimental Archive (BWRA)

Barwood, diary	0203/1
Cameron papers	0186
Cooper, diary	0212
Coveny, 'Letters from Egypt and the Soudan'	0204
Gordon, diary	0127
McIntosh, diary	0421
MacRae-Gilstrap, diary	0202
Mowbray Berkeley papers	0396/2
'Record of Service of the 42nd Royal Highland Regiment'	0080
Scott Stevenson, 'Account of the Battle of Tamai'	0641

| Sinclair, diary | 0808 |
| Stewart, diary | 0196 |

British Library

Campbell-Bannerman papers
Asia, Pacific and Africa Collections, White papers

Gordon Highlanders (GH) Museum

Denne correspondence	PB 64/1
Esslemont, diary	PB 625
'Extracts from Arbuthnott S. Dunbar's Letters during the Afghan Campaign 1879'	PB 75
field telegrams, Dargai 1897	PB 1215
Ford, diary	PB 92
Gordon, 'Diary of the Tirah Campaign'	PB 2476
Hawkins correspondence	PB 1832
Macready, diary	PB 175
Mackenzie, 'A Retrospect' (An Account of the Tirah expedition & battle of Dargai August 1897–February 1898)	PB 167
McRae correspondence	PB 173
Marr, diary	PB 180
Press cuttings on the storming of the Malakand Pass	PB 378/132
Seton-Karr, diary	PB 228
'The Assault of Delhi' (1857) transcribed from the diaries of Lieutenant-General R. Barter (75th Regiment)	PB 1657

King's Own Scottish Borderers (KOSB) Museum

| 'The Suakim Diary of Lieutenant-Colonel Andrew Charles Parker Haggard' | T4/35 |

National Army Museum (NAM)

Bly, diary	Acc. No. 1973-10-85
Cameron papers	Acc. No. 1983-05-55
Grant, diary	Acc. No. 1983-05-97
Grieve papers	Acc. No. 1979-06-139
Lygon Cocks papers	Acc. No. 1988-06-29
Officer of the Gordon Highlanders, n.d.	Acc. No. 1973-07-39

Paterson papers   Acc. No. 1972-08-8
Preston papers   Acc. No. 1977-04-56
Roberts papers   Acc. No. 1971-01-23

National Library of Scotland (NLS)

Haig papers
Haldane papers
Rosebery papers

National Register of Archives for Scotland

Monro of Williamwood Muniments

Royal Pavilions Libraries and Museums (RPLM), Brighton and Hove City Council, Hove Library

Wolseley Collection

The Highlanders Museum

Williamson papers

The National Archives (TNA), Public Record Office

War Office papers   WO 33/26
          WO 33/34
          WO 33/38
          WO 33/42
          WO 32/7870
          WO 32/7966

Wiltshire and Swindon Record Office

Methuen papers

PARLIAMENTARY PAPERS (PP)

Further Correspondence respecting the Ashantee Invasion, No. 4, C. 893 (1874), XLVI.
Report of Her Majesty's Commissioners Appointed to Inquire into Military Preparations and other matters connected with the War in South Africa, C 1789 (1904), XL.

Report of the Commission appointed to inquire into the system of purchase and sale of Commissions in the Army, with evidence and appendix, C. 2267 (1857 Sess. 2), XVIII.

Report of the Committee on the Terms and Conditions of Service in the Army, C. 6582 (1892), XIX.

Report of The Committee of Council on Education in Scotland, 1899–1900, Cd. 170 (1900), XXIV.

NEWSPAPERS

Aberdeen Journal
Aberdeen Weekly Journal
Abingdon Herald
Argyllshire Herald
Ayr Advertiser
Ayr Observer
Banffshire Journal
[Batley] Reporter
Belfast News-Letter
Blairgowrie Advertiser
Bradford Daily Argus
Brechin Advertiser
Bridge of Allan Reporter
Bristol Times and Mirror
Broad Arrow
Cornish Times
Cornubian and Redruth Times
Crieff Journal
Daily Chronicle
Daily Mail
Daily News
Daily Telegraph
Derby Daily Telegraph
Derby Mercury
Derbyshire Times
Dorset County Chronicle
Dover Express
Dover Telegraph
Dumbarton Herald
Dumfries and Galloway Courier and Herald
Dundee Advertiser
Dundee Courier & Argus
[Dundee] Weekly News

Dunfermline Journal
Edinburgh Courant
[Edinburgh] Daily Review
Edinburgh Evening News
Educational News
Elgin Courant and Courier
Evening Standard
Evening News
Falkirk Herald
Fife Herald and Journal
Fife News
Fifeshire Journal
Gainsborough Leader
Galashiels Telegraph
Glasgow Evening News
Glasgow Herald
Glasgow News
Grantham Journal
Graphic
Greenock Herald
Grimsby News
Haddingtonshire Advertiser
Hamilton Advertiser
Hamilton Herald and Lanarkshire Weekly News
Hampshire Observer
Hampshire Telegraph and Sussex Chronicle
Helensburgh News
Hereford Times
Highland News
Highland Times
Horncastle News and South Lindsay Advertiser

Huntly Express
Illustrated London News
Invergordon Times
Inverness Courier
Irish Times
Isle of Wight Journal
John O'Groat Journal
Kilmarnock Standard
Kinross-shire Advertiser
Leamington, Warwick, Rugby and
  County Chronicle
Leeds Mercury
Lincolnshire Chronicle
Manchester Courier
Manchester Evening Chronicle
Manchester Evening News
Manchester Guardian
Montrose, Arbroath, and Brechin
  Review
Morning Advertiser
Morning Post
Nairnshire Telegraph
Newcastle Daily Chronicle
North British Daily Mail
Northern Chronicle
Northern Scot and Moray & Nairn
  Express
Northern Weekly
North Star and Farmers' Chronicle
Oxford Times

People's Friend
Perth Constitutional & Journal
Perthshire Advertiser
Portsmouth Times
Reading Mercury, Oxford Gazette,
  Newbury Herald and Berks
  County Paper
Ross-shire Journal
Rothesay Express
Scotsman
Scottish Standard
Sheffield Daily Telegraph
Shurey's Illustrated
Somerset Standard
Staffordshire Advertiser
Stirling Observer and Midland
  Counties Express
Strathearn Herald
Sussex Daily News
The Times
Warwick & Warwickshire
  Advertiser & Leamington
  Gazette
Westcott's Local Press
Western Mail
Western Morning News
[York] Evening Press
York Herald
Yorkshire Telegraph

BOOKS

Allan, S. and Carswell, A., *The Thin Red Line: War, Empire and Visions of Scotland* (Edinburgh: National Museums of Scotland Enterprises Limited, 2004).

Allen, A. and Hoverstadt, J., *The History of Printed SCRAPS* (London: New Cavendish Books, 1983).

Anderson, R. D., *Education and The Scottish People 1750–1918* (Oxford: Clarendon Press, 1995).

Bahlman, D. W. R. (ed.), *The Diary of Sir Edward Walter Hamilton 1880–1885*, 2 vols (Oxford: Clarendon Press, 1972).

Baird, W., *General Wauchope* (Edinburgh: Oliphant Anderson & Ferrier, 1900).

Barthorp, M., *Afghan Wars and the North-West Frontier 1839–1947* (London: Cassell, 1982).

Bartlett, T. and Jeffery, K. (eds), *A Military History of Ireland* (Cambridge: Cambridge University Press, 1996).

Bates, D., *The Abyssinian Difficulty* (Oxford: Oxford University Press, 1979).

Beckett, I. F. W., *The Victorians at War* (London: Hambledon, 2003).

——, *Victoria's Wars* (Aylesbury: Shire Publications, 1974).

Beckett, I. F. W. and Simpson, K. (eds), *A nation in arms* (Manchester: Manchester University Press, 1985).

Bennett, E. N., *With Methuen's Column on an Ambulance Train* (London: Swan Sonnenschein, 1900).

Bennett, I., *A Rain of Lead: The Siege and Surrender of the British at Potchefstroom 1880–1881* (London: Greenhill Books, 2001).

Blake, R., *Disraeli* (London: Methuen, 1966).

Bond, B. (ed.), *Victorian Military Campaigns* (London: Hutchinson, 1967).

Booth, B. A. and Mehew, E. (eds), *The Letters of Robert Louis Stevenson*, 8 vols (New Haven and London: Yale University Press, 1995).

Boyd, K., *Manliness and the Boy's Story Paper in Britain: A Cultural History, 1855–1940* (Houndmills, Basingstoke: Palgrave Macmillan, 2003).

Boyden, P. B., *Tommy Atkins' Letters: The History of the British Army Postal Service from 1795* (London: National Army Museum, 1990).

Boyden, P. B., Guy, A. J. and Harding, M. (eds), *ashes and blood: The British Army in South Africa 1795–1914* (London: National Army Museum, 1999).

Brackenbury, Captain H., *The Ashanti War: A Narrative*, 2 vols (Edinburgh: Blackwood, 1874).

Bradby, D., James, L. and Sharratt, B. (eds), *Performance and politics in popular drama* (Cambridge: Cambridge University Press, 1980).

Bredin, A. E. C., *A History of the Irish Soldier* (Belfast: Century Books, 1987).

Buchan, J., *The History of The Royal Scots Fusiliers (1678–1918)* (London: Thomas Nelson & Sons, 1925).

Burleigh, B., *Desert Warfare: Being the Chronicle of the Eastern Soudan Campaign* (London: Chapman & Hall, 1884).

——, *Khartoum Campaign: or the Reconquest of the Soudan* (London: Chapman & Hall, 1899).

Butler, E., *An Autobiography* (London: Constable, 1922).

Butler, Colonel Sir W. F., *The Campaign of the Cataracts: Being a Personal Narrative of the Great Nile Expedition of 1884–5* (London: Sampson Low, 1887).

Cage, R. A. (ed.), *The Working Class in Glasgow 1750–1914* (London: Croom Helm, 1987).

Campbell, George Douglas, 8th Duke of Argyll, *Scotland as it was and as it is*, 2 vols (Edinburgh: David Douglas, 1887).

Cane, M., *For Queen and Country: The Career of Harry Payne Military Artist 1858–1927* (Kingston, Surrey: private, 1977).

Castle, I., *Majuba 1881: The Hill of Destiny* (London: Osprey, 1988).

Charlot, M., *Victoria, The Young Queen* (Oxford: Basil Blackwell, 1991).

Cromb, J. (ed.), *The Majuba Disaster: A Story of Highland Heroism, Told By Officers of the 92nd Regiment* (Dundee: John Leng, 1891).

——, *The Highland Brigade: Its Battles and its Heroes* (London: J. Shiells, 1896).

Cromer, Earl of, *Modern Egypt*, 2 vols (London: Macmillan, 1908).

Cunningham, H., *The Volunteer Force: A Social and Political History, 1859–1908* (London: Croom Helm, 1975).

David, S., *The Indian Mutiny* (London: Penguin, 2003).

Davidson, Major H., *History and Service of the 78th Highlanders (Ross-Shire Buffs) 1793–1881*, 2 vols (Edinburgh: W. & A. K. Johnston, 1901).

Devine, T. M., *The Scottish Nation 1700–2000* (London: Allen Lane, Penguin Press, 1999).

Dewar, T. F., *With the Scottish Yeomanry* (Arbroath: T. Buncle, 1901).

Donnachie, I. and Whately, C. (eds), *The Manufacture of Scottish History* (Edinburgh: Polygon, 1992).

Duff, D. (ed.), *Queen Victoria's Highland Journals* (Exeter: Webb & Bower, 1980).

Dunlop, J. K., *The Development of the British Army, 1899–1914* (London: Methuen, 1938).

Dunn-Pattison, R. P., *The History of the 91st Argyllshire Highlanders* (Edinburgh: W. Blackwood & Sons, 1910).

Emery, F., *Marching Over Africa: Letters from Victorian Soldiers* (London: Hodder and Stoughton, 1986).

Erickson, C., *Her Little Majesty: The Life of Queen Victoria* (London: Robson Books, 2004).

Fairrie, Lieutenant-Colonel A., *'Cuidich 'N Righ': A History of the Queen's Own Highlanders (Seaforths and Camerons)* (Inverness: Regimental HQ Queen's Own Highlanders, 1983).

Featherstone, D., *Khartoum 1885: General Gordon's Last Stand* (London: Osprey, 1993).

——, *Tel El-Kebir* (London: Osprey, 1993).

Findlay, B. (ed.), *A History of the Scottish Theatre* (Edinburgh: Polygon, 1998).

Finlay, R. J., *A Partnership for Good? Scottish Politics and the Union Since 1880* (Edinburgh: John Donald Publishers, 1995).

Fletcher, I. and Ishchenko, N., *The Crimean War: A Clash of Empires* (Staplehurst: Spellmount, 2004).

Foot, M. R. D. (ed.), *War and Society: Historical Essays in Honour and Memory of J. R. Western 1928–1971* (London: Paul Elek, 1973).

Forbes, A., *Chinese Gordon: A succinct record of his life* (London: Routledge & Sons, 1884).

——, *Colin Campbell, Lord Clyde* (London: Macmillan, 1895).

——, *The Black Watch* (London: Cassell, 1896).

Forbes-Mitchell, W., *Reminiscences of the Great Mutiny 1857–9* (London: Macmillan, 1893).

Franklin, M. J., *British Biscuit Tins 1868–1939: An Aspect of Decorative Packaging* (London: New Cavendish Books, 1979).

Fraser, W. Hamish and Lee, C. H. (eds), *Aberdeen 1800–2000: A New History* (East Linton: Tuckwell Press, 2000).

French, P., *Younghusband: The Last Great Imperial Adventurer* (London: HarperCollins, 1994).

Fry, M., *Patronage and Principle: A Political History of Modern Scotland* (Aberdeen: Aberdeen University Press, 1987).

Gardyne, Lieutenant-Colonel C. Greenhill, *The Life of a Regiment: The History of the Gordon Highlanders*, 3 vols (London: The Medici Society, 1903–29).

Gildea, Colonel Sir J., *For Remembrance and In Honour of Those Who Lost Their Lives in the South African War 1899–1902* (London: Eyre & Spottiswoode, 1911).

Gooch, J. (ed.), *The Boer War: Direction, Experience and Image* (London: Frank Cass, 2000).

Gordon-Alexander, Lieutenant.-Colonel W., *Recollections of a Highland Subaltern* (London: Edward Arnold, 1898).

Gordon-Duff, L., *With the Gordon Highlanders to the Boer War & beyond* (Staplehurst: Spellmount, 2000).

Grierson, Major-General J. M., *Records of the Scottish Volunteer Force 1859–1908* (Edinburgh: Blackwood, 1909).

Groves, Lieutenant-Colonel P., *History of the 93rd Sutherland Highlanders now the 2nd Battalion Princess Louise's Argyll and Sutherland Highlanders* (Edinburgh: W. & A. Johnston, 1895).

Hamer, D. A., *John Morley: Liberal Intellectual in Politics* (Oxford: Oxford University Press, 1968).

Hamilton, General Sir I., *Listening for the Drums* (London: Faber & Faber, 1944).

Hamilton, V. M., *Things That Happened* (London: Edward Arnold, 1925).

Harrington, P., *British Artists and War: The Face of Battle in Paintings and Prints, 1700–1914* (London: Greenhill Books, 1993).

Harris, Mrs G., *A Lady's Diary of the Siege of Lucknow* (London: John Murray, 1858).

Henderson, D. M., *Highland Soldier 1820–1920* (Edinburgh: John Donald Publishers, 1989).

Hensman, H., *The Afghan War of 1879–80* (London: W. H. Allen & Co., 1881).

Hibbert, C., *The Great Mutiny India 1857* (London: Allen Lane, 1978).

Hichberger, J. W. M., *Images of the Army: The Military in British Art, 1815–1914* (Manchester: Manchester University Press, 1988).

Hindley, D. and G., *Advertising in Victorian England 1837–1901* (London: Wayland, 1972).

Hobsbawn, E. and Ranger, T. (eds), *The Invention of Tradition* (Cambridge: Cambridge University Press, 1983).

Holme, N., *The Noble 24th* (London: Savannah, 1979).

Holt, P. M. and Daly, M. W., *A History of the Sudan: From the Coming of Islam to the Present Day* (Harlow: Pearson Education, 2000).

Holt, V., *Picture Postcards of the Golden Age: A Collector's Guide* (London: MacGibbon & Kee, 1971).

Home, Lieutenant W., *With the Border Volunteers to Pretoria* (Hawick: W. & J. Kennedy, 1901).

Hughes, M. and Johnson, G. (eds), *Fanaticism and Conflict in the Modern Age* (London: Frank Cass, 2005).

Hunter, A., *Kitchener's Sword-Arm: The Life and Campaigns of General Sir Archibald Hunter* (Staplehurst: Spellmount, 1996).

Hutchinson, Colonel H. D., *The Campaign in the Tirah 1897–1898* (London: Macmillan, 1898).

Hutchison, I. G. C., *A Political History of Scotland 1832–1924* (Edinburgh: John Donald, 1986).

Jeal, T., *Baden-Powell* (London: Hutchinson, 1989).

Johnson, P., *Front Line Artists* (London: Cassell, 1978).

Johnston, S. H. F., *The History of the Cameronians (Scottish Rifles) 26th and 90th*, 2 vols (Aldershot: Gale & Polden, 1957).

Judd, D. and Surridge, K., *The Boer War* (London: John Murray, 2002).

Keown-Boyd, H., *A Good Dusting: A Centenary Review of the Sudan campaigns 1883–1899* (London: Leo Cooper, 1986).

Knight, I., *Brave Men's Blood: The Epic of the Zulu War, 1879* (London: Guild Publishing, 1990).

——, *The Sun Turned Black: Isandlwana and Rorke's Drift–1879* (Rivonia: William Waterman Publications, 1995).

——, Castle, I., *Zulu War 1879* (London: Osprey, Campaign Series 14, 1994).

Kochanski, H., *Sir Garnet Wolseley: Victorian Hero* (London: The Hambledon Press, 1999).

Koss, S. (ed.), *The Pro-Boers: The Anatomy of an Antiwar Movement* (Chicago: University of Chicago Press, 1973).

Laband, J., *The battle of Ulundi* (Pietermaritzburg: Shuter & Shooter, 1988).

Lehman, J., *The Boer War* (London: Buchan & Endright, 1985).

'Linesman', *Words by an Eyewitness* (Edinburgh: Blackwood, 1902).

Linklater, E. and A., *The Black Watch: The History of the Royal Highland Regiment* (London: Barrie & Jenkins, 1977).

Lloyd, A., *The Drums of Kumasi* (London: Longmans, 1964).

Loeb, L. Anne, *Consuming Angels: Advertising and Victorian Women* (Oxford: Oxford University Press, 1994).

McAleer, J., *Popular Reading and Publishing in Britain 1914–1950* (Oxford: Clarendon Press, 1992).

McCaffrey, J. F., *Scotland in the Nineteenth Century* (Basingstoke: Macmillan, 1998).

McCracken, D. P., *MacBride's Brigade: Irish Commandos in the Anglo-Boer War* (Dublin: Four Courts Press, 1999).

MacDonagh, O., *Early Victorian Government 1830–1870* (London: Weidenfeld & Nicolson, 1977).

Macdonald, C. M. M. (ed.), *Unionist Scotland 1800–1997* (Edinburgh: John Donald, 1998).

Macdonald, J. H. A., *Fifty Years of It: The Experiences and Struggles of a Volunteer of 1859* (Edinburgh: Blackwood, 1909).

MacKenzie, J. M. (ed.), *Imperialism and Popular Culture* (Manchester: Manchester University Press, 1986).

——, *Popular Imperialism and the Military, 1850–1950* (Manchester: Manchester University Press, 1992).

——, *Propaganda and Empire: The Manipulation of British Public Opinion, 1880–1960* (Manchester: Manchester University Press, 1984).

Mangan, J. A., *The Games Ethic and Imperialism: Aspects of the Diffusion of an Ideal* (Harmondsworth, Middlesex: Viking, 1986).

Mangan, J. A. and Walvin, J. (eds), *Manliness and morality: Middle-class masculinity in Britain and America 1800–1940* (Manchester: Manchester University Press, 1987).

Marling, Colonel Sir P., *Riflemen and Hussar* (London: John Murray, 1931).

Mason, P., *A Matter of Honour: An account of the Indian Army, its officers & men* (London: Jonathan Cape, 1974).

Massie, A., *The National Army Museum Book of the Crimean War: The Untold Stories* (London: Sidgwick & Jackson, 2004).

Matthew, H. C. G., *Gladstone 1875–1898* (Oxford: Clarendon Press, 1995).

——, *The Liberal Imperialists: The ideas and politics of a post-Gladstonian elite* (Oxford: Oxford University Press, 1973).

Maurice, Major-General Sir F. B. and Grant, M. H., *History of the War in South Africa 1899–1902*, 4 vols (London: Hurst & Blackett, 1906).

Maxwell, L., *My God! – Maiwand* (London: Leo Cooper, 1979).

Melville, M. L., *The Story of the Lovat Scouts 1900–1980* (Librario Publishing Ltd, 2004).

Mileham, P. (ed.), *Clearly My Duty: The Letters of Sir John Gilmour from the Boer War 1900–1901* (East Linton: Tuckwell Press, 1996).

——, *Fighting Highlanders!: The History of the Argyll & Sutherland Highlanders* (London: Arms and Armour Press, 1993).

——, *The Yeomanry Regiments: A Pictorial History* (Tunbridge Wells: Spellmount, 1985).

Miskell, L., Whatley, C. A. and Harris, B. (eds), *Victorian Dundee: Image and Realities* (East Linton: Tuckwell Press, 2000).

Moreman, T. R., *The Army in India and the Development of Frontier Warfare, 1849–1947* (Houndmills, Basingstoke: Macmillan, 1998).

Morgan, K. O. (ed.), *The Oxford Illustrated History of Britain* (Oxford: Oxford University Press, 1984).

Morris, D. R., *The Washing of the Spears* (London: Sphere, 1968).

Munro, Surgeon-General W., *Reminiscences of Military Service with the 93rd Sutherland Highlanders* (London: Hurst & Blackett, 1883).

Murdoch, S. and Mackillop, A. (eds), *Fighting for Identity: Scottish Military Experience c. 1550–1900* (Leiden: Brill, 2002).

Murray, J., *The Art of Whisky: A De Luxe Blend of Historic Posters from the Public Record Office* (Kew, Surrey: PRO Publications, 1998).

Nevill, Captain H. L., *Campaigns on the North-West Frontier* (London: John Murray, 1912).

Newton, N., *The Life and Times of Inverness* (Edinburgh: John Donald, 1996).

Oatts, Lieutenant-Colonel L. B., *Proud Heritage: The Story of the Highland Light Infantry*, 4 vols (London: Thomas Nelson, 1959).

Pakenham, T., *The Boer War* (London: Weidenfeld & Nicolson, 1979).

Petre, F. Loraine, *The Royal Berkshire Regiment*, 2 vols (Reading: The Barracks, 1925).

Prebble, J., *Mutiny: Highland Regiments in Revolt 1743–1804* (London: Penguin, 1975).

Preston, A. (ed.), *In Relief of Gordon: Lord Wolseley's Campaign Journal of The Khartoum Relief Expedition 1884–1885* (London: Hutchinson, 1967).

Price, R., *An Imperial War and the British Working Class: Working-Class Attitudes and Reactions to the Boer War 1899–1902* (London: Routledge & Kegan Paul, 1972).

Prior, M., *Campaigns of a War Correspondent* (London: Edward Arnold, 1912).

Pugh, M., *The Tories and the People 1880–1935* (Oxford: Basil Blackwell, 1985).

Reade, Winwood, *The Story of the Ashantee Campaign* (London: Smith, Elder & Co., 1874).

Reith, Lord, *Wearing Spurs* (London: Hutchinson, 1966).

Richards, J., *Films and British national identity: From Dickens to Dad's Army* (Manchester: Manchester University Press, 1997).

—— (ed.), *Imperialism and juvenile literature* (Manchester: Manchester University Press, 1989).

——, *Imperialism and music: Britain 1876–1953* (Manchester: Manchester University Press, 2001).

Robb, A., *Reminiscences of a Veteran: Being the Experiences of a Private*

Soldier in the Crimea, and during the Indian Mutiny (Dundee: W. & D. C. Thomson, 1888).

Roberts, Field Marshal Lord, *Forty-One Years in India*, 2 vols (London: Richard Bentley & Son, 1897).

Robins, Major C. (ed.), *Romaine's Crimean War: The Letters and Journal of William Govett Romaine* (Stroud, Gloucestershire: Sutton Publishing for the Army Records Society, 2005).

——, *The Murder of a Regiment: Winter Sketches from the Crimea 1854–1855 by an Officer of the 46th Foot (South Devonshire Regiment)* (Bowden: Withycut, 1994).

Robson, B (ed.), *Sir Hugh Rose and the Central India Campaign 1858* (Midsomer Norton, Somerset: Sutton Publishing for the Army Records Society, 2000).

——, *The Road to Kabul: The Second Afghan War 1878–1881* (London: Arms and Armour Press, 1986).

Rose, J., *The Intellectual Life of the British Working Classes* (New Haven and London: Yale University Press, 2001).

Rowell, G., *Theatre in the Age of Irving* (Oxford: Basil Blackwell, 1981).

Royle, T., *Fighting Mac: The Downfall of Major-General Sir Hector Macdonald* (Edinburgh: Mainstream Publishing, 2003).

Rudyard Kipling's Verse: Definitive Edition (London: Hodder & Stoughton, 1946).

Russell, D., *Popular music in England, 1840–1914* (Manchester: Manchester University Press, 1997).

Russell, W. H., *My Diary in India, in the Year 1858–9*, 2 vols (London: Routledge, Warne & Routledge, 1860).

Sandes, Lieutenant-Colonel E. W. C., *The Royal Engineers in Egypt and the Sudan* (Chatham: The Institution of Royal Engineers, 1937).

Shadwell, L., *The life of Colin Campbell*, 2 vols (1881).

Shannon, R., *Gladstone: Heroic Minister 1865–1898* (London: Allen Lane, 1999).

Shaw, T., *Letters to Isabel* (London: Cassell, 1921).

Shinwell, M., *Lead with the Left: My First Ninety-six Years* (London: Cassell, 1981).

Skelley, A. R., *The Victorian Army at Home:The Recruitment and Terms and Conditions of the British Regular, 1859–1899* (London: Croom Helm, 1977).

Smith, G. H., *With the Scottish Rifle Volunteers at the Front* (Glasgow: W. Hodge & Co., 1901).

Somerville, A., *The Autobiography of a Working Man* (London: Charles Gilpin, 1848).

South African War Record of the 1st Battalion Queen's Own Cameron Highlanders 1900–1–2 (Inverness: Northern Counties Printing Company, 1903).

Spiers, E. M., *Haldane: An Army Reformer* (Edinburgh: Edinburgh University Press, 1980).

—— (ed.), *Sudan: The Reconquest Reappraised* (London: Frank Cass, 1998).

——, *The Army and Society 1815–1914* (London: Longman, 1980).

——, *The Late Victorian Army 1868–1902* (Manchester: Manchester University Press, 1992).

——, *The Victorian soldier in Africa* (Manchester: Manchester University Press, 2004).

Spies, S. B., *Methods of Barbarism? Roberts and Kitchener and Civilians in the Boer Republics: January 1900–May 1902* (Cape Town: Hunan & Rousseau, 1977).

Springhall, J. O., *Youth, Empire and Society: British Youth Movements, 1883–1940* (London: Croom Helm, 1977).

Stanley, H. M., *Coomassie and Magdala: The Story of Two British Campaigns in Africa* (London: Sampson Low, 1874).

Steevens, G. W., *With Kitchener to Khartum* (Edinburgh: Blackwood, 1898).

Sterling, Lieutenant-Colonel A., *The Highland Brigade in the Crimea* (Minneapolis: Absinthe Press, 1995).

Stirling, J., *British Regiments in South Africa 1899–1902* (Polstead, Suffolk: J. B. Hayward, 1903).

Stone, J. and Schmidl, E., *The Boer War and Military Reforms* (Lanham, MD: University Press of America, 1988).

Sturrock, J., *The Fifes in South Africa* (Cupar: A. Westwood & Sons, 1903).

Symons, J., *England's Pride: The Story of the Gordon Relief Expedition* (London: Hamish Hamilton, 1965).

Tooley, S. A., *The Personal Life of Queen Victoria* (London: Hodder & Stoughton, 1896).

Trousdale, W. (ed.), *War in Afghanistan, 1879–80: The Personal Diary of Major-General Sir Charles Metcalfe MacGregor* (Detroit: Wayne State University Press, 1985).

Trustram, M., *Women of the regiment: Marriage and the Victorian army* (Cambridge: Cambridge University Press, 1984).

Usherwood, P. and Spencer-Smith, J., *Lady Butler: Battle Artist 1846–1933* (London: National Army Museum, 1987).

Villiers, F., *Villiers: His Five Decades of Adventure*, 2 vols (London: Hutchinson, 1921).

Ward, S. G. P., *Faithful: The Story of the Durham Light Infantry* (Edinburgh: Thomas Nelson, 1964).

——, (ed.), *The Hawley Letters: The Letters of Captain R. B. Hawley, 89th from the Crimea, December 1854 to August 1856* (Society for Army Historical Research), Special Publication No. 10 (1970).

Warner, P., *Army Life in the '90s* (London: Hamlyn, 1975).

Warwick, P., *Black People and the South African War, 1899–1902* (Cambridge: Cambridge University Press, 1983).

—— (ed.), *The South African War: The Anglo-Boer War 1899–1902* (London: Longman, 1980).

West, S. (ed.), *The Victorians and Race* (Aldershot: Solar Press, 1996).

Wilkinson-Latham, R., *From Our Special Correspondent: Victorian War Correspondents and Their Campaigns* (London: Hodder & Stoughton, 1979).

Wilson, H., *Blue Bonnets, Boers & Biscuits* (London: The Rotawise Printing Co., 1998).

Wimberley, Captain D., *Some Account of the Part taken by the 79th Regiment or Cameron Highlanders in the Indian Mutiny Campaign in 1858* (Inverness: private, 1891).

Wingate, F. R., *Mahdiism and the Egyptian Sudan* (London: Frank Cass, 2nd edition, 1968).

Wolseley, Field Marshal Viscount, *The Story of a Soldier's Life*, 2 vols (London: Constable, 1903).

Wood, I. S. (ed.), *Scotland and Ulster* (Edinburgh: Mercat Press, 1994).

Wood, S., *The Scottish Soldier* (Manchester: Archive Publications, 1987).

Woollcombe, R., *All The Blue Bonnets: The History of The King's Own Scottish Borderers* (London: Arms and Armour Press, 1980).

Younghusband, Captains G. J. and F. E., *The Relief of Chitral* (London: Macmillan, 1897).

ARTICLES

Anderson, O., 'The growth of Christian militarism in mid-Victorian Britain', *English Historical Review*, 86, no. 338 (1971).

'Ashantee War. Extract From A Letter From Lieut. H. Jekyll, R. E.', *The Royal Engineers Journal*, 4 (2 March 1874).

Bernstein, G. L., 'Sir Henry Campbell-Bannerman and the Liberal Imperialists', *Journal of British Studies*, 23 (1983).

Brown, S. J., ' "Echoes of Midlothian": Scottish Liberalism and the South African War, 1899–1902', *Scottish Historical Review*, 71 (1992).

Bulloch, J. M., 'The Gay Gordons: A Study in Inherited Prestige', *Blackwood's Edinburgh Magazine*, 163 (1898).

Cowling, M., 'Lytton, the Cabinet, and the Russians, August to November 1878', *English Historical Review*, lxxvi (1961).

Dunae, P. A., 'Boys' Literature and the Idea of Empire, 1870–1914', *Victorian Studies*, 24 (1980).

'Extracts from the Diary of Lieut. H. H. L. Malcolm, 79th Q. O. Cameron Highrs, during the Egyptian War, 1882', *The 79th News*, no. 202 (April 1933).

Finlay, R. J., 'The rise and fall of popular imperialism in Scotland, 1850–1950', *Scottish Geographical Magazine*, 113, no. 1 (1997).

Harrington, P., 'The Man Who Painted THE THIN RED LINE', *Scots Magazine*, 130, no. 6 (1989).

Harvie, I., 'The Raid on Essaman, 14 October 1873: An Account by Lieutenant Edward Woodgate of an Operation during Wolseley's Ashanti Expedition', *Journal of the Society for Army Historical Research*, 77 (1999).

Hill, R., 'The Gordon Literature', *The Durham University Journal*, XLVII, no. 3 (1955).

Jacobson, P. B., 'Rosebery and Liberal Imperialism 1899–1902', *Journal of British Studies*, 13 (1973).

Johnson, D. H., 'The Death of Gordon: A Victorian Myth', *The Journal of Imperial and Commonwealth History*, 10, no. 7 (1982).

Kelley, R., 'Midlothian: A Study in Politics and Ideas', *Victorian Studies*, 4, no. 2 (1960).

'Korosko', *The 79th News*, no. 198 (1932).

McCaffrey, J. F., 'The origins of Liberal Unionism in the west of Scotland', *Scottish Historical Review*, 50 (1971).

McIntyre, W. D., 'British Policy in West Africa: The Ashanti Expedition of 1873–4', *Historical Journal*, 5, no. 1 (1962).

MacKenzie, J. M., 'Empire and National Identities: The Case of Scotland', *Transactions of the Royal Historical Society*, 6th series, VIII (1998).

——, 'Essay and Reflection: On Scotland and the Empire', *International History Review*, XV, no. 4 (1993).

McNeill, Brigadier-General A. J., 'Further Reminiscences of a Subaltern', *Cabar Feidh: The Quarterly Magazine of The Seaforth Highlanders*, 7, no. 49 (1934).

Murray, D., 'Kabul to Kandahar', *Soldiers of the Queen*, 102 (2000).

Savage, D. C., 'Scottish Politics, 1885–6', *Scottish Historical Review*, 40 (1961).

Schölch, A., 'The "Men on the Spot" and the English Occupation of Egypt in 1882', *Historical Journal*, 19, no. 3 (1976).

Senelick, L., 'Politics as Entertainment: Victorian Music-Hall Songs', *Victorian Studies*, 19 (1975).

Stearn, R. T., 'Bennet Burleigh Victorian War Correspondent', *Soldiers of the Queen*, 65 (1991).

——, 'War and the Media in the 19th Century: Victorian Military Artists and the Image of War, 1870–1914', *Royal United Services Institute Journal of Defence Studies*, 131, no. 3 (1986).

——, 'G. W. Steevens and the message of empire', *Journal of Imperial and Commonwealth History*, 17 (1989).

Stewart, J. W., 'A Subaltern in the Sudan, 1898', *The Stewarts*, 17 (1987).

Tucker, A. V., 'Army and Society in England, 1870–1900: A Reassessment of the Cardwell Reforms', *Journal of British Studies*, 2 (1963).

Tylden, Major G. Tylden [translation], 'Majuba, 27th February, 1881: A Contemporary Boer Account', *Journal of the Society for Army Historical Research*, 17 (1938).

INDEX